The Tale of the Dancing Slaughter Horse

Victoria Shade

Amberjack Publishing
New York, New York

Amberjack Publishing
228 Park Avenue S #89611
New York, NY 10003-1502
http://amberjackpublishing.com

This is a work of creative nonfiction. It is nonfiction in that this is a true story based on the author's memories, and creative in that the author has expanded on her memory to build a richer narrative. The events contained herein are accurate to the best of the author's memory. Minor details which do not impact the story have been changed as necessary to protect the privacy of those involved.

Publisher's Cataloging-in-Publication data
Names: Shade, Victoria, author.
Title: The Tale of the dancing slaughter horse / By Victoria Shade.
Description: New York, New York: Amberjack Publishing, 2016.
Identifiers: ISBN 978-0-9972377-7-1 (pbk.) | ISBN 978-0-9972377-6-4 (ebook) | LCCN 2016934588.
Subjects: LCSH Shade, Victoria --Childhood and youth. | Horses --Anecdotes. | Human-animal relationships. | Horsemen and horsewomen--United States—Biography. | Horses --Training. | BISAC BIOGRAPHY & AUTOBIOGRAPHY / Personal Memoirs.
Classification: LCC SF284.5 .S53 2016 | DDC 798.2/092/2--dc23.

Cover Design: Red Couch Creative, Inc.
Cover photo: © www.TerriMiller.com reprinted with permission.

Printed in the United States of America

This book is dedicated to those horses killed in slaughter. One day, "horse slaughter" will be a vile memory, an abhorrent practice banned worldwide, a concept no longer fathomable by the humans who will honor and love their horses for as long as they live. There will come a day when all horses are treasured and no longer tortured.

"I have from an early age abjured the use of meat, and the time will come when men such as I will look upon the murder of animals as they now look upon the murder of men."

Leonardo da Vinci

Reflection

"Your left hand is a *disaster*!" he roared in his thick German accent. He didn't need to yell directly into the microphone; I could hear his bellow clearly from across the arena.

Moonshine was completely unfazed, trotting unapologetically past a speaker as it blew out with a sharp *crack-pop*. He never broke his stride. A wave of snickers and chuckles escaped the audience. I hoped that they were amused by the blown speaker and not by my gaffe, which I had evidently committed one time too many. It was undeniable—I had caused Conrad Schumacher, one of the most prominent dressage trainers in the world, to lose his temper. And yet, I wasn't terribly upset about it.

The opportunity to train with a German Olympic trainer was rare—even more so for someone like me, a hopelessly horse-crazy teenager with a huge dream and measly mount. German equestrians are the best in the world. This guy had trained athletes on the Olympic track! The only track Moony had been on was the racetrack to the slaughterhouse. But I yearned to be an international superstar with my equine partner. I was convinced we could do anything together—even compete internationally—because of our bond.

On the drive to the United States Equestrian Team headquarters in Gladstone, New Jersey, I watched the trailer sway as it succumbed to my angry beast's barrage of furious blows. Moony loved to show, but he hated traveling in a trailer.

Moon, stop, I thought, trying to communicate with him telepathically from the car.

I worried that he would hurt himself or damage the shipper's trailer. Moony had, on a previous occasion, kicked a hole in another shipper's trailer, which my mother had to pay for. I was perpetually reminded of what an expensive sport I had chosen, and acutely aware of any unforeseen expenses. But I didn't choose dressage, just like I didn't choose to breathe. Dressage chose me.

As the trailer driver picked up speed and the kicking subsided, I fell into my usual daydream of competing with Moony in an international arena. I am wearing my shadbelly jacket and top hat, while Moonshine proudly dons his double bridle—attire reserved for upper level dressage. We float into the arena, straight down the center line to the middle of the ring. Moony halts squarely, and stands at perfect attention as I salute the judge to start the test. We breeze through the test as one unit, a centaur. He reads my mind every step of the way. When I think extended trot, he finds the diagonal, leans his weight back and launches us into a lofty, suspended trot. When I think half-pass, he turns his head in the direction I want to go, and starts side-stepping that way. When I think walk, he instantly downshifts. When I think canter, he jumps right into it. The whole test is perfect. Upon my final salute, the massive audience erupts in deafening applause. We win the class, despite his unimpressive movement and non-existent dressage pedigree. We win because he is perfect.

I couldn't wait to show *that* Moonshine off to the German. He would go back and tell all of those German superstars to look out for this up-and-coming pair. The Americans would become contenders on the international scene—and on *our* terms, with American-bred, non-warmblood horses. We would show the world that dressage wasn't exclusively reserved for horses bred for centuries in Germany, Holland, and Denmark. We would show them that a perfect pedigree wasn't a prerequisite to being a serious contender.

But there I was, fantasy dying, the German too exasperated with my uncooperative left hand to be impressed with anything at all. And yet, even as he berated me, I found myself calm, not panicking or embarrassed. I was grateful. I was grateful because I was there—with Moonshine. The horse that had narrowly escaped slaughter was performing in the same arena as imported warmbloods—those fancy, expensive horses bred specifically for dressage. I realized I didn't care as much I thought I would about Mr. Schumacher's opinion of my horse. I already knew Moonshine was extraordinary.

1

We're in a bedroom. Mom is standing, holding me. She smiles at me. I'm happy. Then we float down to the floor. I am sitting in front of her face. Her cheek is on the hardwood floor. Her eyes are closed. A red stream crosses her face. Then another. And another. I don't know what the oozing red liquid is but I do know that her face shouldn't be on the floor. I am worried and reach for her. Her eyes slowly open and she looks right at me. She smiles. My worry quickly fades, and I am happy again.

I am two years old, and my father has just smashed a wine bottle over my mother's head while she was pregnant with my sister.

I don't remember him living with us, but I do remember his frequent intrusions when I was young. They usually went something like this: "Get out! I said *get out*!" my mother screams, her body pressed against the front door of our house while my father, on the other side, pushes his way in. With one sweep, he swings the door open, slamming her into the wall.

As he steps inside, he points at her, "This is *my* house, you bitch!"

"The *girls*!" she shrieks, forcing him to acknowledge that my sister and I are only a few feet away. She is more upset that her toddlers just heard profanity, than by the fact that she has just been thrown into a wall.

As he steps toward my little sister and me, standing on the far side of the living room, he reconsiders his entry. He looks at us, then back at her, and spits at her, "This is *my* house. You're *nothing* without me." Finally, he disappears through the doorway, and the terrifying encounter is over.

"Fafa," she orders me, "go play My Little Pony in your bedroom with your sister."

Fafa was my nickname, after my failed attempts when I was younger to properly pronounce the word "fata," in Romanian, which means "girl."

"OK," I obey, grabbing my sister's hand and pulling her away from the entrance of the house.

I lead her to the safety of our bedroom and help her up to my twin bed, into the mess of My Little Ponies strewn all over. I pick up the closest one, and put another one in front of her.

"Look, Baby, aren't they pretty? Look at their long, flowing tails and the stars on their butts." My sister was the baby, so, naturally, her nickname was "Baby."

I knew she had a short attention span and had probably already forgotten the episode between our parents that had just played out before us, but I needed to make sure; I needed to completely engage all of her attention.

"Your pony is so pretty. She's pink, see?" I cue her. "What will you name her?" I ask.

"Pony," she replies, staring at the toy, but not touching it. Since she would not touch it, I pick them both up and make them run alongside each other.

"OK," I say, "then mine can be called Horsey. And they're sisters. And Horsey will take care of Pony."

"I'm sleepy; can I sleep in your bed tonight?" she asks as she lies down on top of all of my toys.

"Sure," I reply, sliding off my bed and making my way toward her bed, across the room. "No," she whispers, grabbing my shirt, "you stay here, too."

"OK."

2

It was 1985. I was five years old when my mother decided we needed to be out of our house and out of Queens, as much as possible. She said we had to go upstate, for the fresh air. It was the first time she had sent us to a small town in upstate New York to spend the summer with our grandparents and relatives we didn't know.

"Are you coming with us?" I asked my mother after her announcement.

"No, you are going with Nanni and Tati. I have to work. But I will visit as much as possible, every night after work, if I can."

"You're going to visit us every night?" I inquired, dubious. She typically worked well into the dark hours of the night. I rarely saw her. And "upstate New York" sounded like it was far away. I wondered how she would visit us every night after the late hours she worked, and travel the distance to this faraway place she was sending us. It seemed impossible.

"Yes, dear," she said as she hurriedly stuffed my clothes and some of my favorite toys into an old, ugly, brown leather duffel bag.

"But we'll be asleep when you come. Why don't you just stay with us?" I pleaded. I never got to see my mother. She was my favorite person, the only person I wanted to be with. I definitely didn't want to stay with my caustic, cold, and abrasive grandparents. They made no secret about what a tedious chore it was to watch me and my sister while my mom worked.

"Because I have to *work*, Victoria," she repeated, audibly annoyed.

I knew to stop antagonizing her when she used my full name, but I still didn't understand why she would only visit us at night, when we were sleeping.

"And besides, I will stay with you up there every other weekend," she said, softening.

The next morning, we all piled into the car—me, my sister, my grandparents, and my aunt, with my mother at the wheel. I felt relief in leaving the house behind.

As the car droned along highway after highway, I watched the gray, lifeless buildings of the city morph into the vibrant green trees of upstate New York. I rolled down the window and took in the fresh, crisp air. The pure, clean air flooded my lungs. The sweet smell of lush trees and flowers filled the car. All eyes were drawn to the rolling green landscape now surrounding the station wagon. Nobody spoke. We were all captivated by the serenity of our new surroundings. There were no more screaming people, no more traffic jams, no more honking horns—just green tranquility.

When we exited the highway, we continued down a maze of winding little roads without double yellow lines or even white dashes. It was as if someone had recklessly spilled cement down a clearing of trees and called it a road. There were no sidewalks, no traffic lights, not even stop signs. Just trees.

After even more driving, the car then made a left turn onto another bizarre road, one made of small rocks. It seemed like the road-making people had gotten lazier and lazier; the roads were getting smaller and shabbier. The car followed the small road to the front of a large white house. Behind the house, I could see nothing but a hill that rolled high beyond my line of sight. In front of the house, the same hill spilled downward, ending with a border of thick brush, and a large, bright blue pool in the ground.

A stout lady with porcelain white skin and short, dark, curly hair blew open the front door of the house and hurtled herself down the front steps.

"Hi, Mariana!" she screamed at the top of her lungs as she leapt down the last few steps.

Before my mother could respond, she tore open the door to the backseat, and yanked me out. Her grasp was like a man's, rough. Her skin was sandpaper, scratching my arm. On seeing her close up, her nose and cheeks were peppered with orange and brown spots. She was older, but the patches and cherub face made her look young.

"You don't remember me, do ya?" she asked as she squatted on one knee before me.

Before I could answer, my mother made her way around the car and got her attention.

"Anita, she's not going to remember you. She hasn't seen you in two years," my mother explained.

"Pfft!" Anita scoffed, as if to say there are no excuses for not remembering her.

"And who is this?" she said, peeking into the other side of the back seat at my three-year-old sister.

"That's my sister!" I let out immediately.

After a few days of berry-picking, swimming in the pool, and climbing trees, my sister and I were bored.

"Take them horse-back riding," Anita suggested to my mother. "There's a barn just down the road that does trail rides through the woods."

"Yeah, Mom!" I was immediately intrigued, eager for something new to do.

I stood by the entrance of the barn, waiting for my horse to be brought out. As the giant emerged from the darkness of the barn, his shadow eclipsed my body. The sunlight peeked out from every outline of his body, illuminating his entire frame. He was massive, not just to me, but he exerted a commanding presence over his handler. And yet, he was completely obedient and docile. He stopped where his handler had parked him, like a car, and waited for his next order. He hung his head, disinterested in the world around him. Although I stared into his eyes, hoping for him to see me, he never did. I scanned the length of his body. Other than his massive stature, there was nothing striking about this animal—he was light brown, slightly dusty, and had no markings.

As I approached, he grew bigger and bigger. When I reached him, I stood face to face with his chest. The stirrup hung above my head. My eyes traveled up the worn leather of the western saddle as I wondered how I would climb into it.

"Big boy, ain't he?" I heard a gruff but gentle voice ask.

Before I could respond, he continued, "Yeah, he's a Thoroughbred aw'right. See them long legs, like a Daddy Long Legs spider? That means he's a Thoroughbred, and good for runnin'."

My eyes darted from the saddle to the man speaking to me. He looked like a cowboy, except that he wore a baseball hat instead of a cowboy hat. But he had the rest of the uniform—flannel shirt, worn jeans, and old chaps. Just like on TV.

"Aww, don't worry dear, he ain't gonna hurt ya. He's about a hundred years old and can't barely move no more. Plus them big ones, we call 'em the gentle giants. The bigger they are, the nicer they are.

"His name's Big Tom," the imposter cowboy continued. And then, "Alley-up!" he said with one motion, stepping behind me, lifting me by my armpits and dropping me into the saddle.

He must have done this before, because he knew exactly how to throw my body so that I would land in the middle of the saddle.

I instantly disliked the saddle. First, the horn of the western saddle stood as tall as the middle of my torso. The end of the saddle lifted so high that I was sandwiched in. They might as well have taken the couch from my living room, with the indented spot that everyone sat in, and put it on this horse's back. I had no freedom, no room to move. It was like sitting in a hole.

But then I looked around and saw how high I was. Now, the man was looking *up* at *me*. In a matter of seconds, I was no longer limited by my weak, miniscule body; I had become part of a giant, powerful being. A foreign sense of satisfaction and serenity enveloped me. For the first time in my life, I was no longer looking up at people. Now, I was looking down at them. For the first time, nobody could reach me. For the first time, I felt safe.

"OK, now you listen here," the man said, stretching to reach my hands. "These are what control the horse. They're called reins. It's real easy, see, if you want to turn left, you pull the left rein, like this, and if you want to turn right, just pull the right one. If you wanna stop, pull 'em both. If you wanna go forward, squeeze with your legs. If Tom tries to stop and eat some grass or leaves on the bushes, pull one rein and kick, to get him out of there. Got it?"

I nodded. It seemed simple.

"Great, now just stay right there," he said, turning back into the darkness of the barn.

He emerged with a much smaller horse, all blond.

"Come 'ere kiddo!" the man called to my sister. She broke loose from my mother's hold and rushed to her horse.

"This here's Goldie," he said. "Now give him a little pet on his nose to make friends," the man instructed.

"Hi Goldie," my sister said softly, lightly stroking the

horse's soft muzzle.

After making some last minute adjustments to the saddle, the man then hoisted my sister into the saddle, and gave her the same instructions on how to turn, stop, and go.

"Cassey, let's go!" The man hollered into the barn, cupping his hands over his mouth.

Then, a girl emerged, much younger than the old man, leading her own horse. She had on the same uniform, hair tied back in an old baseball hat, jeans, and chaps—except she wore a T-shirt, not flannel.

As soon as she was outside, she threw her reins over her horse's head, lifted her left leg into one stirrup, and pulled herself into her saddle unassisted. She looked like she knew what she was doing.

"How long, hour or half?" she asked him.

"Half," he replied, as he patted her horse on the rump and headed back into the stable.

"Hi girls, I'm Cassey, and I'll be taking you on your trail ride today. What are your names?"

"I'm Victoria," I replied.

"And I'm Mary!" my sister exclaimed, making sure her small voice reached the trail leader.

"Great. Now look, girls, this is how it's going to work," she explained. "I'll be in front, then Victoria, then Mary. Got it?"

"Got it," we replied in unison.

"If you want to stop, you pull back on the reins. If you want to turn right, pull the right rein. If you want to turn left, pull the left rein. If you want to go forward, kick lightly."

"OK," we agreed impatiently.

"But do not ever, *ever*, kick the horse *and* jiggle the reins, OK?"

"OK!" We shrieked in unison, anxious to embark on this new adventure.

"Bye, Mom!" we shouted over our shoulders as our horses followed in line behind our guide's horse.

We meandered through the trails for a while and then got bored.

My little sister rebelliously tested the last rule the guide gave us: never kick and jiggle the reins.

"Ahhh!!" she screamed suddenly as her horse flew past mine in a full gallop.

"Ayyy!!" I screamed as my horse took off after hers. I squeezed my eyes shut and clutched the horn on the saddle. We left our guide behind, tearing through narrow trails at terrifying speeds.

I opened my eyes to see a wooden bridge over a stream and then, just as soon as I saw it, we raced across it, still accelerating. I was scared, but also overcome with excitement over how fast we were galloping through the woods—trees and branches brushed past my face just as I saw them. I was in another world, having never known speed like this.

Then I heard the feverish clambering of hooves behind me and saw the guide frantically kicking her horse to gallop past mine, and then up alongside my sister's horse. I watched as she leaned her whole upper body off to the left, reaching for my sister's horse's reins from around his ears. She was suspended over my sister's horse's head for a few strides, unable to grab hold of the reins tangled loosely around the horse's head and ears. My sister's horse's natural instinct to race a horse running alongside him then kicked in, and he sped up. My horse followed in yet another gear. I saw my sister's body start leaning to the left. She was in danger of falling, which, at this speed, with my horse right on her horse's tail, was bad news.

"Bay, stay in the middle!" I shrieked as loudly as I could. I started calling my sister "Bay" because it was a lot cooler than calling her "Baby," like the rest of the family did.

"Hold on to the horn!" I screamed again.

I didn't know if she could hear me, as the thundering of three sets of hoofs on the dirt trail was deafening. But then I saw her body land in the middle of the saddle after a few more strides.

"Girls, stop screaming!" The guide screamed at us, "You'll scare the horses!"

I thought to myself, *they're already scared! What more could they do?*

I shouldn't have thought that. I looked up and saw that my sister's horse and the guide were quickly approaching a drop in the trail, leading to a wooden bridge, built over a sizable river.

"*No*!!" I was overcome with fear, tears obstructed my vision, I could no longer breathe, my heart was in my throat, and I could not feel my hands.

"We're NOT going down!" the guide yelled, more to herself than to us.

Acting with one more wave of heroism, the girl kicked her horse to speed up, cutting off my sister's horse. Then, as the beast started running into the brush alongside the trail, she leaned over, almost onto his neck, grabbed my sister's reins, and jerked them back with a violent backward thrust of her body. The animal's front legs straightened, causing him to come to a sliding stop, bouncing my sister in the saddle for a few strides. My horse slammed into hers, but didn't push him any further, as his feet were now planted firmly into the earth.

I heard our heroine breathe a heavy sigh. I then succumbed to the fear that had gripped me through the entire episode. My body was shaking, I couldn't breathe, and tears exploded from my eyes. My sister turned around, and was my mirror, her face red and wet with tears.

"Is everyone OK?" our heroine asked.

We couldn't answer, still gasping for breath, clutching the horns on our saddles.

The guide then, still with my sister's reins in her left hand, agilely swung her right leg over her horse's neck and hopped off. During her acrobatic dismount, she maintained a mystical, invisible control over her horse. She didn't even have her horse's reins in her hand, and he obediently stood immobilized while she vaulted off of his back. Once on the ground, she loosely looped her right arm through her horse's reins, and tightly held my sister's reins in her left hand.

"OK, girls, we're just going to walk back to the stables, nice and slow."

My sister was silent. I tried to be polite and answer, but my heart was still pounding, beating against my lungs and interfering with my breathing. I forced myself to answer, though. This girl had saved us. The least I could do was respond. So I took in one large breath, and whispered, "OK."

When we finally got back to the barn, I was still crying.

"What's wrong?" my mother inquired.

"Ask *her*!" as I pointed at my sister, and ran to the car as soon as I was off the horse.

"I never want to see another horse ever again!" I declared. "I hate horses! *Hate* them!" I repeated adamantly as I ran to the car.

A few days passed and somehow that terrorizing fear vanished, leaving only the memory of extreme exultation. I wanted to go riding again.

"Mom, can we go back to the barn?"

I was hooked.

3

September came and dragged me back to the city. School was a tedious blur. Days crawled. I watched minute after minute languidly tick by on every clock in every classroom. One hour in a classroom was an eternity. My gaze was either fixed on the clock, or drifting to the open window. I yearned to be outside, where I could breathe.

The afternoons at home made up for the tedium of the school day. Home was where the action was, for many reasons. First, it was crowded—my mother's parents had moved in to babysit my sister and me while she worked. My grandmother was always angry about something. It was usually my grandfather's fault. When it wasn't my grandfather's fault, it was my father's fault.

On one occasion, amidst a fury of slamming pots and pans because my grandfather had forgotten to buy butter on his grocery run, I asked her, "If you hate him so much, why don't you just get a divorce?"

I had heard the word "divorce" so much, and saw that it meant removing the evil man from the house, so clearly it was a logical solution to her hatred of my grandfather.

"Why bother now? I'm too old! I'm just waiting to die! Oh God, just take me already!" she wailed.

Another contributing factor to the perpetual excitement of my home life was my father's unannounced visits. He had moved out and was not allowed to come over when my mother wasn't home, but that didn't stop him. His visits usually resulted in my grandmother brandishing a wooden spoon at him, ready to attack, me jumping between them, screaming at the top of my lungs, and then the police would show up.

It often went something like this, "Get out of here, you pig!" my grandmother would shout at the intruder.

"This is my house, you fat old whore!" he would snap back. "This is my house, MY house!" he repeated.

"Get away from me!" she would scream.

"I'm going to kill you and your whore daughter!"

The death threats were my signal to intervene. Even though I never called him "Dad," I knew it would appease him and then he might listen to me.

"Dad! Please! Go!"

"No way! This is MY house! *She* needs to go!"

"DAD! Please, stop!" I would then start to cry as he turned back toward the door. He would leave, slamming the door so hard it shook the house.

By the time I was seven, the divorce and all its drama were in full swing. Police were frequent visitors at my house. We even made the front page of the metro section in *The New York Times*.

On one occasion after we had finished eating dinner, the doorbell rang. My mother answered the door, and there they were in full uniform. I wondered why the cops were here at night, because they usually came during the day, when my father intruded on us.

"Hi Mariana, we have to take you down to the precinct for some questioning," one officer began as my mother invited them in, and they stepped into the living room. I watched the intruders smear the dirt from their heavy black boots all over the rug in our living room. I was sitting on the couch in my pajamas, barefoot. My sister sat next to me, also in her pajamas and barefoot. I recognized the silent officer as one of the officers who often visited during the day. When he caught my stare, he looked away and then back at my mother.

Some conversation followed, but my grandmother scurried us to our bedroom. As she opened the door to let us in, I turned and saw my mother's back, her wrists bound behind her in shiny silver handcuffs. With one shove, we were alone in our bedroom.

"What's happening?" my sister asked.

"I don't know," I replied. I should have tried to coax and comfort her, but the sight of my mother shackled helplessly with steel on her wrists sucked the wind out of my lungs. I couldn't speak; a lump in my throat was choking me.

After some time passed, our grandfather opened the door. "Your mother will be back in the morning," he said gruffly. "Go to sleep."

Just as he shut the door, I heard my grandmother crying in the kitchen, over the water running on the clinking dishes she was washing in the sink.

Many years later, my mother told me that she had been arrested because my father had called the police and reported that she had threatened his life. Everyone knew it was a lie, not to mention a ridiculous one, but the cops still had to abide by their policies.

4

As I grew older, my father and the police intrusions after school became less frequent, and instead, my afternoons were filled with extracurricular activities such as piano and French lessons. Even though home life was less stressful, the afternoons were still tedious.

"Mom, I hate piano," I declared to my mother minutes before my weekly lesson was to begin. "And French lessons are pointless; no one speaks French," I continued.

"French eets very important language to know!" she huffed in her Romanian accent. Her articles and prepositions were frequently lost in translation.

"Mom, it's English and Spanish in this country, that's it."

"So what, you just want to sit in front of TV every day after school like a bump? No way!" she proclaimed.

"Bum," I corrected.

"*Victoria*!" she roared. She hated to be corrected, especially when making a point.

"Mom, I just want to ride," I pleaded.

"Ride? *Ride*?" she repeated with extra emphasis. "*How* am I supposed to find a horse in Queens?" she mumbled to herself, picking up the yellow pages.

"Mariana!" my grandmother howled, overhearing the conversation about horses. "Girls do not ride horses!" she commanded.

"Mama, this is my child, if she wants to ride, she will ride!" she returned in Romanian.

"So she can break her bones like you did? I do not want to hear it!" my grandmother exploded.

"Then don't listen!" my mother shot back.

The following Saturday, my mother gave me her old riding boots and gloves and I put on my least favorite pair of jeans. Then she drove me to Leslie's Riding School—a barn fifteen minutes away from home, in Queens. One trail ride, and I was hooked.

I didn't meet Leslie for a while. She was usually off tending to things more important than horse-crazed ten-year-old girls. But when I did meet her, she was not the warm, caring horsewoman I expected. She was curt, gruff, and mostly kept to herself. Being around her felt like being in the military—she only spoke to dole out orders to her staff. However, if she could do something herself, she would. Her staff both feared and respected her. She was an accomplished horsewoman, having been raised with horses and inheriting her barn from her father, who was another well-known horseman and blacksmith, as the newspaper clippings on the walls revealed.

I found her extremely intimidating because of how much she knew and how cold she was. But I wanted to be like her. She rode in jeans and chaps like a cowgirl, defiantly breaking the rules of what it means to be a girl. I desperately wanted a pair of cool chaps just like hers—black with fringes. But my mother couldn't afford chaps like Leslie's, so I rode in old boots and torn jeans. I looked like a cross between a homeless person and an equestrian. Leslie, on the other hand, was every bit the cool and confident horsewoman in her jeans and chaps.

Two people could not have been more opposite than Leslie and I. She carried her sturdy five-foot seven-inch frame with purpose and pride. I barely came up to her rib cage and just tried to stay out of the way. My long, dark hair was always tied into a braid, while Leslie had brazenly cut her sandy-blonde hair as short as a man's. Her clear, blue eyes pierced their victim. My brown eyes, on the other hand, had no such intensity. What I appreciated about her, though, was that she never spoke to me like I was a child, as everyone else did. She treated me like an adult.

I searched for any reason to spend more time at the barn. I volunteered to do any chore to extend my barn time and score some free rides. The staff and regular trail riders nicknamed me "barn rat." I had fallen deeply in love with horses.

On the back of a horse, I was whole. On the back of a horse, I was not insecure, anxious, and unsure. On the back of a horse, I was confident, connected, and centered.

In the barn, I felt at home. The sounds of the horses chewing their hay, blowing their noses, and swishing their tails washed away my worries. When I walked past a horse offering his nose for a pat, his breath brimmed with the sweet smell of fresh hay. The feel of their soft coats and muzzles under my hands planted me firmly in their world of innocence, acceptance, honesty, and love. After I groomed the horses, a film of dust and hair coated my clothes, leaving me with my very own piece of the barn to take home.

The barn had a small indoor riding ring, but the main attraction was riding in the trails out in Queens Park. Eventually I came to know all the horses in the barn, but I had a few favorites: Topper, Star, Dusty, Red, and Flash. I had learned to ride in English saddles, which meant I no longer needed the security of a horn on Western saddles to hang onto in case I got scared. I wasn't scared anymore, not even when I rode Blaze.

Blaze was bigger than most of the other horses. And he had blue eyes, unlike any of the others. He was white with splashes of brown and gray. I thought he was ugly. And mean. Blaze bucked off a lot of people—more than half of those brave (or ignorant) enough to climb onto his back. I was scared the first time I got on him. But then I thought he could sense my fear and would definitely buck me off. So I got on and told him (and myself) that I wasn't afraid.

I'm not afraid of you, Blaze. I'm not afraid. I'm in charge, I'm the boss, you listen to me, I repeated to myself.

Amazingly, that horse never bucked me off. He didn't even try.

Topper was my favorite. He was a Palomino, so he was all blond. He was sweet, too. He always nuzzled my hand before I got on, as if to say, "Hey buddy, nice to see you again." Topper was totally reliable. He was like a machine; if I pushed the "go" button, he went, if I pushed the "stop" button, he stopped. He never did anything bad. But I wasn't allowed to ride him all the time. Leslie made me ride all of the horses.

Even though I had dogs, goldfish, and parakeets at home, I desperately wanted my own horse—a horse that only I could ride and that I could spend all day with. A horse that everyone knew was mine, not just borrowed until the next person came to ride it. This wish became an obsessive yearning, and I was not quiet about what I wanted.

"I wish I could have my own horse," I sighed to Sherwin on a trail ride. Sherwin was a short, eccentric Filipino who came every Saturday to ride his favorite horse, Star. He never wore the same outfit twice, and he was the only man I ever saw who wore a printed scarf, like the ones my grandmother wore on her head. He was always so happy. He was the happiest person I knew. I was fascinated by his everlasting good mood.

Star was cute, like a toy. She was a short, sassy white Appaloosa with brown spots. She had a thin, frayed white tail and a huge rump. Whenever she cantered, she helicoptered her small, wispy tail around her rotund behind, completing a full circle with every stride. I could never really concentrate on my own ride if I had to ride behind her because her hilarious canter was too distracting. She was perpetually perturbed, always pinning her ears back and gnashing her teeth at other horses. I couldn't quite understand why Sherwin, who was unendingly jovial and carefree, took such a liking to one of the moodiest mares in the barn. But as long as she had someone who doted on her, I was happy. Every horse deserved their own person to make them feel special and important.

Unfortunately, Leslie overheard my wish to Sherwin and huffed, "Ha! You want a horse now? Just so you can forget about it when you discover boys in a few years? Don't waste your time, you're just like all the other little girls who want a horse until they discover boys."

I was stunned. I couldn't even think of anything to say. I never thought about boys or even my friends, outside of school.

"Don't mind her, darling. She's having a bad day," Sherwin whispered, flashing his bright white teeth through his smile.

5

As I got older, people started to get more and more aggravating. Everyone had an opinion. Everyone told me what to do, or why what I did was wrong or right, for whatever reason.

I started to see adults in a new light. They were not always right, they did not always know what to do, and they did not always have the right answer. My mother was not perfect. She was no longer the confident, single parent I knew when I was younger. She was always scared and worried. She started asking me for advice. Me! I was about ten when I became her confidante.

My grandparents were narrow-minded, judgmental, and relentlessly unhappy. My father was just nuts. He insisted that everyone was out to get him and that he was the greatest thing to walk the face of the earth. I was the second best thing, because I was his daughter.

I also lost a great deal of respect for most of my teachers when I discovered they all had an answer book that went with their lectures. How could I trust a history teacher to teach me history when she didn't know where King Tut was buried without the answer book in her hand? I started to feel alone, because I couldn't and wouldn't trust adults. They weren't better or smarter than me. They were just older.

Then, finally, I met Mrs. Edwards in the fourth grade. She taught writing. She was the only black teacher in the school, and my father's attempts at indoctrinating me with his racism failed because of her.

She was composed, she was patient, and she was smart, really smart. I knew she was brilliant, not just because she could recite lines from the books we read from memory, nor because she was impressively eloquent. She was intelligent because no matter what opinion I articulated in class, she had a seemingly magical skill of molding it to whatever she wanted. I had never before met someone who could take hold of my thoughts and manipulate them as she wished. My father tried, but he was too obvious about it. Mrs. Edwards had finesse. She was graceful and elegant. I was fascinated by her ability to lead my mind in any direction she wanted, like it belonged to her instead of me. That didn't mean I gave in to her. On the contrary, I tried harder and harder to resist her mind control and actually persuade *her* to agree with *me*. What set Mrs. Edwards apart from most adults is that she invited my challenges. She forced me to think, rather than memorize.

I once engaged her in a debate (or she engaged me, I still don't know who started it), which was a great thrill for me, because I felt like I was able to challenge an intellectual.

"You know, kids, my teenage daughter insists that I not go into her room, which I think is ridiculous, since it's my house she's living in," she vented.

"But Mrs. Edwards, you yourself just said it was *her* room," I argued.

"Yeah, so?" she continued.

"Well, if it's *her* room, doesn't *she* get to say who's allowed in or out?" I persisted.

"No, because I own the whole house, and that room is one of the rooms in the house that *I* own. Therefore, *I* own that room too, and since it's mine, *I* should be able to determine who is allowed in or out," she clarified.

"But you keep calling it *her* room. That means you know it's not your room. So, since you know it's not your room, and you even call it *her* room, it really belongs to her, and she should be able to do whatever she wants with it." I didn't really feel argumentative; I just thought she was wrong and I felt like she needed to know.

She smiled and proceeded with the lesson of the day.

In school, I had made two really good friends, Hanna and Sabrina. Both were outgoing, social, and smart, and we had a lot of fun. We ate lunch together every day except every other Wednesday. For some reason, the school enrolled Sabrina, me, my little sister, and a few other students in a lunchtime seminar with the guidance counselor, to talk about divorce. I had been grateful to have school as an escape from my home life, so I really resented how divorce now followed me to school. I never really had much to say about divorce, and didn't feel like I was being deprived of anything, so I wasn't terribly interested in sharing my story.

I was stunned when, in one of the lunch sessions, Sabrina suddenly broke down and started sobbing, as she was talking about her father. I had no idea what to say. She was my friend, so it was my job to soothe her, but I had nothing comforting to say. All I could do was pet her hair as I wondered, *what's the big deal? Isn't everyone better off with their father out of the house? Why is she crying?*

Either there's something really wrong with me, or really wrong with her, I thought to myself as I walked home with my sister that afternoon. I was nowhere near as upset by divorce as she was. *It's got to be her*, I concluded.

6

Tango. I knew he was special from the moment he burst out of the horse trailer, like an over-amped boxer ready for the ring. He hopped back and forth, as if waiting for the perfect opportunity to throw out the first jab. Every signal he gave was a clear "stay away from me," but everything about him drew me in.

First, he didn't seem threatening, as he wasn't a large horse. He was unlike any horse I had ever seen, as his dark brown body contrasted with a bright blond mane and tail. Bright blond hair on a dark horse! It just never happens. He was the most exotic horse I had ever seen. Everything about him was stunning. His yellow hair slashed the air with every furious toss of his head. He reared up and struck out with his front legs at whoever approached him. I stood just a few feet away from him, mesmerized.

"You're riding this one until he's calm enough for trail riders," Leslie told me, as she wrestled him from his handler and struggled to get him into the barn.

Yes! My heart leaped at the thought that he would be mine, even if just temporarily, but I coolly responded, "OK." Still, I couldn't control the huge smile that took over my face.

Tango had an attitude, even with me. He wasn't dangerous to ride. He was just annoying most of the time. He was disobedient and pretty much did whatever he wanted, whenever he felt like it. If he tired of trotting, he stopped in the middle of the arena. When I kicked him, he went backward instead of forward. I was more like an ornament on his back than his rider. But after a few weeks of lessons with Mandy, Leslie's best trainer, second only to Leslie, I got the green light to ride Tango outside.

I first took Tango out on the trails with a large group, about ten horse and rider pairs, under Mandy's supervision. I managed to keep him under control through the hour-long ride, until the final stretch, when we let the horses canter. As soon as the horse in front of me disappeared around the bend, I squeezed Tango's side with my right leg, to cue him to pick up the left lead canter. He exploded into the gait. I wrapped my hands and reins in his mane, just as Mom told me she used to do with crazy horses.

Suddenly, I found myself crouched low in the saddle, in the half-seat position, giving the horse the green light to go faster. I knew I should have sat back and slowed him down, but I couldn't help myself. I wanted to fly just as much as he did.

As soon as I leaned into half-seat position, his body flattened, and we were galloping through the trail. The ends of his long yellow mane tickled my face, and the wind forced me to squint my eyes, but this ride was like no other. I felt alive, awake, free. Even though I was sitting on a runaway horse tearing through the woods, this ride was nothing like my first riding experience. I wasn't completely in control now, either, but I was much older, almost eleven years old. This time, there was no fear, only exhilaration. I had been riding many hyper horses at Leslie's for the past year and a half, so I knew I could handle Tango. But beyond that, I trusted him. So I let him go. I inched my hands forward to let his head extend and his body stretch in the run. Even though I was totally out of control, I had never felt so united with a horse; we were one. We took the same breath, we moved with the same purpose. Then I saw the huge puddle that spanned across the entire bridle path.

"OK, buddy, let's see if you jump," I whispered in his ears. Suddenly, my sure-footed powerhouse seemed unsteady and when his ears pricked forward at the sight of the puddle, he wavered. In one moment, he was heading straight for the middle of the puddle, but in the next moment, he seemed to head to the outside of it. He didn't know where to go, and I wasn't sure where to go, either.

But just as we were one stride in front of the seven-foot puddle, his hind legs slammed into the earth, catapulting us both over the hurdle. And then we were flying. Everything stopped. I couldn't hear, breathe, smell, feel . . . nothing. The world was on mute. It was like hitting pause during a movie. Then, when he landed, I realized I was no longer holding the reins—they were tangled around his ears!

Holy crap! If Leslie sees me galloping without reins, I'll be in so much trouble! I panicked. *I need to stop him before we clear the bend, and get to the clearing where everyone else is waiting.*

I couldn't grab hold of the reins; they were too far from my reach.

How am I going to stop without any reins? I hope he doesn't crash into one of the other horses!

I knew the best way to stop an out of control horse was to turn him, but since I didn't have my reins, I tried to use my body to turn, shifting all my weight to the right. I grabbed a big chunk of his mane, and pulled back, like I would have on the reins. It worked! He stopped right in front of a tree, nowhere near any of the other trail riders. But Leslie saw it all.

"*Victoria*!" I heard the anger already in her voice. "You had no reins!" she roared.

"Yeah, sorry," I mumbled.

"Yeah, *sorry*?" she mimicked. "You are not allowed out on the trails with that horse anymore until you can control him!"

"OK," I said, accepting my punishment.

She then turned in a huff and trotted away on her horse.

We were grounded. We had to work on his training in the indoor arena until he was obedient enough to go out on the trails again. Mandy gave us more lessons.

In one of our lessons, Tango started prancing. He seemed to tense up every muscle in his body, coil his now muscular neck so that his nose was practically in his chest, and gather his front legs close to his hind legs. I could feel he was building up the power to bound forward at any moment. It was as if his body was an accordion, compressing each end. Since I had never experienced anything like this, I asked Mandy what he was doing. I was fascinated by the lightness in the reins and the energy building behind me. It was as if I were sitting in an airplane, and the more power that the engine generated in the back, the higher the plane would rise in the front. I sensed that if I gave him the slightest hint that I wanted to go, the energy in his hindquarters would slingshot us forward.

Oh, that's why he took off, I realized, remembering when he took off with me in the woods. *I leaned forward and gave him the reins!* I felt enlightened.

And yet, here, in the indoor ring, as long as I sat straight and kept some contact with the reins, it was like sitting on an idling engine that was ready to go at the first cue.

"It's this sport called dressage, where the horses do prancing movements," Mandy explained.

"Do you know dressage?" I inquired.

"Yeah, a little," Maureen replied.

"Can you teach me?" I asked.

"I have to ask Leslie first."

After Leslie approved, we began working on the dressage that Tango knew.

"The prancing thing he does is called piaffe. That's when they trot in place," Mandy explained.

Wow, I thought, *trotting in place . . . how does that even happen?*

"You don't want to do any jumping?" she asked.

"Why? All we ever do is just make the jumps higher. That's not as fun as this stuff. It's kind of like he's dancing, which is way cooler than jumping fences," I reasoned.

When my mother picked me up at the end of the day, I asked her, "Hey Mom, ever heard of dressage?"

"Yes," she smiled slowly, as if I had just discovered a precious secret, "dressage is like dancing with a horse. It is the most elegant sport. Me, I was too stupid as a kid to understand it; I always preferred the excitement of jumping. But I did compete in dressage at the highest levels for two years in Romania, after I broke my collarbone."

"You broke your collarbone?" I asked.

"Yes, at the National Jumping Championships in Romania. The horse, she fell into the jump and got her legs tangled in the poles. It was bad, she died at that show."

"I'm sorry, Mom. Was she your favorite?" I asked, knowing I would be devastated if anything happened to Tango or any of my other favorites.

"No, she was just assigned to me for that show by the army. But I was very sad . . ."

"Wait, you were in the army?" I interrupted.

"No, I just rode on the army team. They had a stable open to the public, like Leslie. So if you wanted to ride and compete, you had to wear the army uniform."

"Oh," I said, intrigued about this other life my mother had led. She was apparently more than just a dentist.

"Anyway, the doctors said not to get on a horse for a year. So I started riding dressage two months later. I have a good book on dressage, you want to read it?"

"Yes!" I exclaimed.

As soon as we got home, she gave me the book and I was immediately intrigued by the cover. It had a picture of a proud Olympian astride her elegant horse, executing an advanced dressage movement called the passage, a highly elevated trot.

That picture spoke to me on so many levels. For one, I could tell she had the same lightness in the reins as I had with Tango when he was doing his prancing thing. I could envision his hind legs pushing his body off the ground, and imagined how lofty it would look in real life.

I skimmed through the 250-page book in an hour and then started again, slowly, from the beginning. The next day, I asked Mandy to teach me all of the dressage movements I had read about.

"Well, I don't know everything, kid, but I'll teach you what I do know."

That was good enough for me. I felt privileged to ride Tango, and was eager to learn how to dance with my horse.

7

Even though I was at the barn all day every Saturday and Sunday, the weeks grew longer and longer. Five days without riding was too long! So my mother let me go riding on Wednesdays too, after school. I was delighted.

Since I had a regular presence at the barn, I had become friendly with all of its different sets of visitors. I was friendly with the Saturday morning crowd, the Saturday afternoon crowd, the Sunday crowd, the Wednesday night crowd, and the staff.

The end of the cold winter was punctuated by my twelfth birthday. It had fallen on a Sunday, and I could think of no better way to spend the day than to be at the barn all day. Even though it was the end of March, it was frigid and snowy, so most of the regular trail riders skipped that day of riding. But all of those horses still needed to be exercised, so I got to ride more horses than usual. By the end of the day, I was physically cold but my heart was warmed with contentment, having spent my birthday doing exactly what I wanted—riding.

Then, as I was sweeping the barn floor at the end of the day,

Mandy called me into the office. Only the staff were allowed in the office, which made the invitation to the perpetually off-limits room all the more intriguing. I set down the broom and walked over to the office, noticing that I was the only one in the barn, a strange sight on a Sunday afternoon.

As I turned the doorknob and slowly pushed the door forward, I heard "SURPRISE!" I froze. Everyone was there! I was too overwhelmed to say anything, and luckily everyone began singing the "Happy Birthday" song. I looked around the room, filled with my favorite people: most of the staff, some of the most dedicated, regular trail riders, my mother, and even Leslie. Mandy came to me with a box full of ice cream cones decorated with smiley faces. They even knew I preferred ice cream to cake!

At the end of the song, they all exclaimed, "Happy Birthday, Victoria!" in unison.

"Wow, thank you," was all I could muster, overwhelmed by all of the attention.

"Dig in, kiddo!" Mandy encouraged, and she lowered the box of ice cream to me.

"No, wait! Before she gets ice cream all over herself . . ." Leslie said from the back, coming toward me with another, larger box.

Mandy stepped aside, and Leslie took her place in front of me, lowering another big box. This one was wrapped with a beautiful, huge white bow.

I stared, not expecting any of this, and not quite sure what to do.

"Well, don't you want to see your present?" Leslie asked.

"Yes, thanks," I mumbled as I took the box from her. It was large, but light. I wondered what it could be as I carefully undid the wrapping, so as not to tear the paper—I wanted to save it.

"Just rip it!" someone urged. I looked up and was met with multiple sets of eyes.

Leslie crouched in front of me, with her back to the crowd,

and helped me unwrap it on the floor.

Once I had taken off the wrapping paper, I admired the big, blank white box, just touched that they had bought me a present. And birthday ice cream cones. How did they even know? Why had they gone through all this trouble?

"Open it already!" someone else shrieked.

"Just give her a minute!" Leslie hissed, spinning toward the offending voice.

"Take your time," she said to me quietly. I looked up at her, into her captivating blue eyes. I had never been this close to her.

I broke from Leslie's stare, slipped my index finger under the fold of the box, and lifted the lid. The powerful smell of new leather erupted from the box. I lifted the black suede fabric, and then saw the fringes. I stood up as I lifted the entire gift out—they had bought me a pair of black suede chaps, with fringes! It was what I had wanted for so long, but I couldn't remember telling anyone. I had wanted these *exact* chaps, and now I had them. Tears welled up and a lump grew in my throat. I couldn't speak. I looked up at Leslie, and she simply stared down at me. I noticed the slightest hint of a smile lift one corner of her mouth.

"So? What do you think? Do you like them?" some of her staff began to inquire, curious at my silence.

Then Leslie turned around, facing them in front of me.

"She likes them. Have some ice cream," she ordered.

Everyone swarmed the box of ice cream cones. Leslie then turned back to me, and asked, "You want to try them on? See if they fit?"

"Yeah," I said as I wrapped them around my body and fastened the front buckle. I zipped one leg, then the other. They fit perfectly, as if they were made just for me.

"Perfect," she said, satisfied.

"Yeah," I beamed. "Thank you so much," was all I could say.

She smiled subtly, then cleared her throat and hardened again.

"You're welcome. Now, go get a cone before they're all gone," she instructed.

I wore my new chaps with unbridled pride. Now I was a real horsewoman, just like Leslie. I was one step closer to being as good a rider as she was.

The fact that she got me a present made me believe that Leslie didn't hate me. I cared deeply about her opinion of me, because I respected her so much. I wanted to be exactly like her—always sure of myself, and able to handle any horse.

Nevertheless, Leslie remained distant and continued to turn me down when I asked her for lessons. She insisted that I take lessons with Mandy. But I could see the way Leslie rode and the way Mandy rode. Leslie knew something that Mandy didn't. Mandy sat on top of her horse, but when Leslie was on a horse, they became one. I wanted to learn from Leslie. I couldn't understand why she wouldn't teach me. She was the most knowledgeable instructor there and nothing I did could impress her.

Then, one day, she told me to grab Firefly—another favorite horse of mine—and get on. She was getting on her horse, Illusion, a majestic white Lipizzaner, and she was going to give a lesson to a woman I had never met. I was the lead rider, and they would follow. I loved being in the front, being the leader.

I easily ignored most of the chattering behind me, until the final stretch of the trail ride, when Leslie told her student, "You see that kid up there? You could ride all day, every day, for the rest of your life, and you'll still never be as good as she is."

Wow! All these years I wondered whether she even liked me, and now she just said I'm a good rider! I marveled to myself.

"But she'll never make it to the Olympics."

The wind was knocked out of me. *What the hell?* I thought. I was so confused. *Why would she say that?* I wondered silently. *Why not even give me the chance?*

When the person who I most idolized announced that I would never be a top competitive rider, I was overcome with a desire to prove her wrong.

OK, Leslie, I'll show you, I thought defiantly.

8

Fifth grade was spent in total anticipation of sixth grade, because I was part of the "cool crowd," and the "cool kids" in sixth grade ruled the whole elementary school. I had waited years for the chance to be in the coolest grade, and I would enter it with my cool friends. But unfortunately, my mother had other plans for me—braces and private school.

"I hate you, I hate you, I hate you! You're ruining my life! You're not my real mother, my real mother wouldn't do this to me! I *know* I'm adopted!" I protested upon learning her plans for me.

Meanwhile, my sister would get to stay in public school while I had to start sixth grade in private school.

I had to wear a stiff, ugly uniform. And I had to wear a skirt—a big change from the jeans I had been living in for the past several years. The variety of the outfit consisted of either a wool skirt or a polyester skirt. I opted for the wool skirt, since it actually moved a little and didn't feel like I had wrapped my waist in rigid brown paper. Also, for the first time since I was a little kid, I had to wear tights. Once again, I was forced to endure the scratching of itchy fabric directly on my skin. To top it all off, I had to button myself into a rigid, white blouse.

I looked at myself in the mirror. *This isn't me. I don't belong in a skirt or tights or a buttoned up white blouse.* But I was already dressed in the ridiculous costume so I felt utterly defeated. There was no going back to my friends, my school, my *life*.

I drifted to the living room, waiting for my mother to gather her things and drive me to school. I had to depend on her for a ride, rather than walk to school on my own.

"You look so cute! Let's take a picture!" she gushed.

"No, I look like a dork," I fumed.

Then my sister came in. "No, you don't. You look like a nerd!"

"See?" I said to my mother.

"Baby! Get out!" she yelled at my sister.

But it was true. The uniform was horrible. Judging by the hideous outfit, I was sure the school would be even worse. And the braces made me feel hideous. I had to meet new people, who would ridicule me. I missed my friends. I wondered what they were doing. How would their first day of school be? I was sure they would roam the halls like they owned them, and command respect from all the younger kids.

My mother dumped me in the front of the building, and left me to fend for myself. I found my homeroom. I saw an empty desk near the door and sat down.

"You can't sit there," protested a stout, imposing Asian boy.

I stayed where I was. I hated this place and was ready to face my first enemy. I was so consumed with rage over having been ripped away from my old, wonderful life, that I didn't care about making a single friend here. In fact, I welcomed a fight with anybody, everybody—it would make it easier not to have to talk to anybody. I could never be friends with these rich, snobby kids, whose parents dropped them off in Mercedes and BMW cars. I even saw a *limousine* drop off one kid. A limousine! For a *kid*! It was obnoxious. I was not like these kids, and never would be, I vowed to myself. I resented my mother for trying to force me to be like these people.

I turned to look him right in the eyes.

"Tough," I seethed.

"Yo, man! That's messed up!" he said, exasperated.

"Mike! Be quiet, she can sit wherever she wants!" the teacher reprimanded.

I turned to him again, and deliberately curled my lips into a sinister smile, just for him.

"Yo, man . . ." he began to mutter, shaking his head at the notebook on his desk.

The two girls who sat in front of me kept turning around to smile at me.

Why the hell do they keep smiling at me? I wondered.

It made me uncomfortable. Nobody in Queens smiles at strangers. You're not even supposed to make eye contact with strangers. Everyone knows that.

At the end of the class, the first girl turned around in her chair and said, "Hi, I'm Evelyn, we can be friends if you want."

"OK," I answered cautiously, not enthused by the invitation, but also unwilling to hurt this girl's feelings. She seemed nice enough.

"Yeah, me too, I want to be friends too, I'm Andy."

"OK, hi," I replied.

I felt like sixth grade dragged on and on, but I took solace in my horse-filled weekends at Leslie's. Unfortunately, my mother had different plans for that part of my life as well.

"So you know Yvette who rides Shiloh?" my mother asked me on the way to the barn one Saturday morning.

"Yeah, so?"

"Well, she said there is a bigger barn upstate where you can really learn to ride, and be better."

"So?"

"Well I think you should start riding there instead of at Leslie's."

"No!" I protested.

"Do you want to be a trail rider all your life?"

"Why are you trying to ruin my life!" I shrieked, now in tears. "What about Tango, and Firefly, and . . ."

"Tango and Firefly will be fine without you," she retorted, sternly.

"I can't believe you're doing this to me. Why are you doing this to me!" I cried.

"It's for your own good. You're too young to understand now, you'll understand later."

I knew I had no choice. She had made up her mind—again. Life at Leslie's was over; my life was over.

After my final weekend of riding at Leslie's, that Sunday evening, I tearfully kissed all of horses on the nose for the last time, lingering on my favorites. I hugged the staff I had come to know so well. I even hugged Leslie. Leslie's piercing blue eyes had been dulled by the red around them. After we hugged, she turned on her heel and shut the office door behind her.

I was left alone in the barn, devastated and unwilling to leave the safety and warmth of this home. I would never love any place more than I loved Leslie's.

9

My mother booked me an 8:00 a.m. lesson with Pam the next Saturday at the new, fancy barn. The distance between the new barn and home meant we had to leave at seven o'clock in the morning—on a Saturday. This was a huge difference from the quick fifteen-minute drive to Leslie's. I already hated this new barn.

"Where the hell is this place, on the other side of the country?" I started, getting into the car at about the same time I would normally be waking up for school.

"You can sleep in the car," Mom said.

"This is bullshit," I declared.

"No cursing," she scolded.

"Don't give me anything to curse about then. Just let me go back to my old school and old barn."

"Victoria!" she screamed. "It's enough!"

And that was the end of that discussion.

As we pulled into the driveway of Oakwood Farm, my eyes scanned the perfectly groomed arenas, the green fields, and the abundant space. Surprisingly, I felt calm and safe, the feeling you get when you come home after a long trip. It looked very different from Leslie's small barn in the city, but somehow, familiar.

We walked to the office to check in, and behind the glass sat a tall, thin woman. Her hair was as long as mine, but it was bright red.

"Hi, how can I help you?" she asked with a warm smile.

"This is Victoria, she has a lesson at eight o'clock, with Pam," my mother answered.

"Oh, Pam's out sick today, so I'll be teaching you. I'm Cynthia, I'll be right out," she said, crossing something off a page in the book in front of her. She then rose from the desk and came out to the public viewing area.

As she appeared in the doorway, she was taller than I had imagined, about six feet tall. She was thin but not skinny. She looked strong but still feminine. Her lips were red, as were her nails. I could see her long, black eyelashes from where I stood. They fluttered over a pair of perfectly symmetrical emerald green eyes. Her long, red hair was pulled back into a loose braid.

"Nice to meet you," she said, jutting her hand toward me.

"You, too," I replied, taking hold of her hand for a quick handshake.

"Well, Pam normally does the beginner jumpers, but I do the beginner dressage, so we'll do some dressage today. Do you know what dressage is?" she asked.

"Sort of, yeah."

"OK, well, we'll go ahead and give it a shot."

"OK," I replied.

My first lesson was not on a prancy horse at all. Fannie was the exact opposite of Tango. She was huge, brown all over, and lifeless, nothing like my compact, blonde, fiery Tango. Anything could set Tango off, but Fannie moved as if she were barely alive. I tired quickly from the constant kicking and squeezing to get her to move. My short legs did nothing to motivate the beast.

"That looked good!" my mother said, walking into the barn, after watching my first lesson.

I looked up at her, annoyed, already feeling the soreness in my legs.

"What are you talking about? That horse is barely alive, she can't even canter!" I shot back. "Tango can do a flat gallop if I just squeeze him a little!"

"Psht!" she let out angrily, "you are not riding trail horses for the rest of your life!"

I continued taking lessons from Cynthia. The farm's rule was that beginner riders had to take lessons with either Pam or Cynthia. Since Pam was the beginner jumping trainer, and Cynthia was the beginner dressage trainer, I opted to stick with Cynthia.

Cynthia had noticed my frustration with the slow moving Fannie, because for my next lesson, she assigned me a different horse—Bert. He was an equally huge horse, but slightly more alive. Like Fannie, Bert had no special markings, he was just big and red. Nothing like my exotic Tango with his blonde mane and tail contrasted against his dark brown body. I wondered if Tango missed me as I missed him. I wondered if he compared all of his new riders to the girl who snuck him peppermints and let him run.

Cynthia explained to me that Bert knew the basics of dressage, so he would be a good horse to learn on. Bert was a straightforward, uncomplicated, honest horse. I asked for something, and he did it. He was even comfortable to ride, despite his size. He cantered on cue, and taught me how to do leg-yields, a movement where the horse moves sideways, criss-crossing his legs as he moves. All I had to do was apply pressure with my right leg, and he would drift to the left across the arena. As it turned out, Tango and I had already been doing leg-yields in the park, to dodge rocks, logs, and puddles. But at least now I knew that move had a name, and it was a *dressage* movement.

Before I could grow too attached to Bert, Cynthia instructed me to ride Freddie. Freddie was half Bert's size, but he was not a pony. While Bert was tall and lanky, Freddie was short and stout. He was a little taller than Tango, but much more muscular. He was built like a truck, with a big chest and wide shoulders. He also had some markings that made him look cute—he was a light bay color, with the color fading into black at his knees, and then white stockings splashed on his legs, from his knees to his hooves. A white blaze traveled down his face, ending in a small white diamond on his pink nose. His black mane and tail contrasted with his light bay coloring. It was nothing like the blond and dark brown contrast Tango had, but it was not as boring as Bert's all over red or Fannie's all over dark brown coloring.

Before my first lesson on Freddie, I grabbed the saddle and bridle from the tack room to tack him up. I put the saddle on by myself, like I had learned at Leslie's. But any time I tried to put the bridle on over Freddie's ears, he shied and spun away from me in the stall. I was confused by his bizarre behavior, but resolved to get the bridle on myself. After many failed attempts, I realized I would be late for my lesson, and went to find Cynthia for help.

After slipping the bridle on, she said, "Some of these horses were rescued from slaughter, so they might have some issues. It looks like somebody hit Freddie around his ears and he never got over it. Don't worry, it has nothing to do with you," she coaxed.

That was the first of many times that Cynthia would comfort me. Even in my lessons, she was encouraging, understanding, and patient. After a few months, I had grown attached to her, and I worked hard to win her approval and impress her with my riding. I insisted on riding through the winter, as this farm had a sizable indoor arena. Even though the trek out to the farm was an hour long and being at the barn took up almost all of Saturday and Sunday, I couldn't imagine not riding. It would be like not breathing.

By February, Cynthia had taught me the basics of riding and I was learning preliminary dressage movements. Then I was dealt another unexpected blow. After my Saturday lesson, my mother explained to me that I would have just one more lesson with Cynthia.

"Cynthia is going through a really expensive divorce right now, so she is going to have to quit riding and get another job. She has two little girls to take care of."

I understood, but I was still devastated that I would have to let go of yet another person I loved.

The next Saturday, I maintained my composure both in the barn and during my lesson with Cynthia. But at the end of the day, when it came time to say good-bye, I cried. I cried hard. I prided myself on being tough because I never cried, but this was too much.

Cynthia was technically just my coach, but I could feel my heart breaking, there was a lump in my throat again, and I felt the blood rushing to my head. I would never see her again. I was about to lose Cynthia, just like I lost Leslie and Tango.

"Sweetie, please don't cry. I know you're sad but you're going to train with Carol, who is a whole lot better than me. She knows more, she's been training dressage longer," she said as she stroked my hair.

The ringing in my ears was deafening. All I heard was something about Carol, one of the other instructors at the farm.

Then Cynthia grabbed my hands from behind her waist, and held them at my sides. She knelt down to look me in the eyes. I looked down. I couldn't look her in the eyes. I hated that she saw me like that, weak and vulnerable. But I couldn't stop sobbing.

"I want you to meet her, now," she said seriously. I tried to pull myself together to meet my new trainer.

Carol walked into the viewing area from the office. She was as tall and slender as Cynthia. She was also pretty, with clear blue eyes and dark brown hair. However, she had none of Cynthia's femininity. She had short, unpolished nails, where Cynthia's nails were long and red. Her hair was short and dark brown, pulled into a ponytail. Cynthia's hair was bright red, wavy, and flowed down to her waist. Cynthia wore makeup, Carol's face was bare.

As Carol stood next to Cynthia, Cynthia began the introductions.

"Victoria, I want you to meet Carol. Carol, Victoria," she said formally.

As Carol extended her arm down to mine, I noticed the prominent veins in her forearm. Her skin was darker than Cynthia's, but I could clearly see the veins bulging from her arm. Her grip was firm, and her hand rough. We shook hands.

"Hi Victoria," she said cheerfully.

"Hi," I replied uncomfortably, knowing my face was still visibly wet with tears.

After the introductions, I hugged Cynthia one last time, and followed my mother out of the office, to the car waiting outside in the bitter cold rain.

If only I had known then how Carol would change my life . . .

10

Training with Carol turned out to not be so bad—it was pretty great, actually. She teased me endlessly, pulling me out of my shell of pre-teen insecurities. Our lessons were filled with jokes, challenges, and were usually topped off with a life lesson. At the end of every lesson with Carol, I walked away knowing that I had learned something, knowing that she had pushed me to my physical limit, and knowing that I had had fun. I knew Carol would be important to me after my first lesson with her.

I was twelve years old when I started training with Carol. I was still a novice dressage rider, riding only the farm's school horses, horses that were available to the general public. I told Carol about my adoration of Freddie, and that he was my favorite school horse. She let me ride him in most lessons, but insisted that I ride other horses.

"Why do I have to ride the other school horses? Freddie's the best and he's my favorite, so why bother with the other ones?" I complained.

"Because you can only improve if you ride other horses and challenge yourself. Don't you want to be the best rider you can be?" she rationalized.

"*Fiiiine*," I let out overdramatically so she would know I was joking, "I'll get Scooter."

Scooter was an average school horse—average size, average coloring, dark brown all over, average temperament, and he knew a little bit of basic dressage and basic jumping. I had never ridden him before, but I had seen other people less skilled than me ride him, so I wasn't particularly excited about the lesson I would have on him.

"Good posting trot," Carol instructed during my lesson. "Now, going into the corner, try to find a clear spot to ask for more bend and pick up the canter."

When the arena was filled to capacity with horses, like it was on that day, I had to look for an open spot to pick up the canter. I couldn't do it too close to another horse, because it might set off that horse. Since I was picking up the canter, the fastest of dressage's three gaits, I also had to get on the rail. The rule was that the faster moving horses got the rail when going to the left, but very novice riders got to ride on the rail for all three gaits. Since I was riding on a Saturday, the ring was packed with novice riders, which made it more difficult to find a good spot to pick up the canter.

I found a clear spot in the second corner, just before the long side. I gave the horse the cue to pick up the left lead canter, squeezing with my right leg. When he ignored that, I kicked him with my right heel. Apparently that offended the animal, prompting him to launch himself forward into a buck, catapulting his hind end in the air. I had developed a strong lower body from years of riding horses just as spirited as this one, so my body knew what to do. Even though the force of the buck had propelled me forward, my legs automatically gripped the saddle, my core muscles engaged, and my hands landed at the base of the horse's neck. I wasn't coming off. But I was afraid of hurting anyone behind me, so I kicked him with both legs to make him run forward, which would force all four of his legs back to the ground. Then he bolted. Now, I was pissed. He was being a jerk for no reason. So, I was a jerk back. I yanked hard on the reins, knowing that I was hurting his mouth, the meanest thing a rider can do. He then threw his head up and reared, rising up on his hind legs.

"GET UP!" I snarled in his ears, now four inches from my face. I grabbed his mane, slammed my legs hard against his sides, and he bolted down the next long side of the arena.

"HEADS UP!" I yelled. Everyone stopped and gathered in the middle of the arena, waiting for a riderless horse to start running around the ring, not an uncommon occurrence.

Now furious that I had caused a scene, I took it out on the beast. I kicked him hard, and aimed him directly for the wall. I didn't care if he ran right into it. I wasn't going to fall off no matter what he did. But the animal had enough sense to lock his front legs just before hitting the wall. I knew he would try to pull this stunt—stop short right before hitting a wall to send his rider sailing over it. Too bad I had ridden this ride one too many times at Leslie's. I sat back, and pulled on the reins.

"You OK?" I heard Carol ask, approaching me from the middle of the arena.

"Yeah, but this horse is such an *asshole*!" I fumed, completely unraveled.

"No cursing," she smiled. "And don't ever yank on the reins like that."

"But—" I objected.

"Pick up the posting trot," she interrupted. "Let's try it again, without the rodeo."

11

After a year of training with Carol, she announced, "You're riding Patches from now on."

"Patches? Doesn't he live in the boarder barn?"

The boarder barn was off limits to anyone who didn't own their own horse, so I rarely set foot on that exclusive part of the property.

"Yep," she beamed.

"But isn't he owned by someone?" I asked the obvious question.

"Yep," she smiled, now obviously taunting me with her cryptic answers.

"*So*, how can I ride him?" I continued.

"His owners don't ride him anymore," she simply concluded, "his tack is in the boarder tack room. Meet me in the indoor in ten minutes."

Patches was a small horse, smaller than Freddie. Maybe even smaller than Tango. He was aptly named because of his coloring—his white body was splashed with patches of black. He was unique, just like Tango.

As I set his tack in front of his stall, and turned the latch to open his door, I heard a voice amongst the murmurings in the boarder barn.

"Hey, aren't you that kid who rides all the schoolies?" a woman asked, peeling herself away from a conversation she was having with another woman by one of the stalls in the barn.

I recognized her. She was always chatting with the barn manager, Kim. I didn't know her name.

"Yeah."

"Victoria, right?" she asked.

"Yeah, I'm Victoria."

"I'm Helen, Mandy's mom."

"Mandy, get out here and meet Victoria," she called into the stall next to Patches's.

Mandy emerged, she was shorter and younger than me, I estimated about five years younger.

"Hey," she said, popping her head out of her pony's stall.

"Hi," I said.

"This is Sweet Pea," she said, struggling with the pony attempting to escape the stall.

"She's yours?" I asked.

"Yep, just got her a few months ago," she smiled proudly.

"She's cute," I said.

And she really was cute. She was petite, about 12 hands tall, she had a diamond shaped blaze on her head, and tiny ears that poked out through the fluffiest forelock and mane I had ever seen. Her dark bay coloring faded to black on her knees, going all the way down to her tiny hooves.

"She sure is, but a real pisser though, nuthin' sweet about her so far," Helen said, blocking the pony's escape route from the stall. "Get back in there, mare!" she hollered, throwing her hands up to scare the pony back into her stall.

"Three year olds!" she huffed.

"Watch out for that old geezer you're about to get on!" she let out.

"He's old?" I asked.

"Oh yeah, about 22 or 23, I think. Still has plenty of pep, though! Bucks off everyone who tries to ride him."

"Great," I muttered, grabbing the saddle pad.

Patches wasn't polite about getting tacked up. He insisted on doing laps in the stall while I tried to put on the saddle pad and saddle. When it came time for the bridle, he threw his head up beyond my reach. He was even less polite about being ridden. He insisted on doing two things all the time: 1.) trotting, 2.) with his nose defiantly in the air. No amount of rein, bending, or leg aids could persuade him to do anything else. His blatant disobedience was embarrassing. I couldn't even get his head down. *What kind of good rider can't even get a horse's head down?*

When I could no longer feel my fingers and arms, I stopped and asked Carol, "Why do I have to ride this horse?"

"Because he's a dressage horse, and you're learning dressage."

"This doesn't feel like dressage."

"Might be because you're not doing dressage," she needled.

"Great, thanks," I said, growing frustrated with Carol's unyielding philosophy that every mistake is the rider's fault. This horse's issues were clearly not my mistakes. After all, this was my first ride on him, how could it be my fault?

"Just keep riding. Sitting trot on a twenty-meter circle around me," she instructed.

The advantage of riding Patches was that he allegedly knew all of the high level dressage moves. I learned that he was a Grand Prix dressage horse back in the day. The disadvantage was that he had no desire to do anything remotely resembling dressage when I was on his back.

Carol insisted that I continue riding Patches through the spring. My reward for a half-decent ride on Patches was a lesson on Freddie. The lessons on Freddie were effortless, especially after the body-wrestling matches with Patches.

"Guess what," Carol said to me playfully at the beginning of a lesson on Patches.

"What?" I asked, knowing from her devilish grin that she had something up her sleeve.

"You're doing your first show next month!"

"*Really*?" I let out.

I was elated. Last summer, I watched most of Carol's students, the private boarders, compete in each of the farm's summer shows. I watched ride after ride. Each rider got to dress up in a fancy outfit, fancier for the higher levels of dressage. Their horses were also dolled up, getting their manes braided, hooves painted, and coats shone to a sparkling sheen. For each five-minute ride, they would get the chance to show their stuff to the judge and every spectator watching.

I was even more envious of the riders who were advanced enough to compete at shows off the property. Every time the boarders trailered their horses to go to a horse show, I imagined they were going to an elite show, reserved only for superior riders. Only the best riders at the farm competed off the property. I was painfully aware that I was not included in either group of riders allowed to compete.

"How come I can compete now?" I asked Carol. "I still don't have a horse," I stated, knowing that a basic prerequisite to competing in a horse show is having a horse to compete with.

"You got special permission to compete two schoolies," Carol explained.

"Freddie?" I asked optimistically.

"And Patches," she ended.

"But he doesn't even go on the bit, Carol!" I complained.

"Well, now you have a month to figure out how to get him on the bit," she advised.

"I can't, Carol. I really can't!" I insisted.

"Yes, you can," she responded.

"Carol, I—"

"I want you to read a book on visualization," she interrupted. She told me the title of the book and where to buy it.

"Why?"

"So you can be a better rider," she answered. "I want you to *visualize* a move before you actually do it."

"Halt," she ordered. I wrangled Patches to a stop. She came to him, and held him by a rein to keep him still.

"Close your eyes. Picture the perfect leg yield. Imagine how it feels. Think of a perfect trot, with the energy coming from his hindquarters, traveling through your body, into your hands, and to his mouth. You already know how to let that energy pass through your body and you know how to use that energy to control the horse. That's your talent. See, for me, I have to think about everything I need to do to get the horse to do something. If I want go from a trot to canter, I have to think about bending the whole horse's body, sitting on the inside, squeezing him with the outside leg, and be ready to push him into the canter with my seat, all at the same time. To you, that's all one move, and I know you don't think about it, your body just knows what to do. Some people call it the 'feel,' but I call it talent. What we have to do now is teach you how to use it. Because you have a natural feel for the horse, you need to feel every movement before you do it. Then, when it comes time to do that movement, your body will just know what to do. Does that make sense?"

"I guess so," I replied, recognizing that I had never really consciously dissected what I was doing when I was in the saddle. I just kind of did it.

"Keep your eyes closed," she continued.

"Now, picture the perfect leg yield on Patches. You're coming down the long side, and he's moving forward into the bridle. Your seat is going with his movement, keeping the impulsion going into the corner. You use the corner to create the bend in his body needed for the leg yield. Now you're set up for the leg yield. You turn down the center line of the arena, you apply a little pressure with the outside leg, and let him drift away from it. Feel him stretch his front right leg out, reaching for the ground. Feel the suppleness in his body, feel the impulsion continuing forward."

"Now. Open your eyes and show me," she said, releasing the reins.

12

The morning of my first show was electric. I didn't understand why so many of the boarders were so excited, since they had shown before. In my mind, I was the only one who was justifiably excited, since it was my first dressage show.

"Are you nervous? I'm so nervous!" one of the boarders exclaimed more to herself than to me.

"Umm, I don't know. I don't think so," I replied tentatively.

"Well, why not? It's your first show, right? And you're only twelve years old, aren't you? I would be so nervous if I were you! Hell, I'm nervous already!" she continued.

"Yeah, you sound pretty nervous." I couldn't help myself.

"How are you not nervous?!" she suddenly fumed at me.

"I don't know. I guess I haven't had a chance to think about it," I concluded, dismissively. I didn't enjoy talking to most of the boarders. Some of them acted like owning a horse made them better than everyone else. I know people thought I was shy and quiet, but really, I just didn't want to talk to most of them.

I hustled through the excitement in the boarder barns, and

made my way to the school barn in the back of the property. Freddie stood in his stall, patiently waiting for me, clean and braided. I had bathed him thoroughly the night before, and one of the girls had braided him for me since I didn't know how to braid yet.

"Good boy," I cooed at Freddie through the bars of his stall, beaming with pride over my little gentleman for staying so clean overnight. I bet he knew it was my first show and it was important for him to stay clean and not rub out his braids. I gave Freddie some carrots since he had clearly already earned them. Then, I went to check on Patches in the boarder barn.

I had also scrubbed Patches to a gleaming sheen the day before, taking pride in how the blackness of his spots leaped out of his snow-white coat. I even sponged his nose, painstakingly wiping off the dirt and grime, which ultimately revealed a pink muzzle. I finished him off with a coat of clear hoof polish, to let his tan hooves shine in their natural color, rather than stain them black with an artificial black hoof polish.

When I got to his stall, the first thing he showed off was a massive manure stain on his right cheek. The dark brown stain was painfully obvious against his white coat.

"Patches! What did you do!?" I steamed, before I realized I was talking to a horse.

After inspecting my treatless hands and pockets, he turned to his hay in the corner, exposing an even more massive brown stain on his left hindquarter. And finally, the brute turned yet again and showed off his mangled mess of a mane. What used to be braids were now tortured knobs of hair jutting straight up and out, in different directions, from behind his ears, all the way down to his withers.

"Oh, Patches," I sighed, already defeated.

Despite Patches's attempt to win a prize for worst presentation, I was still excited to finally be competing in a show. I was proud to have earned the privilege of riding the most educated school horse, and even more proud to have earned the honor of competing him in a show (despite his appearance).

Unfortunately, the judges did not share my enthusiasm. We lost points as a result of Patches's insistence that he trot around the arena with his nose as high up in the air as he could get it.

"Cute horse and rider pair, need to go back to basics," the majority of the judges' comments read. We got the lowest scores for submission, mostly 4s (on a scale of 0 to 10, with 0 being the lowest).

"Let's see your score sheet," Carol insisted whenever the scores for one of my classes were announced over the loudspeaker.

I watched her face as she scanned my score sheets, with the judges' scores and comments, waiting for the disappointment. But her grin never faded. It was as if she was sharing the fun of my first show right along with me, despite the low scores.

I put more hope of doing well at this show into Freddie, but Freddie was stiff and I didn't know what to do other than to just sit, smile, and steer. I didn't have Carol in the competition ring telling me what to do. Freddie and I won mostly third and fourth place ribbons, which I expected to get on him. Still, a small part of me was disappointed because after all the love I had showered on Freddie, he didn't magically transform into a superstar dressage horse on show day.

I continued to show Patches and Freddie that summer, in the three shows hosted by the farm, at Carol's insistence. We continued to collect the pastel-colored ribbons rather than the blue and red ones, for first and second place. But I still displayed the ones I had earned proudly in my bedroom. After all, I had beat *someone* to earn most of those ribbons. I wasn't the best, but I also wasn't the worst.

13

I had adjusted to my new barn, new horses, new coach, and even my new school. As 6th grade came to an end, I looked forward to my second show season. Home life had even stabilized with my father's mysterious four-year disappearance. I didn't ask what happened. I was afraid that any talk or thought of him would bring him back.

And then, just when summer vacation began, my mother announced that we would have to spend two entire weeks with him at a resort called Lake George. Right smack in the middle of show season. I was devastated, confused, and angry. I felt helpless and betrayed. I expected things like this from my father, but my mother, who was supposed to be our protector, was just letting this happen.

"Why are you doing this to us?" I demanded, watching her pack my bag. "I thought you loved us," I tried to lay on the guilt as heavily as possible.

"I do love you, but he's your father, and you have to go," she said conclusively.

"Why? The court, again?" I asked.

"Yes," she ended.

"This is *so* unfair!"

"I know, I know," she said, exhausted, "but he is your father, and you will be able to watch the Olympics while you're up there."

"I can watch the Olympics here, *and* keep riding!" I spat at her.

"I know, Victoria, I know," she concluded.

And that was it. If the court said I had to go with my father, I had to go.

As he drove us up to Lake George, I remembered how he and my mother had battled through the legal system. My sister and I missed a lot of school to go to court. My mom was in court a lot more than we were, frequently leaving us with babysitters, most of whom were total freaks. There was the one with nine fingers. Then there was the huge, fat one who attacked the kitchen with a perpetually voracious appetite, but never cooked a single meal for us. And then there was my grandmother. She was a brilliant cook, but a terrible babysitter. She was clear about how miserable she was and how it was everyone's fault, including my sister and me. The wooden spoon was always within her reach if we ever talked back to her.

At eight years old, I began realizing that it was breaking my mother's heart to leave us with these babysitters, and also that it was beyond her control. She was always either at work or talking to the lawyers, because of him. I never saw my mother, and we were always stuck being babysat by my grandparents, because of my father. Why couldn't he just disappear again?

Seething in the passenger seat, the countless hurtful memories of this stranger that I refused to call "Dad" flooded my mind. I remembered how once, in the hallway of the court, before it was our turn to go in the courtroom, my mother was talking to her lawyer. I was lingering nearby, holding my sister's hand, when I saw my father down the hall. He walked directly to me, unnoticed by my mother. I held my ground, stepping in front of my sister. I wasn't afraid.

When he reached me, he pulled something out of a pocket hidden inside his jacket, and bent down, opening his fist in my face. It was a watch—an ugly, old watch.

"I'll give you this shiny new watch if you tell the judge your mother hits you and you want to live with me," he said sweetly.

Blood rushed to my head, and all of a sudden I felt like I could strangle his fat neck with my own hands. I knew what he was trying to do.

I plucked the old watch from his hand and chucked it hard across the hall.

"You can keep the watch and I'm going to tell the judge the truth—that I *hate* you and I *never* want to live with you!" I yelled as loud as I could. I knew I was safe if I shouted. It was a lesson I learned from his many unannounced visits when we were home alone with our grandparents. He always left when I screamed.

The hall suddenly fell silent and my mother rushed to me. She grabbed my hand to pull me away as she chastised my father.

"What did you do? This is your own child!" she chided. Then we hurried into the courtroom before he could respond.

The judge declared that he wanted to see just my sister and me in his chambers.

He softened once we were in his office. It smelled like old leather. He smelled old too, like my grandparents. His old man cologne could not mask the stench of his stale, weathered skin. Pale white skin hung from his face, like the drapes over the living room window at home. His expensive looking gold-rimmed glasses slid down his greasy nose. He removed them, revealing gray-blue eyes.

"So, girls, are you hungry? Thirsty?"

"No," I said sternly.

"I want an ice cream!" my sister declared.

"Oh, Sugar, I'm sorry. I'm fresh out of ice cream. How 'bout a lollipop?" he asked my sister in an unfamiliar, but distinctly American accent.

"Yeah!" she said happily as he handed her a lollipop and supervised her as she tore off the wrapping.

"Would you like to sit on my knee, darlin'?" he asked me.

"No," I replied.

"I do, I do!" my sister jumped in. He then laughed as he hoisted my little sister up on his knee.

I knew what the purpose of this meeting was, so to get right to the point, I started.

"We want to live with our Mom," I proclaimed.

"Oh, really? Did someone tell you to say that?" he asked.

"No. My mom told me to just tell you the truth. And that's the truth," I said.

"Why is it better to live with Mom than with Dad?" he asked.

"He doesn't love us," I said.

"I'm sure he loves you," the judge said.

"No, he doesn't! He makes us eat the slimy part of the meat!" my sister chimed in. "Mommy cuts off the slimy part, and she *never* makes us eat it," she explained.

"That's when one of his girlfriends comes over and cooks. If no one else is there to cook when we're at his apartment, then he buys a box of cookies for us to eat," I revealed.

"Cookies don't sound so bad," the judge countered.

"For *dinner*?" I asked.

"Hmm," he let out.

We answered an unending number of questions. I was amazed that I had to spend such a long time explaining such a clearly obvious situation and what would be the best resolution to the old man in the important black robe.

"OK girls, let's go back to Mom," he said, as he took each of us by the hand and walked us to the guard, who then escorted us to sit beside our mother.

Custody once more was awarded to my mother.

"This isn't over, you bitch!" my father threatened, as we exited the courthouse.

"*Victor*! Not in front of the girls!" my mother retaliated.

"It's OK, Mom. He already taught us all the curses, in Romanian and English," I said, trying to comfort her. But judging by her hard grip on my hand, I wondered if I had done more harm than good.

I was most excited for summer to begin because it was the year of the 1992 summer Olympics. I was curious to see what the big deal was about this event, and to try to understand why Leslie had declared it outside of the realm of possibility for me.

I was lost in thought for the entire drive up to the resort. How could someone be so sure of my limitations? Why was Leslie, of all people, my biggest doubter? Shouldn't she have been my biggest supporter? What's the big deal with the Olympics, anyway?

Suddenly, the car slowed and pulled into the parking lot. I saw the "Office" sign. We would see Kevin, the owner. We knew Kevin because my mother brought us up here years ago. We liked Kevin, he was always nice to us.

He was sitting in the office when we went to check in.

"Hi Kevin!" we said simultaneously.

"Hi girls!" he said, as we rushed over to give him a group hug.

"Wow, you got big! How old are you now?" he asked us.

"I'm twelve," I said, importantly.

"And I'm ten!" my sister exclaimed.

"Where is everyone?" he asked as he looked over our shoulders for our grandparents, mother, and Chihuahuas.

"Oh, it's just us and our dad this time," I said.

My father puffed out his chest, carefully rolled each "r" and enunciated each vowel in our ridiculous last name while he pompously declared, "Yes, hello, I am Victor Radulescu!"

"Hi, there. I'm Kevin Daniels. How long will you be staying?" "Three weeks, and put it on my ex-wife's credit card," my father ordered.

Kevin looked at me quizzically. I rolled my eyes to let him know how unhappy I was with this situation.

"OK, I'll have to call her to make sure she's on board with that, sir," Kevin replied.

"Oh, she's eets on board, don't vorry!" my father cajoled in his thick Romanian accent, visibly amused.

"Right, well, here are your room keys, enjoy your stay. Girls, I'll be down by the beach later if you want to go out on the boat."

"Yeah!" we exclaimed in unison.

"OK! First we go to the room," my father interrupted as he herded us out of the office.

I knew what my father's favorite pastime was—drinking until he passed out in front of the TV. Fortunately for me, I had the diversion of watching the Olympics. I knew he would want to watch it as well, since it was a sporting event.

The summer Games opened the day after we arrived at the vacation resort. I was still annoyed that I had been torn from my horses, but was glued to the television for the entirety of the Olympics. Dressage was not televised, but I still watched all of the major events—gymnastics, swimming, diving, basketball, rowing, and track and field. I was in awe of the athletes and the skill and athleticism they had achieved from years of rigorous training. Even though this event highlighted physical prowess, I thought about what mental toughness they must also have to win, lose, fall, get back up again. I watched the men's basketball where the "Dream Team" earned their name—they were undefeated, invincible, the best. I watched the women's gymnastics where girls not much older than me tumbled to glory and fulfilled a lifelong dream.

It was during this Olympics that I remembered the movie, *Nadia*. I was five years old when I saw the movie, and it was only a distant memory at this point, but I remembered a particular scene in the movie that illustrated how much Nadia Comenici wanted to reclaim her Olympic glory in her second Olympics. The scene zeroed in on one end of the balance beam and caught her hands as they were about to fall on the apparatus, so that she could handstand onto it and begin her routine. But her forearm was wrapped in a white bandage, and blood began to spill out of the wound, soaking the wrapping in red blood. An open injury on a crucial part of her body didn't stop the gymnast from proving to herself and to everyone else that she was still the best. For me, that scene made the entire movie. It showed me that nothing can stand in the way of what you want.

I almost always got to watch the Games, as my father was usually passed out on his bed by the time my sister and I came in from spending the day on the lake with Kevin. This diversion made the days fly by. We got to spend all day without him, and then I got to watch the Olympics at night.

On our last day, a few of the other kids whom we had befriended invited us to play a game of badminton that evening.

We went up to the hotel room to change and ask our father for permission, since it was an evening activity, but he was passed out. I saw more than his usual bottles of alcohol, and was in no mood to spend my last night listening to his deafening snoring.

"Whatever, the court is right outside so if he wakes up, he'll see us playing. We'll come in before dark, it will be fine," I reasoned to my sister.

I was doubtful that he would even wake up, so we headed down to the court.

We played until it began to get dark, and then went back to the room. I saw that the lights were on.

I entered first.

"Where the *hell* were you?" he yelled.

"We were just downstairs, playing badminton," I replied.

"Your mother called and you weren't here, do you have any idea how bad that makes me look?" he shouted.

"You don't need any help from us to look bad," I replied, getting angry and louder.

"You fucking bitches are just like your mother!" he spat. And with that, he simply rolled over in his bed and started snoring.

"Don't listen to him, he's an idiot," I whispered to my sister. "Come on, let's just brush our teeth and go to bed."

"OK," my sister complied.

"I'll be right there," I said. I went directly to the telephone and called my mother.

"Mom?" I said as soon as I heard the line picked up.

"Hi Fafi! How are you doing? I miss you!"

"Mom, you have to come get us. Victor is drunk and we don't feel safe, you have to come get us tonight."

"Put him on the phone," she said, her voice slow and deliberate.

I slapped the side of his head hard with the telephone receiver.

"Hey, wake up. Mom wants to talk to you," I said, putting the receiver down on the nightstand. I walked over to the bathroom.

"What," he said slowly, picking up the receiver.

"Oh shut up, you stupid old whore," he said after a long pause. After another pause, "Yeah? If you come here tonight or if I see any police, I will throw them in the car and drive them to Canada and then you really never will see them again."

"Go fuck yourself!" he said, slamming down the receiver.

And with that, he simply rolled back into bed and the snoring resumed.

I went back to the phone and again called my mother.

"Mom?"

"Hi Fafi," she sighed from the other line.

"So, are you coming to get us?"

"No, your father will drive you home tomorrow," she said, matter-of-factly.

"Ugh! But, Mom!" I objected.

"I want talk to your sister, is she still awake?"

"Yeah, hold on."

My sister stood motionless in the doorway of the bathroom. I waved at her to come over.

"Hi, Mom," she said into the receiver.

"Yeah, I know."

After another long pause, "OK, love you too. Yeah, hold on," she said, handing me the receiver.

"Hi, Mom," I said, taking back the phone.

"Fafi, just look out for your sister tonight and I'll see you tomorrow," she instructed.

"Fine," I sighed, annoyed that she wouldn't come get us.

"I love you," she said.

"Love you too. Bye, Mom," I said, and then hung up the phone.

"Let's go to bed," I said to my sister, putting my arm around her shoulder.

I was so disappointed in both of my parents.

14

My father did drive us back. I was grateful to be home, and eager to get to the barn. My mother told me she would do her best to never again put us in the custody of our father, but it was up to the court. I was annoyed that our lives would again be in the hands of so-called experts who had to be convinced over and over again of what was so clear—that we were better off with our mother.

I was relieved to finally be back at the barn. This was my world, and once I returned to it, I felt normal again. Carol immediately immersed me back into my old routine of riding either Patches or Freddie. But now, I was her working student. I got one free lesson a week in exchange for helping her with the legion of horses under her training. I cleaned tack, tacked horses up for her, brought them to her, and was eventually allowed to warm them up and cool them down. Plus, I got to watch her ride on my lunch break.

Watching Carol ride was the highlight of my day. As soon as she told me to grab lunch, I hightailed it to the viewing area and was glued to the glass while she rode. I couldn't imagine a more perfect rider. No matter what any horse did, she was always calm and composed. I never saw her lose her cool. I was fascinated by this superhuman power she had to always stay in control. No matter how bad the horse was, she just kept riding. She just kept moving forward. Her position was perfect—she was always looking up and straight ahead, carried her hands squarely in front of her, kept her rib cage centered over her hips, and maintained her legs right underneath her. Leslie's mantra was always "ears, shoulders, hips and heels." And that's the way Carol rode. The way she trained was textbook perfect. She somehow knew what each horse needed to shine. And she brought it out of all of them. She made the most average horse look like it belonged in the show ring.

I absorbed every stride, felt the bend in every shoulder-in, floated across the arena with every one of her leg yields. We were together all day, every day, and it was perfect. We never discussed what happened at Lake George. We actually never discussed anything but riding and I loved that about my coach. Training with Carol was a complete break from my reality. It was like being in a whole other world—nothing else existed. The fear of the courts handing us over to my father was paused, my mother's constant anxiety was quelled, and all the fighting was silenced.

I loved being at the barn. The extra bonus was that I got to be Carol's student. She made everything fun and interesting. There was always a new horse to ride, a new movement to learn. And she was often delightfully unpredictable. True to her fondness for surprises, toward the end of that summer, Carol instructed me to tack up a horse named Moonshine.

"*Moonshine*?" I asked, to make sure I understood.

"Moonshine," she confirmed.

15

I knew nothing about Moonshine other than the location of his stall, which was in one of the boarder barns. He didn't live in the school barn, so he couldn't be a school horse. But I also never saw any boarder come to ride Moonshine. I had ridden all of the school horses, so I knew what they were like. As for the boarder horses, I saw most of the horses' owners when they came to the barn to ride their horses, so I knew something about them and their mounts. But nobody ever came for Moonshine.

Nevertheless, I gathered his bridle and saddle from the tack room and headed to his stall. He was dozing with his head held low in the dark corner of the stall. He almost blended into the shadow of that corner, as he was a deep brown color, almost black. When I opened the sliding stall door, his head snapped up. He pinned his ears, turned, and lunged at me with gnashing teeth. I pulled the door closed in an instant, watching as his teeth bit at the metal bars of the stall door. I had never been attacked by a horse before.

What did I do? I wondered.

I stood, frozen, on the other side of the stall, as Moonshine continued biting at the bars. I looked to my left and then to my right. No one was around to help me, or to explain this crazy behavior. I stood there, alone and confused. I waited a few minutes for the animal's fury to subside. He eventually tired of attacking the dead metal bars of the stall and moved back to the same corner in which I found him. Succumbing to my curiosity and perpetual urge to overcome challenges (and an apparent death wish), I entered the stall again, approaching the animal with a saddle pad to put on his back. He stood still while I approached.

Maybe I caught him off guard? Maybe that's why he freaked out? I wondered as he stood still, now that I was I was about to tack him up.

But as soon as I drew my arm over my head and flung the saddle pad over his back, I was instantly pinned in a corner of the stall. With unexpected speed and agility, he had twisted his body so that he barricaded me. Now I was in the corner! This was the first time I was afraid of being hurt by a horse. His ears were again pinned flat to his head, revealing his rage. His body squeezed and pushed me as hard as he could to keep me in the corner. I was afraid of him moving slightly forward and having perfect aim at my body with one of his powerful hind legs. I knew that one good kick would be all that it would take to either kill me or put me in a lot of pain for a very long time. That realization turned my fear into anger. I was suddenly fearless.

"Get OFF me!" I shrieked as I shoved against his heavy body.

He started whipping his tail from side to side in another sign of irritation, which only antagonized me further. I pushed him off of me and, when I was free, amazingly, he didn't kick me. He didn't even lunge at me. He simply went to his feed bucket in another corner of the stall.

What the hell? I racked my brain to try to understand what was going on. *He ignores me when I get mad? That doesn't make any sense. This horse is totally nuts,* I concluded.

Nonetheless, I went to the stall door to get the saddle on the floor right by the door, always keeping an eye on the beast in the corner. I lifted the saddle onto his back while he stood motionless, ears still pinned. When I put on the girth and tightened it around his belly, however, he turned his menacing face around to bite me. Just when his mouth opened, I raised my hand and lunged slightly back at him, to reciprocate the attack. He jerked back around, ears flat on his head and tail swishing during the entire episode. Then it was time to put on the bridle. I knew this would be a struggle. There was no way this beast would let me strap leather all over his head and slip a metal bit into his mouth. As soon as I got the brow band in front of his nose, he jutted his head out and tossed the entire bridle out of my hand. It landed against the wall, and slid down into the shavings. After I picked it up and tried again, he decided he would lift his head high beyond my reach and nod, almost taunting me. All I could do was sigh. I had a feeling that getting angry wouldn't expedite the tacking up process.

Well, you gotta bring your stupid head back down sometime, I thought. I stood there, trying to look disinterested, but waiting for the perfect chance to slip the bridle over his head. As soon as he brought his head down, I grabbed the front of his nose with one hand, jerked the bit into his mouth, and pulled the bridle up past his ears, slipping each ear through as quickly as I could. I was generally careful and gentle when putting bridles on horses, conscious that I was slipping a harsh, cold, tasteless piece of metal into their mouths. But since Moonshine had been such an exceptional pest, I was unyielding and forceful with the bridle. His antics had earned him none of the kindness I showed the other horses.

My arms were already sore from the fight—he had still pulled me off the ground—but I didn't care. I had won.

"Haha, you jackass!" I let out, too overcome by my victory. I didn't care that I was taunting a horse; this one really deserved it.

As soon as the tack was all securely on, I marched him out of the stall and toward the mounting block outside. I positioned him near it so that I could slip my foot into the stirrup, throw my free leg over his back and ease into the saddle. But, just when my left foot was in the stirrup, the beast trotted off!

"Damn it, horse, stop!" I yelled, holding on to the left side of his body with all my strength. I would not let him get away with this! I pulled myself up to the saddle and threw my body over it. Then, I swiftly swung my right leg over his back as I pulled the reins in my left hand and sat back. But the animal kept building speed, and was making his way to the back field, so then I threw my right hand over my left hand on the reins, to pull back with more force.

Moonshine then came to a grinding halt.

In my frustration, I whipped his head around to turn him in the direction of the indoor arena, where Carol was waiting for us. Her dog, Max, a sleepy, old Labrador Retriever, lay at the entrance of the arena, his usual spot. When he noticed Moonshine and me approaching, he stood up to get out of the way. Just as he started to shift out of Moonshine's path, Moonshine flattened his ears and lunged at the dog. I grabbed the reins in just enough time to spare Max.

What the hell is wrong with this horse? Why is he so vicious? And why do I have to ride him? I wondered as I entered the arena, looking for my trainer.

As I approached Carol aboard Moonshine, ready for my first lesson on this animal that had just tried to kill both me and her dog, she remarked, "I see you're still in one piece," she smiled mischievously. Then, she gave me my first tip on how to ride Moonshine.

"If you can ride this horse, you can ride any horse."

Oh great, I thought, *this will go well.*

I squeezed Moonshine with both legs, giving him the cue to go from walk to trot. But he dipped his head down and sped backwards, exactly the opposite of what I wanted. I kicked him to stop the moonwalking, trying to save some face in front of my trainer, and everyone else, but then the jerk bolted forward in a gallop! As I scrambled to collect my reins, I realized that he wasn't just bolting, he was aiming for a target—another horse and rider in the arena, and he was charging the pair! "*Moonshine!*" I whispered loudly through my gritted teeth, hoping my voice would snap him out of his sudden rage. But he wasn't stopping. We were racing to the other horse and rider. At this point I realized there would be no grace or dignity in this lesson, so I resorted to the cowboy maneuvers I had picked up riding crazy horses on trails, and yanked his head hard to the right. I then threw all my weight to the right to at least throw off his balance. Then came the brakes. Instead of turning to the right, Moonshine grabbed the bit with his teeth, leaving me with no control. However, he did stop—like a cow pony, he dug his hind legs and heels into the ground, lowered his haunches, and bounced three times to a sliding stop.

I was grateful for the multiple lessons I had at Leslie's, when other horses tried to pull this on me and I somersaulted over their heads. My body knew to sit down deep in the saddle, my heels knew to pull themselves down for more balance in the stirrups, and my legs knew to hold on tight.

This horse had just taken me for a ride. My ego was crushed. I would show him not to do it again. My frustration bubbled to the surface, and I scolded him with a tap of the whip on the haunches. His immediate reaction was to simulate a handstand, bucking his hind legs defiantly in the air, almost in a perfect gymnastic handstand.

I fumingly tapped again, and kicked him to move forward, only to be met by another recalcitrant buck. Then I kicked hard and he bolted forward.

"It's OK, Victoria, just keep riding, ignore his antics," Carol instructed.

Just before my second lesson aboard Moonshine, Carol gave me some extra insight into Moonshine's personality.

"If Moonshine were a person, he would be the troublemaker smoking a cigarette on the street corner, in the leather jacket, trying to pick up girls," she said. "Just think of him as a punk," she concluded.

Great, I thought cynically.

Moonshine more than lived up to Carol's assessment. My second ride on him was also a disaster. If I squeezed with my legs to go forward, he shuffled backward; if I kicked him again to reinforce the squeezing aid, he bolted like a racehorse out of the holding pen; if I tapped him with the whip to reinforce the kicking cue, he bucked. Steering proved just as problematic as going forward—if I pulled the left rein to go left, he grabbed the bit and went to the right. Moonshine would not be told what to do or where to go. No amount of coaching or coaxing from Carol would ease my frayed nerves. This horse was going to do whatever he wanted and I was incapable of persuading him otherwise.

I walked him back to the barn after the performance, ego bruised and severely humbled.

I'm obviously not as good I thought, if I can't even make this stupid, piece of crap horse go forward, I thought to myself, looking down at my feet as I led the horse back to the barn.

Why the hell does Carol want me to ride this stupid horse? He doesn't know anything, he hates every living thing, and he's nuts. What does she want me to learn from him? How to ride in a rodeo? I could do that at Leslie's, five minutes from home, instead of all the way out here, I thought.

As I untacked the animal in his stall after my ride, I was swimming in anger, confusion, and defeat. I hated this beast, I didn't understand why Carol wanted me to ride him, and the ride was a disaster. I cursed him out while doing all the necessary chores after a ride, including cooling him out. I slipped on his halter, and led him outside to the patches of grass around the barn for him to graze.

As I watched him plucking mouthfuls of grass out of the earth, I fell deep in thought about how much I hated him and wracked my brain, trying to understand why my trainer wanted me to ride him. I was suddenly pulled out of my musings when a rider I had never seen before approached me and exclaimed, "You guys looked really good out there!"

My mouth dropped. *What? Does she realize who we are? I think she's confused, she can't possibly mean Moonshine and I looked good.* But there was only one other horse and rider pair in the indoor and they looked like our polar opposites—the rider had long blond hair and her horse was white. My horse was dark brown, as was my hair.

"Ummm . . . thanks," I muttered and looked down. I didn't want to make eye contact and witness her realization that she was paying a compliment to the wrong person. It was nice, though. I let myself play along with the mistake and gave Moonshine a carrot when I put him back in the stall.

That fall, I transitioned from riding any available school horse, to riding Moonshine exclusively.

16

It wasn't until months after I started riding Moonshine regularly that I started to understand his ceaseless hostility.

Some of the other boarders and trainers were huddled in conversation around Moonshine's stall when I got to the barn one day. I exchanged the usual hellos with all of them as I made my way to Moonshine's stall. Moonshine had trained me in the type of greeting he deemed acceptable in order for me to avoid an attack. First, I had to announce myself before I reached his stall, so that I wouldn't surprise him.

"Hi Moony," I called as I approached the stall.

Then, carrots in hand, I opened the stall door and let him crunch off a carrot top as I held the bottom of it. As long as his teeth were occupied, he couldn't bite me.

Then I petted his neck, quickly scanning his body for any cuts or scrapes that hostile horses like him were prone to acquiring. Since Moonshine shared his turnout paddock with another horse, checking for cuts and scrapes was part of our routine.

After our greeting, I headed to the tack room to get my

stuff—saddle, saddle pad, bridle, and grooming box. When I came back, I noticed the same group I had passed earlier, still in conversation. On my return, however, I noticed a few stolen glances thrown my way, plus hushed voices. I was too preoccupied with preparing for my lesson—physically and mentally—to wonder if I had become their new topic of conversation. However, once I was again in Moonshine's stall, grooming him for the lesson, I noticed all five of them lined up against the other side of the stall door.

"So, uh, Vic, how much do you know about Moonshine?" Nora, one of the dressage instructors, inquired.

Nora was a lower-level dressage instructor, who also trained with Carol. We didn't interact much, other than passing each other when riding together in the indoor arena.

"Well, just that he's owned by this guy, George Beck, who doesn't come here anymore, and he's a First Level horse," I answered robotically. I knew Moonshine knew the basics of equitation and dressage, but he didn't know any of the cool upper level tricks and movements.

"No, I mean do you know what happened to him before George got him?"

"No."

"OK, well, Moony's an off-the-track racehorse from Iowa," she started. "Want to see his tattoo?"

"Tattoo?" I asked.

"Sure, every racehorse gets the inside of his upper lip tattooed," Nora informed.

I pressed my lips together, cringing at the thought of tattooing the inside of my mouth. Poor Moonshine.

"Here, I'll show you," she said, stepping up to Moonshine and grabbing hold of his head. He immediately objected, thrashing his head around, trying to get her off his face.

"Hold still, man!" she let out, struggling to curl his upper lip inside out.

"It's OK, Nora, I believe you," I said, wanted her to stop

antagonizing Moonshine.

"No, no, I almost got it!" she persisted.

"OK, I saw it!" I let out, having seen some numbers on one of the outside corners of his lip.

"So there ya go, proof that he really raced," she beamed, proudly having proven her point.

"Anyway, he never won anything because he's so small and stiff. The people on the track there really beat him to win but he just couldn't. See how short his back is and how close together his front and hind legs are? I don't even think it's physically possible for a horse with such a short back to win any races. But anyway, he never won and so they sent him to auction," she explained.

I remember from my experience riding auction horses at Leslie's that those horses either lived or died after the bidding ended. If someone bought them, they lived on with their new owners. If they were not purchased, they were sent to slaughterhouses and killed.

"Richard was at an auction and bought Moony to make him a school horse when he was three or four years old," she continued. "I heard he bought Moony for only a hundred and fifty bucks."

Richard Snider owned the farm with his wife, dressage diva, Gunilla, who was training with world class coaches in Europe when I started riding at Oakwood Farm. Even though she was gone, she still had a strong presence at this barn, as she was often the topic of conversation amongst the riders and trainers.

"Well, then Richard tried a couple of working students on Moony to see how he would do with different riders on his back," Nora explained. "Moony hospitalized the first three people who tried to ride him—one broken arm, another concussion, and another bruised his back and we never saw him again." Her gray-blue eyes scrutinized my own, waiting for my reaction. But I had none. I wasn't really surprised that young

Moony had hospitalized three people, so she continued telling the story.

"After Richard realized no one here could ride him, he sent Moony to a 'correctional' training facility," she said, throwing her fingers into air quotes.

"What's that?" I asked, and heard snickers, scoffs, and sneers from the rest of the group. My question prompted them to prattle off stories they heard about correctional training facilities.

"They chain horses' legs together!" one voice let out.

"I heard they beat them with whips until they bleed and have welts!" another revealed.

"Me too. I heard that too," another one chimed in.

"Well, I heard they starve the hyper ones," yet another one shared.

"I heard they keep them in the dark all the time and put weights on their heads and legs," another voice expressed.

"I heard that too," yet another one agreed.

Nora began loudly, as if to silence the chattering and take the stage again, "Vic, they really mistreat horses at those places. Moony was in pretty bad shape. I remember. See that scar right there on his heel and how hair never grows on it? You don't want to know how he got that. Poor guy, he looked worse and worse every time he came back."

"Every time?" I asked.

"Yeah, he went back and forth three times. Every time he came back he was skinnier, had more bruises, and was more hostile," her bright eyes clouded and she looked down as the memories rushed back.

"Carol saw it too," her tone changed, slightly more optimistic. "She thought it was horrible that Richard kept sending Moony back to the correctional facility and they would send him back here when they couldn't fix him. She wanted to stop yo-yoing the horse, so she started riding and training him for free. She stuck to him like glue, Vic, you should've seen it. Any time Moony would throw a buck or lunge or rear up on his hind legs, she just sat there and let him have his fit. She rode him for a while, a few months or maybe even a year, I think, until she thought Moony would be a good match for one of her students, George Beck. George wasn't rich but he married into money, and bought Moony so he could brag to his country club friends that he had a boat *and* a horse," she sneered at the memory. "Such a jackass," she said to herself after a long pause.

"Anyway, after about a year and a half or two, George's wife divorced him and he was broke. He stopped coming to the farm and just stopped paying the board. Since no one was paying Moony's bill, he just stayed in the stall—no training, no turnout, no nothing. He just rotted away in his stall until you came along."

The others chimed in, "Yeah, *no one* took him out of the stall, poor guy."

Learning Moonshine's story was enlightening. So I managed to stay on his back after he hospitalized so many other (presumably more advanced) riders. I took some pleasure in knowing that. But I also felt so sorry for him. How rough his life had been. How unfair.

"Thanks, Nora," I said.

"Sure, kiddo," she beamed.

I didn't know what sparked her sudden interest in Moonshine or me or both, but I really was appreciative. I was thankful because now I knew Moonshine and I weren't all that different. Of course he hated people; he had never known a kind hand. Of course he preferred to be left alone; that way, no one could hurt him. It all made sense now.

17

Moonshine and I clashed regularly. Every ride was a fight. I insisted that he work like every other horse—I gave the cue and he should automatically do whatever I wanted. That was rarely the case. With Moonshine, the more forceful the cue, the more inclined he would be to ignore it completely. The more he resisted my cues, the more frustrated I became, and the more we battled. Were it not for Carol's coaxing, soothing, firm, and confident training (and sense of humor) we probably would never have gotten along.

"He's just not listening to me!" I let out in total frustration during countless lessons.

"Just keep asking, Victoria," she frequently encouraged.

"No, Carol, I can't . . . he's not listening; he won't even go straight!" I insisted.

Anytime I applied a cue with my legs, Moonshine either bucked with his hind legs or drifted so close to the rail of the arena that he squeezed and dragged my leg against the entire length of the wall. I had scratch marks on both boots to show it. Luckily, my boots were cheap.

"Yes, he will, Victoria," she coaxed. "Be persistent, don't give in. Just keep asking the same way, and stay calm."

I always followed Carol's instructions exactly. I trusted her completely. But also, I idolized the way she rode and wanted to be just like her, both as an equestrian and as a person.

She was perpetually calm, patient. I found it fascinating that nothing rattled her. She was always in control. Even though she spent most of her waking hours in a barn, she was the most elegant person I had ever known. She carried herself with an effortless grace and poise. She didn't just walk through a barn like everyone else, she glided through it. What was amazing to me was that even with all the elegance she exuded, there was not a shred of arrogance. She treated everyone the same. And she was always in the same good mood.

When she rode a horse, she became part of it. They were so united that it was difficult to imagine one without the other. And even though it didn't look like she was doing anything, somehow that horse picked its legs up higher, floated across the ring, and seamlessly transitioned from one movement to the next. Not only did she have a secret language with every horse, but every horse performed its absolute best when she was on its back—even Moonshine.

"Carol, I can't get him to bend," I let out, exasperated and in a full sweat, in January. "I can't feel my left arm!"

"Hop off," she said, taking off her jacket.

Yes! She's going to fix him! I was jubilant.

I loved when she would jump on, like a plumber fixing a deep clog, and then hand me the finished product.

"But don't get used to this, Victoria. I'm training you not just to be a rider, but to be a good trainer. I won't always be around, so you have to be learn to fix these things on your own."

"OK," I said, not expecting that harsh dose of reality.

"Inside leg to outside rein," Carol repeated over and over in probably every one of my lessons. *How does she never get tired of saying the same thing over and over?* I marveled. *I would have killed me by now.* Not Carol, she always smiled and joked with me.

In spite of her consistent and clear directions, I frequently dropped my outside rein and used both legs when she told me to use just one. It didn't matter. When I disobeyed, she never got angry or yelled at me. All she did was calmly repeat the instruction.

I think I disobeyed for two reasons. First, I stopped thinking about those basic dressage cues and let myself get caught up in everything else that was going wrong. If Moonshine was bent too much to the inside, I would pull his head to the outside. Then his shoulders would fall to the inside and he would bend the wrong way! Too many things would go wrong all at the same time, and I needed to fix them all. How could I ignore everything that was going wrong and just focus only on inside leg to outside rein?

The second reason I didn't listen is that I wanted to test Carol's theory. Did I really *have* to always apply pressure with my inside leg and hold on to my outside rein? Was that really the *only* way to ride dressage? Would it make any difference with a horse as terrible as Moonshine? He would always be impossible to ride, so why bother doing all that work?

"Inside leg, outside rein," I heard again. "You know, Victoria, pretty soon you'll be hearing this in your sleep."

"I already am!" I let out, trotting past her, still wrangling with Moonshine.

"Aww, I'm flattered. Dreaming of me every night?" she joked.

It was true, I heard it so much, I dreamed her voice. It was powerful and calm, loud but close, "Inside leg, outside rein, inside leg, outside rein . . ."

I didn't just hear her voice when I slept; I heard her all the time. I heard her when I brushed my teeth, on my way to school, and when I sat in class.

Even though I heard her repeating the same instruction

over and over, at virtually all hours of the day, I still resisted. It didn't register, my body wouldn't do it. I continued to drop my outside rein and my inside leg would hang loosely by Moonshine's side. Nevertheless, she continued to repeat calmly, patiently, and cheerfully the same instruction. I was grateful that she was so calm—if she had been as emotional as I was, that would have surely pushed me over the edge.

Another show season was going by, and I again noticed that most of Carol's students went to away shows. I still yearned to be considered one of Carol's advanced students and be good enough to compete off the property. I was thirteen, I had been riding for years. I was ready.

"Carol, when can I go to the away shows with everyone else?" I asked.

"When you're ready," she replied.

"I'm ready. I want to go to away shows, too," I insisted.

"I know, you're ready for the Olympics," she teased. "Away shows are very different from the shows we have here. You would have to compete against top, imported European horses and professional riders and trainers. It's a different world."

"I don't care. I'm ready. I hate being stuck here when everyone else gets to go," I insisted.

"How about this—when you hold on to your outside rein for an entire lesson, then we'll talk," she bribed.

"Fine," I sighed.

That summer slipped by without us going to any of the elite away shows. I was more frustrated than ever. Moonshine didn't make it any easier. He kept me honest in my riding, which means he never cut me any breaks, like a nice horse would have. Trained horses will sometimes cover up a rider's mistakes. When I rode Carol's horses, it didn't even matter that I was on their backs, they would still go through the entire routine by themselves. Needless to say, if I made a mistake, they just kept going as if it were business as usual.

Not Moonshine. If I ever dropped my outside rein, he would turn his head away from it and broadcast to everyone watching, "Look everyone, she dropped her outside rein again!" Not even the school horses would sell me out like Moonshine did—and school horses take any shortcut they can get. Moonshine seemed to do whatever he could to piss me off. His attitude only fueled my irritation. But I trusted and respected Carol, so I did whatever she said.

Months rolled by, and we weren't progressing. I didn't get to do the fancy upper level dressage movements like some of Carol's other students. It was the same lesson, over and over, every weekend. For almost a year, I was only allowed to canter in a circle. If Moonshine ever saw a straight line at the canter, he would take off running. It was so frustrating being forced to ride on a circle, when Carol's other students got to do pirouettes and flying changes—and it looked so easy. I felt like we would be in training wheels forever.

I was particularly envious of Beth. She was 17 and her parents had bought her a huge, beautiful warmblood—the type of horse that was bred specifically for dressage. Their whole bodies were designed to do all of the upper level dressage moves. Moonshine, on the other hand, was an Appendix—half Quarter horse, half Thoroughbred—which was really half cowboy's horse, half racehorse. Moonshine's long hind legs and short back were all wrong for dressage. Beth's horse, Lugano, with his elegant long limbs and high neck, had the perfect conformation for high level dressage. Plus, he was sweet. He never slapped his ears back on his head or tried to kick people, horses, and dogs, like Moonshine.

Beth had everything I wanted—the superstar horse, the loving parents, and the stable family. She even had the car I wanted, a brand new Toyota RAV4. She was also Carol's most advanced student. Lugano knew how to do all the cool tricks in upper level dressage. Not only was Lugano already trained to the highest levels of dressage, but he also adored her. She didn't have to bribe him to like her with bags of carrots like I did with Moonshine. Lugano always nickered as soon as she stepped in the barn. I wouldn't dare open Moonshine's door without a carrot, certain I would be greeted by gnashing teeth. And then, I would be on the never ending twenty-meter circle in one of my lessons with Carol, while Beth floated by on her spectacular horse, doing trick after trick.

Comparing Beth and Lugano to me and Moonshine made me question why I should keep riding. Maybe it wasn't just that Lugano was better than Moonshine, maybe Beth was also better than me. Maybe everyone was a better rider than me. Maybe I was a terrible rider and no one had the heart to tell me the truth.

Why am I doing this? I started asking myself. *What's the point? Even if Moonshine is perfect, he'll never compete against a horse like Lugano.* I couldn't answer. It seemed as though I was riding whenever I wasn't in school because it was the schedule I created for myself. Was I riding so much just because this had become part of my routine, or did I really love it? *Sure, I love being at the barn, but what's the point of riding if I'm not getting any better?*

On the hour-long drive to the barn, I would daydream about doing pirouettes in my lesson. And on the drive back home, after having spent the entire lesson on a twenty-meter circle, I would wonder if I would ever be good enough to do a pirouette, or any other advanced dressage move.

18

Spring brought another show season. The barn was buzzing with boarders getting ready for the big show in April, in Washington, D.C.

"So, Vic, don't you want to do the D.C. show?" Nora inquired when I was grooming Moonshine in his stall, getting ready for a lesson. I always groomed Moony in his stall because he was too dangerous to be on cross-ties in the barn aisle; he would either lunge at people or kick at horses, even if he was tied up. I didn't mind grooming him in his stall, except that if someone wanted to chat while I was in the stall, I was forced to talk to them, instead of spending every precious moment at the barn exclusively with Moony. All of my barn time was spent in a bubble with Moony, and intrusions were generally not welcome.

"Yeah, but I can't," I replied, still brushing Moony.

"Why not?" I heard Carol's voice, and then saw her face appear in front of Moonshine's stall.

I was at a loss. Was this a trick? Was I supposed to say out loud, in front of Nora, how crappy a rider I was?

"Umm . . ." I stammered, "because I'm not ready?"

"You're ready," Carol said conclusively.

"Seriously?" My heart jumped.

"Seriously," she said, turning back toward the indoor ring.

Nora's eyes met mine, and she smiled. "Moony will ride in the big trailer, with all the other horses that are going."

We were finally part of the team!

I was thrilled that I would be able to compete off the property. I was now good enough to ride in a big, important away show, just like all of Carol's advanced students!

I trained harder than ever, obeying Carol's instructions and making every effort to ride with my inside leg to outside rein.

"This show will be a good start for you because they have an equitation seat competition only for Juniors," Carol informed me after one of my lessons.

"What's that?" I inquired.

"It's a class just for kids between fourteen and eighteen, where you ride around the arena. The hitch is that the judges are only judging the riders' positions, so they don't look at the horse at all. I think it would be a good class for you, now that you're fourteen." Carol said.

"OK, I'll enter it," I responded.

The date of the show was fast approaching, but for me, it couldn't come fast enough.

Then, finally, it was time.

Richard told everyone that he would ship all of the horses himself. But we would have to get our horses on his six-horse trailer ourselves and we had to pack all of our equipment in our own cars and drive down with him in a caravan. Load time would be 4:00 a.m.—sharp.

"If you're late, I'm leaving without you," he warned.

Shipping day finally came. I arrived a half hour early to make sure I wouldn't be late. Luckily, my mother didn't object too much to being woken up at 2:30 a.m.

When I got to the barn, I threw a bag of carrots into

Moony's feed bin, and immediately wrapped his legs, to protect them while he was in the trailer. I finished just in time—I had secured the last wrap when he stopped crunching on his last carrot.

"Good boy," I whispered. "Ready to go to a show? Let's go!" I said, slipping his halter on his head.

He followed me out into the darkness, to the end of the property, where the trailer was parked and waiting. As we approached the huge rig, I sensed Moonshine getting tense. He was nipping at my jacket, and slowing down his stride. His ears pricked forward and his neck shot up when he heard the voices and then the loud echoes of hooves on the trailer's ramp. He stopped walking shoulder to shoulder with me, and started to pull on the lead rope, to go back to the barn. I learned this maneuver and how to trick him into moving forward by allowing him to move in circles around me. I would move the center of the circle closer and closer to my ultimate destination. But when he saw the trailer, he started snorting, pawing at the ground, and dragging me backward.

"It's OK buddy, you're OK," I coaxed.

Richard stormed toward us, and ripped the rope from my hand.

"Moonshine, GET ON!" He screamed as he marched toward the ramp with Moonshine pulling back on the lead rope. As soon as Moony resisted, he bellowed, "Beth! Get me the whip!" Beth immediately complied.

As soon as he had the whip in his hand, he cranked his arm back and whipped Moonshine hard on his shoulder.

"No!" I screamed.

Moonshine reared up on two legs and struck out at Richard's head. He missed by a small margin. The small crowd of the five other horse owners did nothing but gawk.

"Damn good-for-nothing piece of shit!" Richard shouted as he raised his hand again.

"Stop!" I shrieked.

"Shut up! This horse is getting on the trailer NOW!" he yelled back at me.

"He won't if you keep whipping him!" I yelled but was ignored and Moonshine continued to struggle with Richard on the other end of the lead rope.

I knew Richard wouldn't listen to me, so I started toward Moonshine.

"Victoria, *no*, stay *here*," my mother commanded, as she grabbed my shoulders, but I easily slipped through her fingers. I was by Moonshine's hindquarters in an instant. I had always been told never to stand by a horse's hindquarters because you could get kicked, but I knew Moony wouldn't kick me, not even now, as he was battling with Richard.

"Moony," I called softly, in stark contrast to Richard's yelling. I made sure to pet his hindquarters just after I called him, to let him know I was there, and he wasn't alone. I knew he sensed me when I saw his left ear flip back toward me, on his left side. I had at least half of his attention.

"Moony, I'm right here, you're OK, it's OK, buddy," I talked to him, petting the left side of his body, making my way up to his head.

"Get *away*! I'm *handling* this!" Richard bellowed at me.

I ignored Richard, knowing that I had Moony's focus with that one ear. I had initiated a dialogue. Now I had to ask for what I wanted. I had no idea whether Moony trusted me as much as I trusted him. Would he follow me into a dark trailer, the thing he hated, the thing that used to take him back and forth to those correctional facilities? I had no doubt that he had only bad memories of trailers. I also had no doubt that Richard's antagonizing him would not encourage him to step right in. But I did doubt that those two things would overpower the bond I had created with him. So, I tested that bond.

"*Moony*," I called long and sweetly, trying to make my voice sound exactly like it did every time I greeted him in the barn.

I tried hard not to let my voice quiver, and to hide how upset I was. I knew that if Moony sensed danger in my voice, he would never get in the trailer. I turned toward the ramp, facing the inside of the trailer. Out of the corner of my eye, I caught his eye watching me, as he continued to struggle with Richard. I knew I had him. I then shoved my right hand into my pocket, which Moony knew was always filled with treats. Moonshine could never resist those treats. Then, with my hand in my pocket, jiggling the treats inside, I walked up the ramp.

As Moonshine watched me amble leisurely up the ramp, he lowered his head and approached the ramp himself. He gingerly put one foot on the steep ramp while Richard brushed past him, to "lead" him up. Richard was clearly no longer part of the dialogue, even though he was holding the lead rope. I called Moony, and now my horse was coming to me.

Richard started up the ramp toward me. From inside the trailer, I turned my back to Moonshine, shaking the contents of my pocket, as if to tell him, "If you don't catch me, I'm giving these treats to someone else." When Moony saw me turn my back and walk away into the darkness of the trailer, he scrambled up the ramp. As soon as he was inside, Richard shoved him into the last empty stall and hooked his halter up to the cross-ties.

"Good boy!" I praised, bursting with pride, as I fed him the carrot in my pocket. As he crunched the carrot from my hand, I couldn't help but admire my horse. I searched his eye for some sort of acknowledgement that he knew I would do anything for him, but he was totally focused on the treat he was devouring. It didn't matter. I knew we were a team now; he did trust me as much as I trusted him. As much as he drove me crazy, we were bonded. He was my horse, and I was his person. It was now me and Moony against the world.

As I made my way down the ramp to let Richard latch up the door, this escapade reminded me that adults don't always know best. I was proud that I disobeyed both my mother and Richard. I was glad to have been brave enough to do what I knew I had to do to get Moony in the trailer. I was disappointed that no one else tried to help. I was also surprised that I somehow knew what to do, and yet nobody else did, not even Richard.

"We're leaving now!" Richard announced to everyone watching. As he began to close up the trailer, I heard kicking and watched the entire trailer rattle with each blow. I knew it was Moonshine.

As Richard brushed past me to the driver's seat, he said, "If he breaks anything, you're paying for it."

The four-hour drive was relatively uneventful, despite the unyielding barrage of kicking coming from the stall in the back left side of the trailer—Moonshine's stall. I watched the changing landscape on the drive down and marveled at the wide, open fields I saw from the highway. I rolled down my window and took in the fresh, clean air. I daydreamed of winning all of my classes at the competition. I couldn't wait to get in the show ring.

The show grounds were like no other farm I had ever seen. It was massive—the show organizers said it was 300 acres and there were 500 stalls. It took ten minutes just to drive through it all and get to the barn reserved for our team.

When the trailer finally parked, I jumped out of the car and ran to my horse. As Richard lowered the ramp, I asked, "Can I take Moonshine out?"

"Don't let him step on you, and stay in the middle of the ramp. And go down slowly," he ordered.

I know how to handle my horse, jackass, I wanted to say, but simply responded, "OK."

I hopped into the trailer and petted Moonshine on his nose as I grabbed the lead rope, and snapped it onto his halter.

I led Moonshine out of the trailer, slowly down the ramp, and he followed me at the pace I had set. When we set foot on the ground, he looked to his right, then to his left, and then started grazing. He was calmer now than before he was in the trailer.

"Victoria, get out of the way! Get him in a stall, and get him a bucket of water!" Richard bellowed from the trailer.

I did as I was told, leading Moony to his stall, and then grabbing a bucket from the car, to fill with water. When all of the horses were unloaded from the trailer, Richard marched to my mother.

Ugh, now what did I do? I thought as I hauled the bucket full of water to Moonshine in his new stall.

"That damn horse kicked a hole straight through the divider. You owe me two hundred dollars," he told her.

I rolled my eyes and stopped listening, shifting all my attention to Moonshine. I found a hook in his temporary new stall on which to hang the water bucket and made my way to the hay and shavings, to give him food and lay down bedding.

I let Moonshine rest for about an hour before taking him out of his stall. Then, I tacked him up, got on, and we walked to the warm up arena. By now, most of the competitors had arrived and many of them were riding in the main warm up ring.

When I got to the warm up ring, I froze at the entrance.

Oh my God, Moony! That's Robert Dover! And Ashley Holzer! And Betsy Steiner!

I was starstruck. I hadn't expected to see big time dressage celebrities in this ring, where I was going to ride. These were the guys in *Dressage Today* magazine! These were dressage's celebrities, my heroes—Olympians, World Cup competitors, international caliber equestrians. And I was stepping into the very same warm up arena as them! It was hard to focus on my own ride, as I was overcome with intrigue at how my idols were training. I couldn't stop gawking at them. My ride on Moonshine was short, about a half hour. I spent twenty minutes letting him walk on a loose rein so that I could watch them train.

After my ride, I walked Moony back to his stall, where my mother was setting up the rest of the equipment.

"Mom, *Robert Dover* is here!" I shrieked quietly.

"So?"

"What do you mean 'so'? It's *Robert Dover*! He's an *Olympian*!"

"I know," she stated flatly.

I sighed in exasperation. I was shocked at her lack of interest. These were superstars! At the same show! In the same ring as me! How did this not blow her mind?

I always hand grazed Moony after I rode, and since there was grass all around the warm-up arena, I figured why not let Moony graze while I watch the superstars train?

I observed with complete focus. The horses floated around the arena. Each horse and rider pair moved like they were one. The equestrians' bodies didn't move at all; it looked like all of the riders were motionless aboard their horses.

How are they so still? I wondered. *Where are the cues?*

I watched until Moonshine started back toward the barn.

"Is it dinner time, buddy?" I asked Moony as we walked briskly back to the barn. Moonshine always knew when it was feeding time, and if any of his meals were ever late, he was one of the loudest protesters in the barn. Food was a definite priority to my horse.

I fed him his grain and tossed him a few flakes of hay for the night.

"Night, Moony," I said as he gobbled the grain in the bucket.

I then realized I was hungry myself, and exhausted, but content. I was so happy.

The next day, I arrived at dawn to feed Moonshine and braid his mane, as I had learned from one of the girls at the farm.

Moonshine was picking at the last remnants of the hay on the ground. I dumped his morning grain into his bucket, tossed in two more flakes of hay, and then filled the water bucket. Then, I grabbed a pitchfork and wheelbarrow to muck the stall as he ate. I finished after about ten minutes.

"I'll be right back, Moon." I had fallen into the habit of talking to him as if he were a person.

I went to the show office to see the indoor stadium that everyone had been talking about. The food vendors were also in the indoor, so I figured it would be a good opportunity to get breakfast. I walked in at the top of a long row of bleachers. As the rows descended from where I was, I saw hundreds of rows of chairs, and then the ring itself. I had just walked into a stadium.

"*Wow.*" The magnificent scene took my breath away. It was beautiful.

It's bigger than Madison Square Garden, I thought, mesmerized.

After a few minutes of scanning the arena, I realized I was hungry. I went over to the food vendors to buy a bagel and orange juice.

"Program!" I heard someone call out.

"Hi, can I have one?" I asked the man with the programs.

"Sure, here you go, kid."

I flipped it open to the first page, to see where my two classes of the day would be held.

"OK, first class is in ring five. Have to find ring five," I muttered to myself.

Equitation class is in the stadium? That can't be right.

"Excuse me, is this the final program?" I asked the volunteer.

"Sure is!"

Why is my equitation class in the stadium? Wait, it's at 8:00 p.m.? Why is it so late at night? I wondered. Normally, all my classes were any time between 8:00 a.m. to 5:00 p.m., during show hours.

Carol had arrived that day and I saw her at the barn when I

got back.

"Hi, Carol!" I was thrilled to see her.

"Hey there, how's it going?" she beamed.

I was immediately comforted by her usual greeting. She always greeted me with, "Hey, there," it may as well have been my name. I had wondered in the past why she never used my name, but this time, I found her usual greeting overwhelmingly appeasing. Perhaps in the midst of all of the newness, I did appreciate the familiar.

"Great! Moony's great! But I have a question. I think my equitation class is in the stadium. And this program says it's at 8:00 p.m. Can that be right?" I asked.

"Sure, why not?" she smiled and winked.

I had no idea what she meant by the smile and wink, so I simply responded with an eloquent, "Ummm, OK."

My first class was in ring five, which I discovered was actually set up on a racetrack at the other end of the show grounds.

I got on Moonshine and we headed for the other side of the property. Moonshine walked calmly through the crowds, vendors, dogs, and horses. It was like walking through a crowded flea market on horseback until we got to the show ring. I assumed that since the crowds didn't faze him, he would be calm during the whole show. But then he saw it—the racetrack. He must have remembered his racing days because as soon as he stepped onto the sand, he bolted. My back snapped as he took off down the track. Amazingly, my legs knew to hold on tight as I worked to gather my reins.

Most horses that I had ridden would take off because they were running away from something. Not Moonshine! Moony's ears were pricked forward, so he was focused on something *ahead* of him, and he was picking up speed. Moonshine was running *toward* something. This was the first time I had ridden a horse that was acting like a predator, rather than prey.

"*Moonshine*! Oh God!" I panicked as I realized that he was running toward the arena with a horse and rider already in it, competing!

"Moonshine, *no*!" I whispered loudly as I yanked his head to the right. I managed to turn him away just as he was about to enter the arena. I thought I had broken his momentum, which would make him stop, but as soon as he was turned around, he took off down the track in the other direction! At least this was going away from the two competition arenas, but I really hoped the judges weren't watching. This wasn't my idea of a respectable first impression.

I realized how strong Moonshine had become from the power with which he ran. I tried and tried to pull the reins and sit back to stop him, but the more he ran, the stronger he became and the more impossible it was for me to stop him.

Well, it's a big track, hopefully he'll get tired soon, I hoped, as the wind whipped me in the face, realizing the futility of interfering with Moonshine's resolve to have some fun.

Luckily, he did; after about five minutes of a flat gallop, he began to slow down, and finally came back to a trot. Then, I turned him around and trotted him back to the show ring.

My mother was still standing by the entrance of the track and when she knew I had caught her eye, she lifted her hands in emphatic applause. She was clearly humored by our performance. Even though my horse had just taken off with me, I couldn't resist laughing and dramatically bowed my head and hand in appreciation of her teasing applause. Luckily, Carol was helping Beth prepare for her ride in another arena, so she wasn't around to witness the mockery I was making of dressage. She did have a sense of humor, but this display of a blatant lack of control may have been too much, even for her.

I waited patiently by the entrance of the show ring on Moonshine, as my ride time was approaching. The rider before me had just completed her final salute. It was my turn. I trotted

Moonshine once around the outside perimeter of the arena to make sure he was comfortable with the surroundings. He was, as usual. Nothing ever spooked this horse.

The judge blew the whistle. I entered and saluted. Moonshine and I executed every movement as precisely and correctly as we could. I had put every ounce of effort I had into performing all of the movements perfectly. I tried to cue Moony to execute every transition crisply, and exactly where the test mandated in the arena. I sat up as tall as I could, keeping my eyes and head up, as Carol instructed. I maneuvered Moonshine as deep into the corners as his stiff body would allow, for extra points. Then, I gave the final salute. I could hear two people applauding (the large crowd for the previous rider having dispersed); I knew one of my two fans was my mother. I petted Moonshine, but I knew we were nowhere near as good as the pair just before us.

"Oh well, we tried," I said to my mother as I passed her, heading towards the barn.

"It was good!" she encouraged.

"Yeah, that was a nice test, sweetie!" remarked the rider who had ridden just before me.

"Thanks!" I was flattered by the compliment from the elegant rider on the talented horse.

The loudspeaker then announced the results of my class, I had received a mediocre score, and had landed in fifth place—out of six riders.

"At least you didn't get last!" Carol joked. I usually appreciated her humor, but this stung a little. Then, more seriously, she added, "You'll get them tonight." And I believed her. If Carol told me I could fly, I would have believed her.

I had to wait six hours for my final class of the day. The rest of the team went to dinner, but I stayed behind. I wanted no distractions. I wanted to be completely focused.

I got on Moonshine a half hour before my class to warm up. Carol came to the warm up arena to supervise.

On my first break, she told me, "Just remember to focus on yourself, Victoria. In this class, they don't look at the horse at all. They're just judging you and *your* riding ability. Remember to ride from your seat."

"OK," I replied.

Then it was time for the class to begin. Unlike other classes where each horse and rider pair ride alone in the show ring, in this equitation class, all of the riders were shuffled into the stadium at the same time. Moonshine was completely unfazed as he descended the long, wide ramp and the magnificent arena swallowed us in.

Carol was waiting for us at the entrance. As we approached her, she said, "Good luck." Then, she stepped closer to me, looked me in the eye and said, "Smile."

I then turned and looked ahead, into the massive, brightly lit arena. As Moonshine and I emerged from the darkness, I smiled.

Moonshine marched proudly onto the sand as if he belonged there. As soon as he stepped into the bright stadium, I could feel him grow bigger. He seemed to puff his chest out like an actor taking his stage.

There were fourteen other young riders in the arena. The announcer said through the speakers, "Riders, please line up and salute the judge." As everyone got into formation, I glanced up at all of the empty seats in the stands.

But, in the middle of one section, I saw everyone from the Oakwood Farm team! I was touched that they had come to watch my class. I saw Carol standing by the entrance and was comforted by having her there, watching. My mother also stood silently next to Carol. I was struck by how white my mother's face looked, in stark contrast to Carol's tanned and flushed face.

The judges then ordered the riders to make their way out to the rail. Then, I heard, "All trot please, all trot!" over the loudspeaker.

All riders picked up the trot.

"Change direction, please, change direction!"

A cluster of horses and riders started to crowd around Moonshine. I feared that he would kick anyone who got too close, which would cost me the class, so I looked for an opening through all of the riders. I waited to get closer to the opening, and then I slowly trotted Moonshine in a big circle, to land in a less congested part of the ring, just like Carol told me to do if this were to happen.

"Now, all canter, all canter please!"

I was happy to pick up the canter with no other horses around, so I wouldn't have to worry about Moony attacking any innocent bystanders.

I noticed that some horses did start kicking out at others, in a more crowded part of the ring, and was thrilled that I was not a part of that mess.

Yes! I missed it! I rejoiced. I was sure that if Moonshine had been around those bucking horses, it would have been worse than the minor scuffle it was.

"All riders please trot and then come to a walk, proceed to center of arena and line up!"

All fourteen riders obeyed immediately.

"The following riders are dismissed. . ."

I braced myself. *Please don't let me be first to lose, please don't call me first*, I closed my eyes and prayed.

"Numbers eighty-seven . . . one-hundred and eighteen . . . fifty-six . . . twelve . . .thirty-one . . . sixty . . . ninety-three . . . one hundred and three . . . two hundred and six!"

"Oh good, that wasn't us, Moon," I whispered, relieved, scratching his withers with my knuckles.

"In sixth place, we have number fourteen. Number fourteen, please approach the judge and accept your ribbon!" The rider did as she was told. The judge hooked the ribbon to the horse's bridle, and then she was directed to stand on the other side of the ring.

I tightened my grip on the reins, preparing to be the next one called.

"In *fifth* place, we have number forty-two!"

Cool! That wasn't us, either! I was pleasantly surprised.

"In fourth place, we have number . . ."

OK, this is us, I know we got fourth, we always get fourth or fifth, I thought.

". . . seventy-seven!"

That didn't sound like my number. I leaned over, and looked down at my right boot, where Carol had hooked my number, to see what it was. *Maybe I forgot my number. Man, that would be embarrassing!* I thought. I saw my number was still thirty-three. *Thirty-three, thirty-three . . .* I repeated to myself. I didn't want to embarrass myself and my team by not stepping up to the judge when he called my number.

"In *third* place we have number thirteen!"

Now I was panicking. *Did they forget my number? Am I actually entered in this class? Why are they not calling me? Was I disqualified and they're going to tell me after they announce the winner? Why am I the only rider left other than this girl to my right? What's going on?*

"And the winner of the 1994 Junior Dressage Seat Equitation class is number thirty-three! Number thirty-three, please come up and accept your prize!"

I was frozen. I stared at the judge, waiting for him to realize his mistake.

"Number thirty-three, please come up and accept your prize!" the announcer repeated.

And then I heard a rumble of cheers, whistles and screams from the Oakwood team, my team, sitting in the bleachers. They were standing, jumping, waving their hands at me. I suddenly couldn't hear. I saw them jumping up and down, but it was as if I were underwater—everything was muffled.

Suddenly, I saw the judge pinning a beautiful blue ribbon

to Moony's bridle. Moonshine objected to wearing the small cardboard number on his bridle, but the huge, flowing blue ribbon was fine with him. He even threw his head up, proudly displaying it after he was pinned.

"Congratulations," the judge said, as he took my right hand off the rein and shook it. My mouth was open, but I couldn't speak. I was in total shock. I simply nodded.

Someone else came up behind the judge and handed me a shiny silver plate, with some sort of engraving that I couldn't read, because my eyes wouldn't focus. And then a third person came up with a sash that she draped around Moony's shoulders. Moony didn't object at all. He stood motionless, waiting to be adorned with more stuff and admired by his public.

"Wave, dear! And smile for the cameras!" the judge suddenly ordered.

I looked up into the stands, to the Oakwood team cheering loudly. I lifted my right arm to wave at them, and was blinded by a lightning of flashes.

Then, I found myself back where it all started, at the entrance of the stadium, with Carol and my mom. Now my mother's face was red, but Carol was glowing. I had never before seen her smile so widely.

"Wow, what's that?" Carol asked as she took the plate from me, so I could have both hands on the reins.

Just then, the Oakwood team rushed to Moonshine, while he still stood calmly, appreciating the attention.

"Let's see it!" I heard Nora command.

"We're posting your ribbons to our 'Oakwood Farm' banner, Victoria!" she announced, as they took the ribbons off Moonshine.

In that instant, they vanished into the night, with the blue ribbons I had just won. I had made my contribution.

"Congratulations, Victoria," Carol smiled broadly, after the others had run off.

"Thanks, Carol."

"Congratulations, darling!" my mother said in Romanian, clearly trying to contain herself.

"Thanks, Mom."

"Cool him out and get to bed, you have another day of showing tomorrow," Carol instructed.

"Thanks for your help today, Carol."

"No sweat!"

"I am so proud of you!" my mom gushed, after Carol left.

"Thanks, Mom."

I dismounted and walked Moonshine back to the barn in the darkness. He wasn't afraid of the dark if I walked on foot alongside him. I petted his neck as we walked.

"Thanks, Moony," I whispered.

The rest of the show was uneventful compared to that first night. We earned our usual fourth and fifth place ribbons. There was no contest against the superior horse and rider pairs. We didn't stand a chance against those fancy horses.

One time, however, I watched the rider before me—Marie Annette Matthews. I knew her from her advertisements in all of the dressage and horse magazines I read. She owned Mountain View Farm, a premier breeding facility full of beautiful warmblood horses. She was in my class, competing on one of her talented horses.

I watched her horse glide across the arena, executing the movements of the test. I did see her make some mistakes, she made one circle too early, picked up the canter depart too late, but still, if dressage was judged mostly on the horse's talent, like Carol said, then this horse was definitely winning this class.

After she saluted, it was my turn.

Moonshine and I trotted in, and saluted in the center. Our test was precise, we executed each movement exactly where it was supposed to be done, our lines were straight, our circles were round and the right sizes. But that was never enough when we were competing against a prancy warmblood. Still, I always hoped for a different outcome.

I saluted at the end, ready for my fifth place ribbon. But this time, we won third place, and Marie Annette Matthews won fourth. *Moonshine* beat the fancy Mountain View Farm horse! I was exultant. We may as well have won the class. I was so happy to see that for once, a judge valued the accuracy of the test over another horse's talent. Our hard work to be precise and perfect in the ring paid off this time!

Even though I only won one blue ribbon at my first away show, I went home feeling exhilarated and ready for more.

19

In my first lesson after the show, Carol asked me what I had learned.

"Well, if Moony and I are going to be competitive with the warmbloods, we have to be perfect in the test," I said.

"OK, what else?" Carol pressed.

"Don't take him out on any racetracks!" I answered, remembering how Moonshine had taken off with me.

Carol laughed.

"OK, but I want you to know that those equitation seat judges recognized your talent and that you have a good seat, so we should work on developing *your* riding skills as much as we can."

I found it curious that Carol emphasized "your" as though I could improve my riding without Moonshine. *It's probably just all in my head*, I thought dismissively.

That summer, I continued in my training with Moony and Carol; I also worked as Carol's assistant in exchange for free lessons once a week. I was content spending every day at the barn and working for Carol. I watched her ride during my lunch breaks, and envisioned the movements as she schooled them.

In one lesson, she told me that she would teach me a more advanced movement called a half-pass, where a horse moves sideways, with his front and hind legs crossing. This was one of the movements I regularly saw her train, so I knew what the cues were. It was different from a leg yield because in this move, the horse had to look in the direction he was going, whereas in the leg yield, the horse's head was kept looking straight ahead.

"So today, we're going to learn how to half-pass," she said.

"I already know how to half-pass," I joked confidently.

"Oh, really? And how do you know how to half-pass all of a sudden?" she questioned.

"From watching you," I replied.

"OK, hotshot, show me what you got. Do a half-pass to the left," she challenged.

I was on one of Carol's client's horses, which was a more advanced horse that knew how to perform the movement. I picked up the trot, found an open spot in the arena, and applied my right leg to his side so that he moved away from it, to the left.

"Not bad!" Carol said when I stopped to obtain her feedback. "But I'm going to explain how to do it, just to be official," she said in a teasing, matter-of-fact way only she could pull off.

I translated the new things I had learned to Moonshine, or I should say *tried* to translate them, as I was often met with resistance. Moonshine was still not an easy horse, as he challenged everything and seemed to say, "make me," with every new movement I introduced.

Despite the fact that Moonshine was still a difficult horse, he had become an integral part of my life, and of me. I spent as much time around him as I could. Our bond was growing, and apparently was becoming evident to others.

Kim, the barn manager, who rarely spoke to me because

I was "just one of the barn kids," even paid me a compliment once that summer. As she passed me in the barn, she said, "You and Moony are coming along pretty fast, kid. Keep up the good work." I was astonished because Kim only spoke to me to reprimand me for something I had done or to reiterate the long list of barn rules.

Then, one evening, the phone rang and my mother picked up.

"It's a man, he says it's for you."

"OK . . ." we both looked quizzically at each other, not knowing who the caller was.

I picked up the line.

"Victoria?" The voice inquired.

"Yes?" I answered.

"This is George Beck, Moonshine's owner."

Moonshine's owner had become a phantom memory to everyone, since he no longer paid the bills for the horse.

"Hi . . ." I said warily, curious as to his sudden emergence from the past.

"Listen, I have to get rid of the horse. You need to buy him by the end of the week or I'm shipping him to slaughter."

The room started to spin.

"Wait, what? Why?" I stammered.

"I just have to get rid of it," he concluded curtly.

I hated him for calling Moonshine an "it." Moonshine was a "him." Moony deserved the proper pronoun. Moony had as much personality as any person I knew. But this was not the time to correct George Beck.

"But . . ." I began, but he interrupted.

"Just call me at the end of the week to set up a meeting so you can give me the money. Bring $3,500 in cash."

"But, I can't, I don't have . . ."

"(845) 932-5555. Bye."

The line went dead. I was still holding the phone to my ear when my mother walked into my room.

"What happened? What's wrong?" she asked. I felt my face turn white, and I could feel all the blood fall from my head to my heart. Tears pooled my eyes. My ears were ringing. I couldn't see, I couldn't hear. An invisible boulder crushed my chest, and I had just been punched in the stomach.

"*Victoria*!" my mother demanded to know what had just happened.

"Moonshine's owner . . . He said we need to buy him by the end of the week or else." I blurted out.

As soon as I got the words out, hot tears poured down my face.

"WHAT?" she yelled. "He said that to *you*?!" she roared.

And then she went back to the phone in the living room, dialed his phone number, and began yelling.

"WHAT did you just say to my daughter?"

She paused and listened.

"I don't care what you want, it's *her* horse now! I have been paying for the horse for the past year! And where were you? You have no right to do this!" she replied.

She paused again, listening.

"There is NO WAY you will get away with this, you fucking pig!" she exploded. She hardly ever cursed, so when she did, it was bad.

She then slammed down the phone and then called her best friend, my godmother, Ava, for advice. I knew she would be a while, so I went to the farthest room of the house—the bathroom in the master bedroom—closed the door, sat on the floor, and sobbed. It was over.

There was nothing I could do. I would lose Moonshine. The fear of losing him, the idea of life without Moonshine, began to plague me. I still had to go to school, and attend my classes. But as soon as the lesson started, my eyes drifted to the window and I wondered what Moony was doing at that moment.

When I sat with my friends at lunch, I envisioned Moony in a crammed auction house, waiting with hundreds of other innocent horses for their doom. I had recurring nightmares. In one dream, I was at a huge show, and there was a big crowd outside of the arena, waiting for me to enter the ring. And then I entered, on foot. No horse, just me.

In another nightmare, I had a vision of Moony being stabbed to death in a slaughterhouse, ropes around his ankles, leaving him defenseless against his assailants. And then I saw his bloodied legs on a steel table.

"NO! MOONY!" I screamed.

"Vicky, Vicky, wake up!" My sister was shaking me awake.

"They're going to kill him."

"No they won't, they won't," she said.

"Yes they will. I know Mom can't afford to buy him, you know Victor cleaned her out with the stupid divorce. There's no way."

"It'll be OK, Vicky," she insisted. Then she called for our mother, realizing there would be nothing she could say to diminish my despair.

The following Saturday morning, my mother drove me to the farm, as usual. However, instead of dropping me off like she usually did, she parked the car, and strode off to the office. I plodded to Moony's barn. I don't know how long she was there, but Carol, instead of coming into the barn at 8:00 a.m. to tell me which horses she wanted me to get ready for her that morning, like she always did, didn't come into the barn until 9:30 a.m. I knew she was at the farm because her car was parked in her spot.

Then, at 9:30 a.m., Carol appeared. Her face was red and agitated. For the first time, I saw her frown lines, most notably two vertical lines between her eyebrows. There were no smiles, no jokes.

"Hey, there. Can you get Solstice now, Sunny after him, and then Prinz?"

"Sure," I said, avoiding eye contact, as I headed for the tack room.

The day was work as usual.

At the end of the day my mother picked me up. Once I was in the passenger seat, she ordered, "You have to call your father."

"What, why?" I asked. I had not spoken to or seen my father since that ill-fated vacation at Lake George. I didn't even know if he was in the country or if he had gone back to Romania.

"It's our only hope," she said. "If you want Moonshine, you have to fight for him. I can't afford it on my own."

"It's not going to work," I said.

"It's our only chance," she insisted.

"Fine." I gave in. I would do anything for Moony, even beg my absentee father for money.

I dialed his number when I got home. My mother listened silently on the other phone.

"Da," he answered in Romanian, almost sounding offended.

"Hi, Dad."

"Faaaaafi?" he replied, addressing me by my nickname. I knew he was drunk when he lingered on vowels like that.

"Yeah, hi Dad." It was strange to call him Dad. Whenever my family and I talked about him, we called him by his first name. But I knew he liked to be called Dad, and I needed him to be on my side this one time.

"Dad, I need help," I started.

"Yeaaah . . . what *kind* of help?" he spoke slowly.

"Well, I've been riding this horse Moonshine. His owner abandoned him a long time ago, so Mom's been paying the bills so I can ride him and have my own horse."

"Sooo . . .?"

"So, now, out of the blue, the owner calls me and wants me to pay thirty-five hundred dollars to keep Moonshine. And the reason I'm calling is because Mom can't pay it all by herself."

He interrupted.

"That's a lot of money . . ."

"Yes, I know. I wouldn't call if I wasn't desperate, Dad. I mean, you don't even have to pay the whole thing, can you just pay as much as you can? Can you maybe split it with Mom?"

"You want me to pay *half*?" he exclaimed, like I was absurd for even asking.

"Can you?"

"No," he said shortly.

I was ready. I knew he was incredibly stingy, so I was prepared for a "no" early on in the negotiations.

"Dad, *please*, this horse means everything to me. Can you pay at least a thousand?"

He laughed.

Interrupting his amusement, I added, "Five hundred?"

He continued his cackling.

"Dad, come *on*."

"Darling," he began condescendingly, as he never addressed me with pet names, "it's just a horse—dog food! Forget about it. Just focus on school."

My mother and sister watched me anxiously.

"Dad, this horse is my life now," I turned away from them, lowering my voice.

He broke out into roaring laughter now.

As infuriating as his dismissiveness was, I continued to plead. "Dad, please, whatever you can help out with, please! Even if it's just a hundred dollars, please help me."

But then the line went dead.

The drone of the dial tone was deafening. My stomach sank all the way through my body. I lost the feeling in my hands, and then I saw the phone receiver drop to the ground. I started to see spots, then I saw the ceiling, and then nothing.

I opened my eyes and saw my mother's agitated face above my own. Her mouth was moving but I couldn't hear her over the ringing in my ears. Then she started to shake me.

"Victoria!" I heard now, she was screaming.

"Oh shit!" my sister let out, standing behind my mother, in the doorway of the bathroom. "She fainted!"

"Get cold water in a glass, and bring a cold, wet towel!" my mother barked at my sister.

As soon as my sister ran off, my mother grabbed me under my arms and pulled me to my bed. She was cursing my father and George in Romanian. I had never heard her curse like that, like my father, before. It was like venom.

She ordered my sister to stay in my room with me, while she went back to the phone. I knew it no longer mattered who she called or what she said. I now felt nothing, I was empty. Then I closed my eyes and fell asleep.

I woke up the next morning, and put on my riding clothes.

When we got to the farm, my mother marched off to the office and I straggled to the stables. This time, Carol was already tacking up Prinz, her first horse of the day.

"Hey there! Get your helmet. You're starting Prinz for me."

"OK." I welcomed the immediate distraction.

"Hey, Moony," I called to Moony as I approached his stall, since it was on my way to the tack room, sort of. I dropped a couple of carrots in his bucket and headed for the tack room, to get my helmet.

As soon as I was done riding Prinz, I made my way back to my favorite spot on the farm, Moony's stall.

Just as I started to open the stall door, Kim flew into the barn in an obvious rage.

"VICTORIA!" she bellowed.

Now what did I do? I wondered.

"Moony's not going nowhere, you hear me?" she started.

Just then, I saw my mother come into the barn. I knew she had just told Kim what was going on.

"Sure, OK," I replied.

"Listen, this is *your* horse and *no* one is taking him away from you. I'll lock him in his stall if I have to," she assured me.

I was touched. Kim had never been particularly warm. In fact, it seemed like the only time she talked to me was to reprimand me. I was moved by her sudden interest.

"See, Fafi, you won't lose Moonshine. Everyone is on your side," my mother started.

"OK, thanks, Mom. I have to get back to work."

I didn't have anything pressing to do, but I was drained and just didn't feel like being around people anymore.

"OK, I will pick you up at six."

"OK."

Throughout the day, I came to visit Moonshine every chance I got. I didn't ride him until the end of the day, though. I didn't want to be rushed. I wanted to savor every last minute I had with him. When all my work for Carol was done, I got on him without a saddle. I just wanted to enjoy a light and easy bareback ride.

Carol was in the indoor teaching when I came in bareback on Moonshine. When I was within earshot, she called, "Saved the best for last today, huh?"

I smiled as I petted Moony's neck, "Yeah."

I didn't work for Carol on Saturdays because those were the days reserved for her teaching those students whose horses she trained during the week. I woke up late that morning, lamenting that I had awoken and would soon have to part with Moonshine.

My mother drove me to the barn in silence; no radio, no conversation, just tense silence. When we arrived, everyone was there, most of the boarders, all of the trainers, Kim, and even Richard, were all in Moonshine's barn. The buzz in the barn was unusual, even for a Saturday. Everyone seemed to be engaged in conversation around Moonshine's stall. I noticed Kim leaning casually against Moonshine's door. Only Carol and a few other busy trainers were outside giving lessons.

"Hey, Victoria!" I heard from the crowd.

"Hey guys," I replied.

"I'm going to the office," my mother declared.

"OK."

I made my way through the crowd. The conversation stopped.

"Hey Moony," I said through the bars of Moony's stall, as he was staring out of his window. I dropped a carrot in his feed bucket, and he came to devour it. I petted him on his cheek. I then headed to the tack room to retrieve my riding equipment.

I tacked him up in his stall. He stood still, knowing the routine. First, pick the feet, then curry, then brush, then wrap the legs, then saddle pad, saddle, girth (he still didn't like it when I tightened the girth, pinning his ears and thrashing his head around, but now he just threatened, and stopped his antics if I scolded him), and finally, the bridle. Kim stood by the door the whole time. She had never done that before.

I led him outside, got on, and we proceeded to the arena in which Carol was giving a lesson. We didn't have a lesson scheduled, I just wanted to be near her.

When I finished my ride, I walked Moonshine back to the barn.

I noticed my mother sitting on one of the benches in front of the barn with my godmother, Ava. When they saw me approaching the barn, Ava said, "Hi honey!" in her thick, Bulgarian accent.

"Hi," I replied.

I walked Moonshine to his stall, and, though most of the crowd had now dispersed, Kim was still engaged in conversation with a few others, by Moony's stall.

As I began to take off the saddle, a short, thin, plain-looking stranger walked into the barn, toward Moonshine. He had curly black hair, an ugly beak of a nose, and glasses. In that instant, Kim went from calm and pleasant to hostile and loud.

"OUTSIDE, BY THE PICNIC BENCHES!" she bellowed as she started toward him, pointing in that direction.

"OK, OK," he said, smiling, and putting his hands up, as if to show he was unarmed. He turned, but caught my stare as he stepped out of the barn, escorted by the angry barn manager.

My mother and Ava followed. I could see the picnic benches perfectly from Moony's window. I immediately pulled off the saddle and bridle, unwrapped his leg wraps, and led him into his stall. I glued myself to the window so that I could watch the negotiations. The setting was too far from Moony's stall to hear anything.

George said something inaudible.

My mother stood up and yelled, "I TOLD YOU NOT TO BRING THE TRAILER!" I heard that perfectly.

I sighed. "It's over, Moony, I love you," I whispered to him as he busily chomped his hay in the opposite corner of the stall. The hot tears started to build and fall quietly.

Then I saw Carol come to the table, and when Kim saw her, she got up, to give her that spot. Kim then went into the office.

They spoke for a long time. Everyone had a turn, although there were frequent interruptions. George looked amused, almost like this was fun. Carol arrived calm, but as the discussion went on, her face ripened to a bright tomato red. The conversation continued for over an hour. I clutched the bars of Moony's window, unable to let go.

Then they all stood up. George offered his hand to my mother for a handshake, but she ignored it and started to march toward the barn. Carol disappeared into the office. Ava simply looked at George and then followed my mother. George then got up and strode toward the parking lot.

I poked my head out of Moonshine's stall, not knowing what to expect, but hoping for a miracle.

"Moony's yours!" my mother and Ava said, almost simultaneously.

"What? But how?"

"The pig just wanted more money, and we'll send it to him," my mother explained.

"Are you sure?"

"Yes, honey, yes!"

They both hugged me tightly, as I sighed.

I had never before felt such joy and relief. I had never before wanted something so badly, and come so close to losing it.

The next day, everyone congratulated me. I swelled with delight as I thanked everyone who offered congratulations. Even Jean came over to Moony's stall to congratulate me.

Jean Schwimmer was another one of Carol's students who mostly kept to herself when she was at the farm. I had seen Jean in passing in the barn and riding in the arenas since I first started riding at Oakwood. I never saw her smile, so I figured she just wanted to be left alone. I also kept my distance since she stabled her two horses in one of the smaller, more exclusive stables on the property, and ignored all of the other boarders. The only person I saw her speak to was Carol. It was only after I had been riding Moonshine for a few months that she would greet me in passing. As time went on, she became even friendlier, to the point where she was my biggest fan. She would watch my lessons, she would offer me praise whenever we learned something new, and she always wanted to know how we did at our last horse show. Maybe it was because she felt sorry for us always getting mediocre scores. I didn't care, it was always nice to hear what she had to say. Having Jean on my side felt like a huge compliment, since she didn't socialize with anyone else on the farm.

"Victoria! Congratulations! I just heard the great news!"

"Hi Jean, thanks," I said, grinning widely, unable to contain myself.

"You guys will do great together," she said as she petted Moonshine and put her hand on my shoulder.

"Thanks," I replied.

"Well, tack up that horse of yours, and go show your stuff!" she said enthusiastically.

My horse, I thought. *Did she really say 'my horse'? Is Moony really mine? No one can take him away from me?* The dream of having my own horse had actually come true; it was surreal.

Everything changed, and yet it all remained the same. I was happier, every day, regardless of what happened. I had a sense of security I had never before known. I didn't care as much when Moonshine was difficult in training, or if he snapped at dogs on the farm. I didn't care if Richard chastised me for letting my horse graze on one of the off-limits patches of grass around the barn, or for letting Moonshine flatten a bush when he tried to sit on it to relieve the itch under his belly, or for letting Moonshine roll in the sand in the arena. I didn't care if I got yelled at, because I wanted to make Moonshine as happy as he made me. And if Moony wanted to eat lush grass and sit in bushes, I would let him.

The training with Carol was the same, but I was different. Before Moonshine was officially mine, I got frustrated with setbacks easily and quickly. I was insecure about others seeing the mistakes I made when I rode. But now, I didn't care what anyone thought, aside from Carol. Moony was my horse and Carol was my coach, and I loved them both.

20

I was the happiest fourteen-year-old on the planet. As soon as Moony was mine, Mother Nature celebrated with me, bringing me my favorite season sooner than usual—fall. The green leaves morphed into vibrant yellows, oranges, and reds. The crisp, cool air was perfect for riding—not too hot, not too cold. But it quickly turned cold, and a heavy blanket of snow buried the city before Thanksgiving. Deep, white paths were shoveled through to the sidewalks. The streets became channels of gray slush, and black ice waited patiently for its victims.

On my way to school one morning, I slipped on an invisible patch of ice in front of the house, and was totally airborne. I saw my feet fly up in front of me, as my heavy backpack pulled me backward. I landed square on my behind. I stood up and felt fine, so I got in my mother's waiting car and went to school.

But, as the car pulled up to the school, I started to feel pain in my tailbone and shooting sensations down both of my legs. I got out of the car and assumed it would work itself out. As the hours passed, the pain in my tailbone intensified, and the shooting pains intensified. My legs turned to lead, and it became almost impossible to move them. I went to the nurse's office, where I lay on my stomach, hoping that I would feel better if I wasn't sitting down. It didn't work, the pain took over my lower body. It became excruciating, and then everything went black. When I woke up, I was in my bed at home.

How am I home? Wasn't I just in school?

I tried to get out of bed, but couldn't move. My legs just wouldn't do what I wanted. It was scary, wanting to move a part of my body, but not being able to. It was like trying to scream, but having no voice.

I still felt pain, only now it was beyond excruciating, right at the end of my tailbone. Any angle I sat in was sheer agony. Even lying on my belly did nothing to relieve the pain.

Then I thought of Moonshine, and the fact that it was winter.

Who's going to ride him? And everything is frozen, so there won't be any turnout until spring! He'll be stuck in the stall and no one will ever take him out! This cannot be happening!

A week went by. The pain remained excruciating.

"We're going to the doctor; we need to get this checked out. It's been too long," my mother informed.

"Mom, I can't move. I don't think you understand. It hurts just when I breathe."

"Exactly why we're going to the doctor right now."

I knew that when she made up her mind, there was no changing it. I sighed in defeat.

She bent over the bed to help me sit up. I bit my lip hard, to keep quiet and not let her know how much pain I was in, but tears escaped and rolled down my cheeks. I put one arm around her neck and she helped me up. She put one arm around my waist and shuffled me to the car outside.

The doctor took X-rays. Then he called us back to his office.

"Young lady, your coccyx is broken. Unfortunately, there is

nothing we can do to speed the recovery. The fragmented bone must fuse back together on its own."

"How long will it take?" I asked.

"Three to four months, at best," he replied.

"What? That's too long!" I was exasperated.

Moony would be abandoned yet again, I gloomed.

I had permission to stay home from school to recover, but I still had to do all of the reading and homework so I wouldn't fall behind. I welcomed the distraction from the physical pain as well as the anguish at being separated from my horse. But every time I would start an assignment, worry seeped in. Nobody's taking care of Moony . . . we're not going to get to Third Level by the spring . . . is he being turned out every day? I felt hopeless and helpless.

The hours crawled. Night stole away daylight almost as soon as it came. And then it lingered ruthlessly. I watched the white snowflakes fall in the dark, outside my window. I would watch one fall from the top of the window, all the way to the bottom. And then I wondered what Moonshine was doing. I missed petting his neck, the smell of the barn, and my lessons with Carol. The constant physical pain plagued me, the inability to use my body tortured me, but being torn from the greatest love I had was the greatest pain of all.

A month full of school work, daydreams, and self-pity dragged on. I finally had enough. *I won't be a victim. This isn't me. I'm done. I'm done being a blob on the couch, I'm done feeling sorry for myself, and I will ride again.*

Commercials and advertisements for the ab roller were inescapable. I knew that a strong core was essential for dressage riders, so I asked for one and got it. Just because I couldn't use my lower body didn't mean I couldn't exercise my abs. And I might as well have a strong core when I rode again.

The first time I rolled onto the ground and set myself up

in the ab roller, piercing pain punished my back and legs. I was so furious with my body for failing me and hurting me, that I wanted to hurt it even more. So, I turned on a half-hour TV show and did crunch after crunch for the whole show. *I need to be strong for when I ride again.*

I was satisfied. I was no longer just sitting there, being useless. I was no longer a victim. I would take my life back. I would ride again. And nothing would stop me, not even pain that made my eyes well up.

I was pleased, but I wanted to do more. I had just shown myself that I could power through the pain, and that I was stronger than it. I relished this new sense of empowerment, and wanted more. I resolved to work my arms out. My once strong arms had become weak, wet noodles. I would get my arms back. Exercise programs dominated daytime television, so I channel surfed until I found a show that focused on arms. I found two water bottles, lay on the ground, and did chest presses and flies, along with the instructor. I still wasn't as happy as I used to be, but I was satisfied. I will ride again.

February did not drag on like January because, now, I was busy. When I wasn't doing schoolwork, I was exercising. And finally, by mid-February, the pain in my back and legs began to subside.

As soon as I could stand it, I tried exercising my legs. At first, I could only do leg exercises lying flat on my back. I had lost the strength I used to have in my quadriceps and hamstrings, as well as all of my inner thigh power I had gained from sitting through Moonshine's bucks. I lay on my side as I lifted one leg up, just like the exercise instructor did on the program I watched. There was a searing pain shooting from my spine into the leg I had suspended in the air. I went from not feeling so much pain when the leg was down, and my muscles relaxed, to the same intensity of pain I felt right after the accident.

I don't care. I can deal with it, I already dealt with it before, I told myself, *just keep going.*

I did repetitions until my body started shaking.

Doesn't matter. Ignore it. Do the other leg now, I forced myself. *I have to do this.*

I was going to ride again soon, and nothing would stop me.

21

When I could walk, I was ready to go to the farm.

"You are not riding yet," my mother insisted.

"I know. I just want to see him."

The hour-long drive out to the farm was uncomfortable. The car seat was much firmer than the couch. I tried to be subtle when I shifted my weight to alleviate the pressure, so my mother wouldn't think I was in pain.

When we arrived, the parking lot was full, as it usually was on Saturday afternoons.

"Victoria! Hi!" Boarders and trainers greeted me as I walked from the parking lot to Moony's stall. I whizzed past all of the distractions and rushed to my horse.

"Hi Moony!" I called as I walked into the barn.

His head shot up, hay sticking out of the corners of his mouth. His ears flew forward, and, for the first time, he nickered at me. I opened the door and gave him a carrot as I petted the white star on his head. He looked different, but the same. He had no scratches or bruises, but he was so dark now, almost black. I had never considered Moonshine a nice-looking horse, but now, with his gleaming white star and almost black fur, he was beautiful. I wanted to take him outside, but there was still a blanket of snow on the ground, and I knew no one would let me do it.

"Hey there! I heard you were here!" I heard Carol say as she approached Moonshine's stall. "How are you feeling?"

"I'm good." I lied. It hurt to stand.

"Great, well Moony's doing well."

"Yeah, he looks good."

"Yep, he can do some tricks now," she beamed.

"What do you mean?" I asked.

"Half-passes, shoulder-in, haunches-in, flying changes . . ." she trailed off.

I knew these were more advanced movements, but Moonshine didn't know them.

"I don't get it," I was puzzled.

"I've been riding him," she revealed.

"Are you serious?" I had not expected this.

"No, just kidding. Of course I'm serious!" she teased.

I knew her training was invaluable; I also knew how expensive it was, and that my mother had not said anything about paying any kind of training bill for the last two months. Carol had trained Moony for free.

I was touched. I didn't know what to say. All I could do was thank her. "Thanks so much, Carol."

"Don't sweat it. So, when can you ride again?" she asked.

"The doctor said not to even think about it until April."

"We'll see how you feel next weekend," she winked, understanding the addiction.

"I think your first ride back should be in a lesson, so I'll put you down just for a half-hour lesson for next Saturday."

"I can do a regular, one hour lesson. I've been working out." I was eager to get back to my life.

"OK, Rambo, we'll play it by ear," she said.

I was thrilled.

I groomed Moony in his stall, smiling as I brushed his dark, soft coat, gleefully breathing in the mixture of hay, dust, and manure that now smelled almost foreign. I had never noticed how strong the smells could be, but they quickly became familiar again. I scratched Moony under his neck, one of his favorite itchy spots, while he continued to munch on his hay. No other horse had breath that smelled that sweet when they chewed on hay.

"I love you so much, Moony Monster," I whispered to him. And then he shoved me in the belly with his head, sending me flying into the wall, like he always did when he saw an opportunity for a good head-butting. I could almost hear him say, "Cut the shit and just scratch my neck, you sap."

22

The following weekend, I could stand up without the excruciating pain that had plagued me for the past few months. What little pain I felt was bearable, so I eagerly put on my riding breeches, slipped on my paddock boots, and headed out to the car.

It was the second week of March, and even though it was normally still cold in March, the past week had brought us a heat wave. The temperatures soared to fifty degrees and melted all of the snow. It was just as warm on Saturday, my first day back to riding. The sky was clear blue, unusual for a winter day.

I got to the farm later than I had wanted and rushed to tack up so that I had at least twenty minutes before the lesson to adjust to sitting in a saddle again and riding my horse.

I put on the saddle, led Moonshine outside to the mounting block, stepped into the stirrup and threw my right leg over his back. In that instant, the pain I first felt rushed back. I plopped into the saddle. My right leg was paralyzed.

Moony, please don't move!

I needed a minute to recover. The aching did not subside,

but Moonshine, growing restless, had begun to paw and shuffle, so I knew it was time to get him going. Luckily, no one was around to see me wincing in agony.

I knew Carol wanted me to go to her in the indoor but I needed to be alone. I was afraid that if anyone saw me, they would pull me off my horse. I pointed Moonshine to the farthest arena on the property.

I insisted he walk slowly. Amazingly, he obeyed. His walk was even less choppy than I remembered. I was grateful. Then, I looked up ahead and realized I was riding again! I was where I belonged, in the saddle, on my horse. I finally felt whole again. The soreness in my back and legs didn't matter anymore. Nothing else mattered now. I turned Moony around and pointed him toward the indoor. I was ready for my first lesson.

I could only ride the walk and rising trot. Most of the fancy movements were done at the canter, but Carol knew I couldn't handle that yet. Although I was elated to be back in the saddle, I was annoyed that I couldn't canter. I wanted to ride those fancy moves!

"I was going to teach you the upper level dressage moves at the walk anyway," she declared, detecting my frustration. Somehow, she had turned my limitation into an opportunity to teach me more. Unlike anyone else, my trainer understood me. She knew what to say and how to say it.

By April, I was riding pain-free. Even though I was riding again, training was still hard. Carol constantly pushed us, challenged us.

"Keep at it," she would say, "Legs on strong, keep your seat strong," she often instructed. She would work us until I had very little strength left, and then offer a walk break. I found it fascinating that she knew what my breaking point was physically, brought me to it, and then let me rest just when I reached it.

How does she know how much to push and when to back off? I wondered. She seemed to have full access to both Moonshine's and my own thoughts and physical capabilities. We were transparent to her.

Moony and I continued to progress, although occasionally my back would freeze up, inhibiting my ability to sit his choppy strides. He would responsively also freeze up. I should have known that he was just reacting to the tension in my back, but instead I immediately got frustrated. Before the accident, I was able to compensate for Moonshine's stiffness by overusing my back, but now, that ability was gone. I would then kick my horse in my annoyance, which set him off on a bucking spree—also not ideal for my weak back.

After a few lessons, Carol sensed my growing aggravation.

"You can't get mad at him when your back gives out. So you temporarily lost one of your tools. Why don't you replace it with another one?" she said.

"Like what?" I asked.

"Your mind. When you get angry, that means you've lost control. That means that that control has shifted over to Moonshine. So basically, every time you lose your cool, the horse is outsmarting you," she said plainly.

And now I felt stupid.

"So how do I avoid that?" I asked.

"You will have to figure that out. But what I can help you do is to gain some advantages," she said.

"Like what?" I asked.

"Little tricks; because dressage is performed in a rectangular arena, you can use geometry to help you reinforce your aids if the horse is ignoring them," she said.

"How?" I asked.

"Let's say you're having trouble with your shoulder-ins, utilize the corners just *before* the movement to establish the bend you need for the shoulder-in on the long side of the arena. It's impossible for him to not bend in the shoulder-in if he's already bent before he starts. Let's try it out. Pick up the trot and bend him before you start the shoulder-in, let's see if he stays bent in the movement."

I squeezed my legs, cuing Moony to pick up the trot, and headed to a corner leading into one of the two long sides of the arena. I bent Moonshine's head and neck to the inside, just as I approached the corner. It was easier to ask for more bend in the corner, as his body was already bending into the sharp turn. As he trotted through the corner, I applied my inside leg to my outside rein, so that I could bring his shoulders to the inside of the track (hence the name shoulder-in). To my astonishment, he stayed bent! It was so much easier to just keep my inside leg on to keep him moving down the long side on three tracks, as opposed to applying my leg and wrestling his head to the inside with my reins.

"It worked!" I let out.

Carol was amused, as usual.

"Let's try it a few more times, just to make sure that wasn't beginner's luck," she coached.

After trying this trick out on both directions to ensure that it wasn't an accident, I was ready to learn more.

"What's another trick?" I asked.

"Oh, now you're ready for all the tricks in the book, huh?" she teased.

"Of course!" I played along.

Now, taking an air of official authority in a very non-serious manner, Carol started, "Well, technically, there are no tricks in dressage. You know all the experts say it's just a matter of hard work."

"Those experts never rode Moonshine!" I retorted.

She laughed.

"OK, back to work, cheater," she joked. "Pick up the trot on a twenty-meter circle around me."

I did as I was told. Moonshine picked up his pogo-stick-like choppy trot. He was almost round in his body, but not quite. He was *almost* working through his back, pushing off his hind legs, but still rigid. He was always "almost" there.

"Ready for your next trick?" she asked.

"Yup!"

"OK, is he totally round?" she asked.

"No," I admitted.

"What's the aid to make him round?" she tested me often.

"Inside leg to outside rein," I let out automatically.

"Good, did you apply that aid?"

"Yes," I said.

"OK, we know he didn't immediately respond to the aid for roundness. So now we need a little reinforcement. Only use this when the first aid doesn't work. This is more of a tip for when you're desperate, like in a class at a show or something."

"I'm always desperate on this horse," I joked, half-serious.

"I know, I know, woe is you," she dished back.

"Back to business, what you can do to reinforce the aid for roundness is to take your inside rein in your inside hand, and sort of move your fingers around softly but firmly, like you're milking a cow."

"Milking a cow?" I asked.

"Yeah, haven't you ever milked a cow before?"

"No," I said.

"What about a goat?"

"I've never milked anything before," I told her. *Did she forget I was from Queens? Where was I supposed to find a cow to milk in Queens?* I wondered.

"Really? OK, well anyway this is what it looks like when you're milking a cow," she said as she lifted her hand and tickled the air with her fingers. It looked like she was playing the piano.

"So when he locks his jaw and grabs the bit in his mouth, you can massage the inner corner of his mouth and unlock the jaw by moving your fingers on the reins like that. But you have to be gentle, you're playing with a piece of metal in his mouth, the most sensitive part of his body," she warned.

"I think I got it, can I try?"

"Sure," she said.

I tried wiggling my fingers slowly and gently on my inside rein. His mouth was rigid and unyielding to the rein. It took a few revolutions around the circle when I noticed that he started chewing, a sign that his jaw had unlocked!

"That was harder than the first trick, but at least it worked," I said to Carol.

"It will get easier," she assured. "When you ride alone, don't let him outsmart you. Don't let him get you riled up, because as soon as you get emotional, the ride is over and you might as well just hop off and go home. Ride more from a technical point of view. If you see a problem, try to figure out how to fix it before getting mad that there's a problem in the first place, because I've got news for you—there will always be problems. Everyone has problems. Even the super star Olympians have problems on their super star Grand Prix horses. The key is how you handle a problem when it creeps up on you."

"OK," I replied, digesting her expert advice.

23

I was approaching the end of my freshman year in high school, and had to shift my focus to school, to do well on my final exams. I didn't find any of my classes particularly challenging, but I still knew I had to get good grades because a good GPA would lead to a good college, which would lead to a good job, which meant that I would be able to support my addiction to dressage. I was acutely aware of how expensive it was to board and train a horse. My mother had grown accustomed to confiding in me about her problems, the biggest of which were finance related.

My mother also urged me to reconcile with my father.

"You only have one father," she reasoned.

"But he's an asshole!" I started.

"No cursing!" she interjected.

"Guess who taught me all the curse words I know—in Romanian *and* English," I shot back at her.

"He's still your father," she insisted.

"I don't care. Besides, family is a group of people who love each other, whether or not they're related. He's not my family.

Never will be."

"No, family it's blood," she retorted, letting her grammar slip as she grew angry.

"I don't think so," I argued.

"Just call your father!" she huffed, ending the conversation.

It started out with short telephone conversations. Even though the court had still ordered him to have weekend visitations with my sister and me, he was no longer interested in having us over to his apartment. Instead, whenever he felt like going for a weekend excursion, he would show up to drive me to the farm. I always accepted, as this would be an opportunity to ask him to pay one month's board for Moonshine, as my mother perpetually lamented how the horse was depleting the family's funds, and my father had not paid child support in years. He got away with it because she could not afford any more attorney's fees.

Even though he was an attorney with his own practice in downtown Manhattan, he insisted he was poor. I knew it was a lie; almost everything he said was a lie. Nevertheless, I was persistent, or desperate, and as soon as I had him trapped in a car for a good solid hour, I went on and on about my dedication to the sport; how it shaped my life; how hard I had tried; and how far I had come, but still did not neglect my school work. I told him how when I wasn't at the farm, I was either in school or doing homework, and how I would be doing this for the rest of my life, etc. I knew he was a selfish, stingy person, but also knew that I was the only person he cared about. He often told me he loved me because I looked like his mother, but was smart like him. He was an egomaniac, so of course I spent the first hour of the drive to the farm telling him what a great father he was and how much I admired him, and the second hour—the drive home from the farm—telling him how much I needed his support.

"Victoria, be serious. This is a joke. This is not serious. Just focus on school. You just work on getting into Harvard," he would say in his thick accent, condescendingly.

"Dad, I am serious. Lots of people say I have a talent for this."

"So? I also have a talent for many things, but I don't do it all. It's a waste of time and money," he would continue.

"Dad, I know you're great at everything you do. But I'm not you. My only talent is for riding."

"So who cares about talent anyway? Will it pay the bills and put food on the table? No, it won't. You need to forget all this hanky panky nonsense, get your head straight, and just focus on school. You are smart girl, Victoria. Don't act like stupid," he would add in his broken English.

On most occasions, he grew frustrated and I knew nothing was going to happen. But after a few drives out to the farm, he took an interest. We resumed our usual conversation regarding my talent for the sport.

"How do you know you have talent anyway? You think you are a superstar at fifteen years old?" he challenged.

I knew I had a chance of convincing him how dedicated I was and how much I needed his support when he challenged me.

"I'm just telling you what other people told me."

"What other people?" he inquired.

"My trainer, for one."

"Who is your trainer?" he asked.

"Carol."

He was silent. I was unsure what to make of it, so I was also quiet until we got to the farm. He always waited in the car, reading the newspaper, while I was at the barn.

On this particular occasion, however, when I was in the middle of my lesson, he entered the arena and approached Carol. He didn't wait until after the lesson to talk to her, like a normal person would have. No, when he wanted to chat, the whole world needed to stop spinning.

Great, here we go. Well, she knows he's a deadbeat so hopefully she's ready for whatever he has up his sleeve, I braced myself.

He whistled at her, and gestured for her to walk over to him. I was horrified.

She held up her hand, until my lesson was over. *Good, Carol, just ignore him*, I thought. But, he remained in the same spot, in the indoor.

Apparently, most people knew of my deadbeat father, even Gunilla, the owner of the farm. She was an international rider, trainer, and judge. Gunilla had a reputation for being a tough, no-nonsense person. She was also riding, at the same time as my lesson, in the same arena. She was instantly annoyed at seeing a visitor inside the arena, where only instructors and riders were allowed. She trotted over to my father.

"You cannot stand here. This arena is for training only!" she huffed.

"Do you know who I am?" he spat, astonished that someone, especially a woman, had the nerve to tell him what he could and could not do.

"Do you know who *I* am?" Gunilla retorted, clearly annoyed.

Carol had me trot in a circle at the other end of the arena, possibly anticipating an explosion. We continued in the lesson, but I couldn't help trying to overhear the exchange between my father and Gunilla; I knew Carol was doing the same.

"I am Gunilla Peterson! This is *my* farm!" she exploded. "You are interrupting serious training here! Remove yourself from this arena immediately!"

"I am Victor Radulescu—Victoria's father!" he exploded back to her in his heavy Romanian accent.

"I don't care if you are the Pope! Get out of my arena now! You are interrupting important training here!" she now reached a higher octave.

"Hmph!" he declared as he turned toward the exit. He then stood in the entrance of the arena, blocking anyone who wanted to get in or out with his corpulent 300-pound frame.

"*Not* there!" Gunilla shouted after him.

I relished the fact that someone finally had enough courage to yell at him.

He moved over to the bleachers, where he stood silently for a minute, until he cupped his hands to his mouth and bellowed all the way across the arena, "CAROL! CAROL I NEED TO SPEAK WITH YOU IMMEDIATELY! PLEASE COME HERE NOW! THAT OLD BITCH FORBADE ME TO COME TO YOU!"

Oh my God, I thought, mortified. I knew Gunilla heard what he said. *Please don't kick me out, please!* I thought.

Carol, with her trademark grace and elegance, simply ignored him.

At the end of my lesson, she walked over to him. I walked Moonshine around the arena to cool him down after the workout.

"Yes?" she said to my father.

"I am Victor Radulescu!" he declared.

"How can I help you?" she asked.

"Listen, just between us, this is all bullshit, right? I mean, come on, isn't it a joke?" he started, loudly. I couldn't believe he was mocking her profession right to her face. I wanted to melt away.

"No, it's not," she responded flatly.

"Why not? Is there money in it, like in the horse races?" he asked.

"No."

"But they still win some money, right?" he asked.

"Rarely," she stated.

"*RARELY*? Then what is the *point*?!" he exclaimed. "Victoria! Get off that horse right now! This is a huge waste of money, just as I thought!" he bellowed to me.

"Sir, with all due respect, your daughter is a talented rider," Carol stated. It was strange to hear her praise me, as I rarely heard it.

"So?" he challenged.

"Well, that is rare."

"So?" he repeated.

"Rare things are often special," she was growing frustrated. It was interesting to see Carol get annoyed, when not even the most obstinate horse could irritate her.

Apparently, Gunilla had had enough as well, so she trotted her horse over to where Carol was standing.

"Sir," she began, "what Carol is trying to say is that your daughter is a good dressage rider. She has talent that others would die for, and if she continues on in her training, the way she has been doing, she will be an international sensation. Don't you think that is special?" she asked.

"You really think she has a chance?" he asked Gunilla.

"Yes!"

Then Gunilla exited the arena and Carol left to teach her next lesson.

I followed after Gunilla, and my father remained motionless.

"Your father is a piece of work, kiddo," she said as we walked to the barn.

"I know, I'm sorry," I said.

"It's not your fault," she said flatly.

Gunilla had a reputation for being tough, so it was strange for her to reveal a soft side.

After I had finished cooling Moonshine down, cleaning tack, and putting everything away, I walked back to my father's car in the parking lot.

"Victoria, please tell me you don't want to be a joke like these crazy women here," he started.

"I don't think the Olympics are a joke," I said.

"What?" he asked.

"That's what I want."

He was silent.

"So, how are you going to get there? How will you pay for

it all? How will you support yourself?" he asked.

I knew the right answer. "I'll be a lawyer, just like you."

He smiled and was quiet for the entire drive back.

When he dropped me off at home, I was greeted by my mother just as I entered the house.

"How was the farm?" my mother asked.

"Oh, you know, the usual. He met Gunilla, called her an old bitch, and said she and Carol were jokes."

She gasped. "OK, from now on, he will drive you only when I absolutely *have* to work."

24

Summer came again and I was ecstatic that I could now ride every day, instead of just weekends. I looked forward to being Carol's assistant again.

"Victoria, I would love to have you as a working student again, but I have to hire an official helper, now," Carol told me at the beginning of the summer.

"Why?" I was confused.

"Just new farm policy," she said. I knew that she wasn't telling me the whole truth, but I simply responded with, "OK." I was disappointed that I wouldn't be able to spend all day every day at the barn with Carol and Moony.

I was still at the barn every day, but now I spent all of my time with my horse. I only had two lessons a week with Carol, but when I rode on my own, I pretended she was teaching me. I practiced the same exact things she made me do in our lessons. When it was too hot to train, I got on Moony bareback for a light hack around the farm. I washed him every day and polished his hooves after every ride. I also practiced braiding his mane once a week, because I wanted his mane to look perfect at horse shows.

Gunilla passed me once, while I was untacking Moonshine in the aisle. He now stood like a statue for me in the aisle. All four legs remained on the ground, and he no longer tried to attack passersby.

"Hey kiddo, when are you going to show me what a superstar you are?"

"Umm, what?" I was genuinely surprised, as Gunilla was almost always stern and short with everyone.

"You're all I ever heard about when I was in Europe. Carol raved about you every time we spoke! Now that you've learned the basics from her, you are ready to take a lesson with me. Carol learned everything she knows from me."

"Umm, OK . . ."

"Hey, good job with this horse, his muscles are really strong," she said as she patted Moonshine on his hindquarters before she walked off.

"Thanks," I replied.

A few days later, the farm organized a clinic. Gunilla was the featured clinician. A sign-up sheet was posted in the tack room.

"What's a clinic?" I asked Betty, who was signing up.

Betty was one of Carol's students. She had the most expensive saddle, bridle, and blankets. She once asked me what brand of breeches I rode in and scoffed when I revealed I rode in thirty dollar breeches. She emphasized that real dressage riders wear the full seat breeches she wore—that were well over one hundred dollars. She also joked that I might win a class one day when I got myself a real horse, a warmblood, like she had. Almost all of the other boarders were dismissive of me and Moony, except Jean. Not only did she talk to me when we saw each other, but also lit up when we spoke. The way she spoke to me was in stark contrast to the gruff attitude she showed most of the other boarders. Also, Jean never passed Moony without petting him.

"Oh, it's a really exclusive event where there is one famous trainer, the clinician, and only a few slots for really good riders to take a lesson from them. It's great because you can learn from watching other people's lessons too, and there's usually an audience. It's for advanced riders, not for kids," she said, looking down at me.

Jean was in the tack room, too, and had just overheard what Betty said to me.

"She's more advanced than you'll ever be, Betty. Quit kidding yourself."

"Hmph!" Betty let out, grabbing her tack and storming out of the tack room.

"Ignore her, Victoria. You sign up if you want to," Jean said.

"So, did you sign up?" Carol said, when I entered the arena for my lesson with her.

"For what?" I asked.

"The clinic, genius," she teased.

"I heard it wasn't for kids."

"I want all of my students in that clinic, including you," she advised. It was nice to be lumped in as part of "Carol's students." It was validating.

The clinic would take place in one week, and it was the talk of the farm. Everyone would participate. I was looking forward to watching Beth's lesson, as I was still pseudo-obsessed with her and her beautiful, huge, sweet horse. Beth was much more advanced than me, so she had ridden with Gunilla on prior occasions. This clinic was a big deal in my world, but probably just another lesson to Beth.

On the day of the clinic, I sat in the bleachers along with almost all of the other boarders, waiting for Beth's lesson to begin. It started with basic work on improving the horse's walk, trot, and canter. When Gunilla told Beth to start schooling some advanced movements, Beth turned to Gunilla and said, "Are you kidding? No walk break?"

Gunilla blew up.

"No, I am not kidding! And definitely no walk break, you spoiled brat! You could use the work!"

The crowd grimaced and winced. I was sitting next to Beth's mother and stayed completely silent.

Beth began to laugh.

"She's nervous. She laughs when she's nervous," Beth's mother said, more to herself than to me.

"What is so funny? I wouldn't laugh if I were you. I don't even know why you still bother riding. You don't have half of your horse's talent!" Gunilla spewed.

Oh my God, she is mean! She is going to rip me and Moonshine apart, I thought, now dreading my lesson.

I left the bleachers an hour before my scheduled ride time, to have enough time to get Moonshine ready. I hoped that grooming him to a spotless sheen would salvage us from the barrage of insults I expected.

As I groomed him, I pleaded with him not to embarrass me.

"Please don't buck today, Moony, be a good boy, OK? If you're good, I'll give you a whole bag of carrots," I whispered to him as I brushed his coat.

I arrived ten minutes early, and had warmed up in one of the outdoor arenas, so I was ready for the lesson.

At 2:00 p.m. sharp, just when the previous lesson ended, Gunilla gestured for me to walk over to her. I complied. When I came to her, she put her hand up and ordered, "Halt."

While Moony stood, she circled us slowly. She scrutinized the buckles of the bridle, the leather of my saddle, his shiny coat, and white leg wraps.

"He is clean. Good girl."

"Have you warmed up?"

"Yes," I replied robotically.

"Good. Pick up the trot on a twenty-meter circle, then do a shoulder-in down the long side," she instructed.

"OK," I said, as I nudged Moonshine with my legs to move off into a trot.

"More, MORE!" she yelled.

I bumped Moonshine with my legs to go faster.

"Not faster, *bigger*! Bigger trot! Open the stride, more expression!"

She didn't explain how to do a bigger trot, unlike Carol, who explained everything before she had me do anything. Carol would explain the movement, how to execute the movement, how the movement was supposed to improve the horse, and how it should look. Plus, she knew what Moonshine and I were capable of and had been trained to do. And finally, she was funny. She was simply the best.

In my next lesson with Carol, she asked me, "So, what did you think of your first clinic?"

"It was OK," I replied.

"*Just* OK?" she asked, astonished.

"I think your lessons are better," I said seriously.

She smiled.

25

It was yet another show season full of fourth and fifth place ribbons. I was growing frustrated again.

Carol told me it was my fault.

"How could it be my fault? All the judges say he's 'limited.'" I was offended.

"It's your fault because there's more in there, and you're not pulling it out."

"So how do I do that?" I asked.

"If you want *him* to be good, *you* have to be perfect," she replied.

"What do you mean by that?" I wondered what was in store for me now.

"You have to be crystal clear in your communication with Moonshine. And how do you communicate with a horse you are riding?" she asked.

"My seat," I answered.

"Exactly," she said. "We have to perfect your communication with Moonshine, and that means perfecting your seat."

"How do I perfect my seat?" I asked.

"I thought you'd never ask!" she seemed delighted, as she grabbed a lunge line, a really long cord, and attached it to Moonshine's bridle.

"I'll lunge him on a circle around me. I'm going to keep Moony on a circle, but you have to control everything else, how fast he goes, slowing him down, and stopping him—using only your seat—no reins and no stirrups.

"What? That's impossible," I said.

"Nothing's impossible," she insisted.

"I can't stop without reins!" I exclaimed.

"Just pick up the trot," she ordered.

"What am I supposed to do with my hands if I have no reins to hold?" I asked.

"Pretend like you're holding them," she stated. "Now, trot."

I squeezed with my legs for Moonshine to pick up a trot. I could make him move forward since I still had my legs to use, but there was no way I would ever stop him without any reins!

"Your seat sets the rhythm of each gait. If you want to speed up, just speed up your seat to set the rhythm you want. If you want to slow down, slow down your seat to the rhythm you want. Keep your back relaxed, but firm. Be adjustable," Carol instructed.

This is so not going to work, I thought.

In order to pick up the pace, I sped my seat up. Amazingly, Moonshine followed my lead by picking up his pace.

Incredible! I thought, as I smiled.

"Good, now, slow it down, with just your seat," Carol instructed.

I slowed the speed of my seat, and Moony instantly slowed down again!

"Let's just try it a few more times to make sure it's not beginner's luck," I heard.

I sped up, slowed down, sped up, slowed down as many times as Carol instructed. Then we tried the same exercise in the other direction, and it still worked! I was amazed. I often felt like Moonshine was a very callous horse, almost like driving an old truck, because he ignored me so much. So, now with none of the extra reinforcements, and using just the most basic communication for dressage, my seat, I was amazed at how sensitive he was to my commands.

"I have a question!" I blurted out.

"What's that?" she asked.

"I don't understand how he's more reactive off my aids when I have no reins and no leg."

"What do you think?" she responded.

It drove me crazy when teachers made me answer my own questions. By now, I was totally comfortable being myself with Carol. And myself could get sassy sometimes, so I said, "Well obviously I have no clue, otherwise I wouldn't have asked the question."

Carol almost doubled over. Her face had turned bright red and her eyes were squeezed shut while she laughed.

"OK smarty-pants, I'll help you out this one time, but I want you to become more independent and start thinking these things through on your own. I won't be around forever, and I definitely can't help you out in the show ring."

"OK, OK," I said impatiently.

"You don't need all the extras. You're a more advanced rider now, so you don't need to steer and stop with your reins, like beginners. Dressage riders control their horses with their seats. That's why in the higher level competitions, the more advanced riders don't look like they're moving any part of their bodies to control their horses. They're still controlling, but just with their *seats*. And if you think about it, that's really the most effective way to ride because when you use the core of your body, you're using the strongest muscles you have—your back, abs, and upper legs."

"Hmmm, that does make sense," I said.

"And the cool part of it is, when an advanced rider and horse are so in tune with each other, the rider can just *think* of a move, and the horse immediately does it," she added.

"Wow, that *is* really cool," I said.

"Yes. Now pick up the canter," she instructed.

I applied the basic aid for canter, which was to squeeze with my outside leg. Moonshine was supposed to automatically pick up the canter; instead, he started trotting faster.

"Why do you think he didn't pick up the canter?" Carol asked.

"To be annoying," I said.

"You weren't clear enough. Remember, everything comes from your seat. Did you ask with your seat or with your leg?"

"My leg. How can I ask with my seat?" I asked.

"Just start cantering with your seat, and he'll pick up the canter," she said.

I did as I was told, convinced it wouldn't work. But it did.

"It worked!"

Carol smiled.

At the end of my lesson, Carol told me there we had a lot more work to do. Apparently, my seat had been pretty bad.

"We'll do lunge lessons for about a month, until you can ride with just your seat," she informed me. "And when we're not in a lesson, when you are riding on your own, I want you to ride bareback—no saddle," she added.

"You want me to ride full workouts without a saddle?" I asked.

"Yes."

"So, I have to do all the movements we practice with no saddle?" I asked.

"What's the matter? Can't hack it?" she challenged.

"Of course I can!" I always fell into her reverse psychology traps. "It's just that I've never seen anyone riding full workouts without a saddle."

"Well, you get to keep the bridle, and you can sit on a saddle pad, so the hair doesn't go up your butt," she winked.

"Great, thanks," I said sarcastically, but smiled.

26

"Beth has to go to a big show in Connecticut next month to get her qualifying scores, and you're coming," Carol informed me. "I want you to sign up for the Second Level qualifying classes, so you can try and qualify for the Regionals at the end of the summer," she instructed.

I was elated that I was finally allowed to move up from First Level, which didn't have any of the more advanced movements that Moonshine and I had been practicing. I was also excited that Carol thought I was good enough to try out for the Regional Championships.

Regionals? I thought. I knew the Regional Championships was a prestigious show at the end of show season, for which riders had to earn at least two qualifying scores. After all, only the best riders from the region (usually a cluster of six or seven states) were invited to compete. I was worried that we would not be able to go, as the requirements called for two scores from two different shows from two different judges of over 60%, and Moonshine and I normally scored between 50% and 55% when we competed.

"So you're tagging along with Beth to the show in Connecticut, huh?" Richard asked a week later, as he passed through the barn.

"Yup," I beamed.

"Be ready at 4:00 a.m.; I'm not waiting," he added.

"I know," I said. I had grown used to his perpetual attitude with me, and was less and less offended by it.

The morning of shipping, I was ready at four. I walked Moonshine to the trailer, where Richard stood by the steep ramp, waiting.

"Give me the horse," he commanded, as he snatched the lead rope from my hand. I never put the chain part of the rope over Moony's nose, as some people did, for more control of the horse. I didn't need it, Moony just followed me everywhere; I didn't even need a rope. But Richard did. I watched as he put the chain over my horse's nose.

Moonshine tossed his head. Richard yanked on the rope to punish Moonshine for tossing his head. Then Richard walked off in the direction of the ramp, pulling on the rope. Moonshine pulled back and moved backwards.

"Quit it!" Richard screamed immediately.

Moonshine remained planted where he was.

"Beth—get me the whip from the trailer," he ordered.

Once he had the whip, he slashed it hard across Moonshine's neck.

"STOP!" I screamed, louder than I had ever screamed in my life. Moonshine exploded; I knew he wouldn't tolerate Richard's whipping him, and he did just what I feared he might—fight back. He reared up, completely vertical in the air, striking out his front legs at Richard. When he was back on all four legs, he threw his ears back and lunged at Richard. Richard dashed out of the way, dropping the rope. When Moonshine was free, he trotted away into the darkness. I ran after him, following the sound of his hooves. He had escaped into the dark field.

"Moony," I called, my voice shaking. I was riddled with guilt for putting him in the hands of someone I knew would hurt him. It was hard to look for him in the darkness with the water building in my eyes. Then I heard him snort, and walked in his direction, talking to him the whole time, so he knew it was just me. I saw his dark outline, and then the white star on his forehead. I walked to him, hand outstretched, with a peppermint candy—his favorite.

"I'm sorry, buddy, you're a good boy," I cooed, petting his cheek, as he crunched the treat. I bent down to pick up the other end of the lead rope, and turned back toward the trailer. I kept my right hand in my pocket, knowing Moony couldn't resist searching my pocket for more goodies.

"He won't touch you again. Come on, let's go to the show," I said as I started toward the trailer. Moonshine followed, and we walked shoulder to shoulder back to the trailer.

"Give me the horse," Richard commanded.

"No," I said firmly. "*I'm* loading him." I didn't care about the consequences of talking back to Richard now. He wouldn't hurt my horse again.

Surprisingly, he simply turned and walked back to the truck.

"OK, buddy, it's just you and me," I said to Moony.

I walked Moony in a circle in front of the ramp, and then, shoulder to shoulder, we scampered up the ramp together. It was so easy, the lead rope was even slack, but Moony was glued to my side. I backed him up into the free stall, next to Beth's horse. Once he was in, he turned his head to bite at the giant horse standing next to him. I hooked him up to a cross-tie, to limit the range of motion he had with his head, and to keep Lugano safe from my tiny terror.

I wasn't sure what happened to Richard, but then I heard his truck door slam shut and the engine blew alive.

I petted Moonshine on his neck and nose and said, "Be a good boy, OK?" I pulled another peppermint out of my pocket and gave it to him, and then ran down the ramp, to my mother's car, idling in the parking lot.

I was thrilled to go to an important away show with Carol and Beth, Carol's best student. She almost always got the qualifying scores she needed. I, on the other hand, did not, and this show was no exception. Our scores improved slightly, but they still were not qualifying scores. I was again disappointed toward the end of the show, but proud of my horse. He was precise and correct in all of the tests. He was performing at his best, and was now completely obedient in the show ring. Yet, most other horses placed above us. I sometimes watched their tests and saw that their performances would be riddled with errors. The rider would forget a movement, the horse would buck, and there were other mistakes that should have been major deductions in their scores. But most of those other horses were talented, unlike Moonshine. They had huge, graceful strides while Moonshine had short, choppy movement. I was growing frustrated with the judging system.

"What's wrong?" Carol said, when she saw me scrutinizing one of my score sheets with all of the judge's comments.

"I got a 55%, again," I replied.

"So? That's good," she encouraged.

"Thanks, but this test I rode had *no* mistakes," I said.

"That's great, good for you!" she stated.

"No, you don't understand," I lowered my voice, as I pulled her closer to me, "the other riders in the class had *lots* of mistakes in their tests, but they all scored higher," my voice went up as I finished the statement.

"Let me see the score sheet," she said.

"Accurate circle, rider has effective seat, horse's gaits—four," she said as she read down the score sheet.

All the movements are individually scored on a scale of 1 to 10, and the end of the score sheet provides four additional general categories to evaluate on the same scale of 1 to 10—the horse's gaits, rider's position, submission, and impulsion.

"Ouch, that was pretty low," she said, "I don't think Moony's gaits are a four."

"Yeah, me neither!" my eyes widened.

She looked at me, quizzically, and thought.

"OK this is done, we can't change it. You have one more class. Be perfect," she said.

"But I *was* perfect!" I interjected.

"Give it everything. Be perfect with something extra. Don't just do the movements, ride the whole test, you have to be perfect for every stride. I want you to visualize all the movements before you do them. See yourself doing them perfectly and fluidly, and then do them how you saw them in your head. Does that make sense?"

"Sort of, I don't know," I sounded defeated.

"Don't get discouraged just because one judge doesn't like your horse."

"It's not just this one judge. I always get low scores on Moony's gait and impulsion."

"And you also always make up those low scores on the high scores you get on your position and submission," she reminded me.

"Yeah, I guess you're right," I said.

Carol gave me a full half hour lesson before my class, which was rare, since she usually focused on her more advanced students at shows.

"You're ready. Let's head over to the show ring," she said.

It was unusual for Carol to escort Moonshine and me to the competition arena. On the way, she reiterated, "Do your best, Victoria. You and Moony are a great team, show the judge how brilliant you are. Take your time. And *smile.*"

I trotted around the arena to give the judge a chance to see that I was on deck and ready to go. She rang the bell. I saw Carol standing just outside of the ring, watching me.

I entered the ring, halted and saluted the judge. I smiled as I raised my head after the salute. I collected the reins, and cued Moony to push off into a trot to begin the test. I tried to elongate Moony's strides by imagining that I was sitting on a big warmblood; the vision must have slowed my seat down, because I could feel Moonshine shift his weight back onto his hindquarters, so that he could have more spring in his gaits, and lengthen his strides. I steered him deeper into the corners that I had ever done before. I noticed the hoofprints from the other horses before me—no one had gone so far into the corners. I kept my inside leg and outside rein on strong, but not rigidly. I pushed Moonshine especially hard in the extensions, to show how much power he had. He opened his stride more than he had ever done before, especially in the last canter extension, where we covered the entire diagonal line across the arena in 10 canter strides, and normally it took 16 to 17. His strides had almost doubled in length! My lines were straight, and I knew the judge would only see two tracks—right and left—when I came down the center line again for my final salute. I also knew my halt was straight and Moonshine's legs were square under me. I saluted as Moony stood motionless.

Then I heard applause. I looked up and saw a sizable crowd peppered around the arena. *Some famous rider must be next*, I thought as I smiled at them and patted my horse.

"Good job," Carol beamed.

"That was a really nice test!" I heard a stranger say.

I looked in the direction of the voice and said, "Thank you."

As I headed back to the show stable to untack my horse, I wondered if I would get a qualifying score for that ride. I was hoping the judge would reward my effort.

An hour later, the announcer came on to reveal the results of my class.

"Second Level Test Four Results!" he started.

"In fifth place, we have number 34, with a 51.22 percent. In fourth place, number 213, with a 53.65 percent."

My number—12—had not yet been called. I closed my eyes, willing myself to have won the class, with any score over a 60%, which is what I needed to qualify for the Regionals.

"Third place, number 67, with a 58.894%."

Oh my God, I got higher than a 58%! I thought, gleefully. *This could be it! We could have qualified!*

"Second place, number 12, with a 59.95%. And in first place, number 112, with a 64.59%. Congratulations, riders. Please pick up your score sheets and ribbons in the secretary's stand."

My mouth gaped. I was devastated; we were a tiny *fraction* away from a qualifying score! I looked around the barn, where was Carol? Then I saw her; she looked worried. She started toward me; I was frozen.

"It's OK, Victoria," she said as she put her arm around my shoulder. The others in the barn gathered around.

"Oof, that sucks," a voice said.

"It's OK, Victoria," others chimed in.

"It happens to everyone," someone else said.

I hated this kind of attention, and Carol knew it. She pulled me out of the barn, as she said, "Let's get out of here."

It always helped to do something else when I was upset, even if it was something as simple as walking.

We walked silently through the back field of the show grounds, where no one would notice us, as it was in the opposite direction of the show rings, warm up ring, and secretary's stand.

I saw cows in a neighboring field. I had not been so close to cows since I was a child. They looked massive.

"Those cows are really big," I said, breaking the silence.

"Yep," Carol said.

"I'm sick of being a loser," I let out.

"You're not a loser," she said.

"Yes I am. I always lose, so I'm a loser," I insisted.

Then she stopped, grabbed my shoulders and leaned down to me. Her face was inches from my own. I had never been so close to my trainer. It was strange to see her so serious, she looked almost angry. It was bizarre to see her not smiling.

"You are doing a great job with Moony. It doesn't matter what these judges say. I know and you know that Moony gives you everything he's got, and you are bringing out his best. Nobody else has been able to do that with this horse, Victoria. But you have to understand that these judges have to judge other horses in the class, and most of them will always be warmbloods. Judges will almost always favor the warmbloods over Moony. I know you want to win, but try to focus more on yourself and less on other riders. You know when he's good and when he's not so good—let that knowledge be your measure. It's good to listen to others' feedback, but sometimes, it's just as valuable to listen to what you know."

"OK, thanks, Carol," I replied.

I went home feeling defeated and deflated, again. I still needed two scores from two different shows, by August, to qualify for the Regional Championships.

"Carol, if I do the Oakwood show in July, would the two days—Saturday and Sunday—count as two separate shows?" I asked, hoping she might say yes.

"No," she said apologetically.

"Well then, I'm not going to the Regionals," I said.

"Why not?"

"Ummm, because I have no qualifying scores," I said, confused.

"So? You can still enter the regular classes. They don't only have Championship classes at the Regionals," she said.

"Oh, really?" I asked.

"Yeah, go ahead and print out an entry form. Bring it to

me, and I'll tell you which classes to enter. But you should still try to get a qualifying score," she concluded.

"Alright, thanks!" I said, refreshed.

I had signed up for the July show at Oakwood, as well as the Regionals in August. I looked forward to competing at both shows. I felt ready. Moony had been good the entire week before the show. I was optimistic; this time I would get a 60% or higher. I checked the weather forecast for that weekend—rain.

Ugh, that will be annoying, I thought, *but no big deal. I can ride in rain.*

Saturday morning arrived. I had been awake since three that morning, not because I was particularly nervous or anxious, but because of the wind and rain. The elements hammered against the house, whipping around garbage cans and the trash they held.

It will die down by the time I have to ride, I told myself.

At five, my mother and I got into the car and headed for the farm. It was worse out there. The sky was black. Once we arrived at the farm, I sprinted to Moonshine's stall. He was inside, clean, dry, and safe. I looked out at the arenas from the safety of the barn, but I couldn't see them through the waterfall.

The show would go on, as dressage shows always do—rain or shine.

I took my time getting ready, as my first ride wasn't until late morning. At around ten in the morning, I tacked up and headed for the indoor arena, where I would warm up.

"Can you believe this rain?" Nikki, a friendly older teenager who boarded in Moony's barn, called as she passed by on her horse.

"No, it's crazy!" I shouted back, over the sound of the pelting rain on the indoor's metal roof.

"Are you still going to ride?" she asked

"Yeah!" I said.

"Well, I don't know if I will. I'll try, though," she yelled.

I barely heard what she said.

Then, Beth's mother appeared through the office window and shouted, "Hey girls—I just checked the weather—this is Hurricane Bertha!" she called out, thoroughly amused.

Nikki and I completed our warm ups and walked out into the rain, together, since we would ride at the same time in the two outdoor arenas.

"Good luck!" I yelled to her.

"Thanks, you too!" she replied.

I walked Moonshine down to the farther arena, where I was scheduled to ride. My leather saddle was soaked, and the wet leather was slippery. I was starting to slide from side to side. I shoved my heels down in my stirrups as far as I could push them, hoping they would anchor my legs. As we walked around the arena, waiting for the judge to ring the bell to begin my test, I saw the worn track in the sand had become a long, deep stream of water. The entire arena was flooded, but at least the small rivers showed me where the tracks were. As I passed by the judge's booth, waiting for her to ring the bell, she shouted, "Good luck! Just think white water rafting!" Then she rang the bell. I noticed a small crowd of boarders and trainers under umbrellas at one end of my arena. *Why are they out here in this rain? Are they crazy? I'm just riding my little Second Level test, this isn't Grand Prix*, I thought.

I entered the arena, and saluted. I couldn't see anything, except Moony's neck and ears. The poor horse had laid his ears flat on his head, not because he was angry, but because there was so much water falling into them.

I can't see anything, I thought, *how am I going to do this?* Moonshine trotted forward willingly, as if he didn't mind the rain beating down on the both of us.

Oh, there's a straight line of water, that must be the center line track, we'll go straight until we see the wall, then we'll turn, I strategized.

The wall came up sooner than I thought. I quickly steered Moonshine to the left, and almost slipped off the saddle. I grabbed his braided mane, which barely helped me to stay on. As Moonshine continued to trot, I struggled to center myself in the saddle. It was as if I were sitting in slick oil, I so easily slid from one side to the other in the wet leather. The next movement was the extended trot down the diagonal.

There is no way I'm going to stay on for this, I thought, as I nudged Moonshine forward into the movement.

I slid from side to side in the saddle. But every time I nearly fell off the right side, Moony swerved right; whenever I almost fell off the left side, he raced to catch me. I couldn't believe it—my horse was not letting me fall! This horse that used to buck so much and tried to throw me so many times in just the past year, was now doing everything he could to keep me safely in the saddle.

The ride was finally over, and I saluted. I patted Moonshine, as he walked hurriedly to the exit. The crowd was applauding.

My friend Sarah, cupped her hands around her mouth and shouted "I can't believe you stayed on!"

"Me neither! Moony was catching me every time I almost slipped off!"

Then Sarah's mother declared, "Victoria, that horse will jump through fire for you."

I believed her.

A larger crowd of boarders had assembled by Moonshine's stall.

"You are crazy, kid!" one said.

"I had to try to get a qualifying score," I reasoned.

"Yeah but this is really nuts, they should cancel the show. You know Nikki disqualified herself right after she started her test—that would have been the normal thing to do," another jumped in.

Then I saw Carol coming toward me and I knew she had

heard, she said, "Don't slam my student for being so dedicated!"

Then, through the sound system, we heard an announcement, "Due to the inclement weather, the rest of today's classes will be held tomorrow, after 4:00 p.m."

Are you kidding, they couldn't re-schedule my class? I thought. *Whatever, Moony was a superstar,* I smiled fondly, as I fed him his well-deserved carrots.

27

August arrived and we shipped off for the Regionals. Richard finally realized that it was easier to let me load my own horse. Moonshine followed me into the trailer without any pressure on the lead rope. We walked shoulder to shoulder everywhere, even up the trailer's steep loading ramp.

When we arrived at the show, Carol told me to take it easy in schooling Moonshine, since it had been a long trip, and he might be sore and stiff. She said I should just do relaxing work like letting him stretch his head down, at the walk, trot, and canter. No collection, she ordered. I was nervous about not doing a full workout the day before the show—it was sort of like not studying the night before a test. But I did whatever Carol said.

The next day, Moonshine was relaxed, fluid, and elegant in his first test. To reward him, I untacked him and led him out to graze. I wanted to watch the top riders performing in the more advanced levels, so I led Moonshine out to graze by the main show ring. There was a crowd seated on the grassy hill around the arena, watching the performances below. I was instantly captivated by the beauty and elegance with which they rode and their horses moved. I let the lead rope slacken so Moony would stop pulling me while he looked for good patches of grass. I didn't want to be distracted from watching the show. Then, all of a sudden, he started charging right into the crowd of people sitting on the grass, causing them to jump up and run out of his way.

"Moonshine, STOP!" I whispered loudly, horrified that he was stampeding these innocent bystanders. I could do nothing to stop him. I dug my heels into the ground and threw all my weight back, pulling against the lead rope, but he continued to plow through to wherever it was that he wanted to go. The mayhem in the crowd caught the attention of the horse performing in the arena. The horse spooked, and took off.

Holy shit! I thought, horrified and humiliated.

Luckily, the horse was being ridden by a skilled rider, who managed to regain control, and resumed her test. She shot me an angry glare.

I wanted to run away and crawl into a hole.

"Damn it, Moonshine! Come on, we're going!" I said as I pulled him back to the barn. I was humiliated. Moonshine, on the other hand, did not seem to care, and followed me nonchalantly back to the show barn.

I was frustrated and furious, and unfortunately, those emotions did not subside quickly. I was angry all the way into the next day, so any little thing that Moonshine did now was totally unforgivable. Our performance on that day was lackluster, even for us. I knew we could have done better, but I was too angry to "ride smart," as Carol put it, and Moonshine just didn't care, as usual.

After my last class, I declared to my mother, "I'm quitting, this is pointless."

"What do you mean?" she asked, bewildered.

"I suck. Moonshine sucks, we never get good scores. So, what's the point?"

She said nothing, which was highly unusual for her. She left me alone in the barn, to clean up and pack for the trip home. Then, Carol appeared.

"What's this I hear about you quitting?"

I was instantly furious with my mother and decided I would never again tell her anything in confidence.

"I never win, we never get good scores, so what's the point?"

She started with one of her usual speeches, which I ignored. I wasn't in the mood for a pep talk or lecture. I wasn't listening. She apparently noticed, and left.

I was alone for an hour until she reappeared.

"Come with me," she ordered.

I walked with her, following her to the warm up arena. An older-looking gentleman, with an old looking horse, stood waiting, in the center of the ring. We approached them.

"Victoria, this is Dr. Max Gahwyler," Carol said.

"It is a pleasure to make your acquaintance, young lady," he said in a foreign accent, as he removed his glove from his hand, and extended his arm down to me for a handshake. As he lowered his body from where he sat on his horse, his thin, loose skin fell toward me.

"Nice to meet you," I said politely.

His horse looked just as ancient as he did. The animal's bones looked large and heavy. The hair on his dark face was peppered with white. The horse did not prick his ears forward at all, like most horses do when they notice new things. Instead, he simply kept them pointed back, toward his rider, almost as if he were listening to his partner as he spoke.

"Dressage is not about the tricks you see in the ring. It is about *the feel*—how united one is with the horse. The tricks are simply a result of the feel. Allow me to demonstrate."

As soon as his horse began to walk, those weathered eyelids unveiled a spark in his crisp blue eyes.

"Did you see me give the walk command?" he asked.

"No," I replied.

"Good, because the communication was not meant for you—it was meant for the horse. Now, lightness," he said as he edged his inside hand forward, showing slack in the rein.

"What changes when I give my inside rein?" he asked

"Nothing," I said.

"Correct. That is because I don't need my reins, I ride from my seat and legs," he stated. "You must also make sure that the horse is using his back when you are riding—by that I mean, he must be rounded over his back, as it is the connection between back and front. Imagine that the engine of the horse is in the rear, the rear legs begin the forward motion, it must pass through the back, and if the back is working, it will be slightly elevated, or, in other words, rounded. When the horse is round, that forward energy passes into the bridle, where the rider then has total control of it, and therefore the horse. Do you understand?" he asked.

"I think so," I said. I actually did understand, since Carol had already explained roundness a long time ago. But then he showed me the difference between a hollow horse, where the horse drops his back and picks up the neck, and a round horse, where the forward motion is coming from the rear end, passing through the back, and going through to the neck. He showed me the difference in all three gaits—walk, trot, and canter. The horse did look a lot harder to control when he wasn't round.

When he finished the demonstration, he asked, "Do you see the difference between round and not round?"

"Yes," I replied. It was remarkable to see how the average looking horse could look so impressive just from becoming round. It was also impressive to see how subtle the rider's commands were on a round horse.

"Good. I wish you the best of luck in your dressage career. It was a pleasure meeting you, young lady," he concluded.

"Thank you, it was nice meeting you, too," I said.

Carol and I turned and walked back to the barn.

"I think I know why the canter is so much harder for me than the trot," I said to Carol.

"Why is that?" she asked.

"I don't think he's really round all of the time," I said.

"We'll work on it," she encouraged.

"Who was that guy anyway?" I asked.

"He judged you in one of your classes. He is also a pretty famous trainer."

The following weekend, everyone who didn't go to the Regionals wanted an update on my experience.

The first person who asked how my first Regionals went was Jean.

"Hi, Victoria!" she seemed elated to have found me by Moonshine's stall the following Saturday.

"So, how were the Regionals? Did Moony strut his stuff?" she asked excitedly.

"They were OK," I stated.

"Are you being modest again?" she beamed. I was struck by her radiant smile. She looked so much prettier when she smiled, I thought. She really should smile more.

"No, we mostly got scores in the fifties, again," I said.

"Well, it takes years and years of practice. Plus, those judges have no clue what a superstar Moony is," she said.

I swelled with pride—nobody ever called Moony a superstar.

"Yeah, those judges can't stand that he's not a warmblood, but I don't care, he *is* a superstar," I said, more to myself than to Jean.

She smiled, patted me on the shoulder, and walked off to her barn.

28

"Your grandmother has stomach cancer," my mother told us. "She will be in the hospital for a while."

The house was different—quiet, without any aromatic smells coming from the kitchen. We no longer heard the angry clanking of pots and pans. There was no more bickering between her and my grandfather. And all of the dogs that previously had tailed her with purpose everywhere she went, now wandered around the house aimlessly.

My mother was at the hospital most evenings and weekends. She insisted that I call my father for rides to the farm, and also Sandra, my sister's classmate, who had a horse at the same barn.

My father, surprisingly, did show up occasionally to take me to the farm.

"Hi, Dad," I said.

"Bonjour!" he said as he donned his beret and driving gloves. He was in his eccentric mood, I recognized. Good, this means he's playful.

"Nice outfit," I teased as I scanned his plaid blazer with

elbow patches, corduroy pants, black beret, and gloves.

"Are you jealous?" he smiled.

"*So* jealous," I joked.

Good thing you're not a woman, you'd be broke with all your crazy outfits and jewelry, I thought. I never saw him in the same outfit twice, and he seemed to have a different get-up for every occasion. Today was his Saturday driving day, so he was in his Saturday driving outfit.

"Is that a new necklace?" I asked noticing the gaudy gold chain strangling his double chin.

"Yes, it is! Do you like it?" He was elated that I noticed his new jewelry.

"Amazing," I said sarcastically. My sarcasm never bothered him if I was paying him a compliment.

"But you're still poor, right?" I asked, annoyed he could buy himself new outfits and wear obnoxious gold jewelry, but always declared how poor he was and that's why he couldn't afford child support, or help with school tuition or Moonshine or my sister's figure skating.

"It was a gift!" he exclaimed.

"From who? You have no friends," I replied.

"Very funny, you know everyone wants to be my friend, that's why they are always buying me these nice things!"

"Right," I said. "So, can you pay Moony's board this month?"

"Nope."

"Half?" I bargained.

"Not possible!" he said gleefully.

"Can you at least pay for a lesson? It's sixty dollars."

"Too much money!" he let out, as he turned up the music. Unlike my mother, who couldn't stand my taste in music, my father actually let me listen to my favorite radio stations, maybe because he learned that it sometimes kept me quiet. But today I turned it down.

"OK, well if you're so broke, why don't you pawn your gold

chain? I'm sure it's worth something," I stated.

"This was a *gift* from a *friend*!" he gasped in horror.

"Is it more important than me?" I asked.

"You are a child, you cannot possibly understand," he stated, as he usually did when he had grown weary of being asked for money.

"I'm not a child, and I think the problem is that I *do* understand."

"Oh, really?" he was amused.

"Yeah, really," I said, getting angry. "I understand Mom is struggling to pay off the house, to pay both of our tuitions, and to pay for riding and figure skating. I also understand that you pay for nothing, you never pay for board even though I always beg you to, and you haven't paid child support since I was eight!"

"Enough! You are making me crazy!" he cried out.

You're already there, you selfish fucking pig, I seethed.

When we arrived at the farm, I leaped out of my father's car, happy to escape his miserable company. I walked into the barn to find Kim, the barn manager, holding my horse still in the barn aisle, while the vet, Dr. Sheila Danberry, was examining Moonshine's left front leg.

"What's going on?" I asked as I approached Moonshine and petted his nose.

"Good, you're here. Here, take your horse. I have to get back to work," Kim said gruffly, handing me the lead rope.

"Kim called me this morning because Moony was lame on his right front. It's not terribly serious," the vet said when she looked up and saw my face.

"Moony just has a condition called Navicular Disease," she said.

"What's Navicular Disease?" I asked.

"There are two bones down here, by his ankle, that are

separated by cartilage. But when a horse has Navicular, that cartilage disappears, and the two bones start to wear against each other," she said.

My eyes widened at the horrific image of two bones grinding away at each other.

"You can help Moony by adjusting his shoeing. Instead of regular horseshoes, I would recommend that the farrier put on bar shoes, which look like full ovals, so that he has support on his heels. You should also ask the farrier to put rubber pads between the hoof and the bar shoe, to give Moony more support on the front legs. The hind feet can still be shod with regular shoes, since he only has Navicular in the front. However, you should also keep an eye on the hind legs, since he has arthritis back there," she advised.

Great, he has no good legs, I thought. *Like I needed another challenge.*

"I'm going to prescribe a medication called Isoxuprine, he'll need twenty pills a day—ten in the morning, and ten in the evening."

Twenty pills? That's so much! I can't believe it's that bad! I thought.

"Thanks so much, Dr. Danberry."

I went to the office to cancel my lesson. I waited for Carol to come in from teaching so I could tell her what was going on.

"Hi Carol, Moony's lame," I said when she came into the office.

"What's wrong?" she asked.

"The vet says he has Navicular Disease."

"Oh, ok. Did she leave you Isox?"

She knew about Navicular Disease. I was comforted.

"Yeah."

"Great, start him on it, we'll give him the week off, and see how he is next weekend."

The following weekend, Carol was her usual chipper self.

"Hey there! How is Moony feeling?" she asked.

"He's not lame!" I exclaimed. I had been nervous all week.

"Always a good starting point," she joked. Then she got serious, when she noticed my feeble smile.

"Look, it's not a death sentence. We just have to watch it. If he starts feeling ouchy, then we'll back off. He's a strong little horse, he'll be OK."

"What about the arthritis in his back legs?" I asked.

"That makes things tricky. With arthritis, exercise helps, but with Navicular, the more he's worked, the more the bone degenerates," she explained.

"Great, so I have to work the back legs and not work the front legs," I stated.

"Basically, yeah," she agreed.

"How do I do that, cut him in half?" I was growing frustrated.

"No, we'll just keep doing the dressage. As you guys progress, you will start to collect more, which means Moony will start rocking his center of gravity from the front half of his body to his butt. That will take more weight off the front legs, and rotate it back to his hind legs."

I was thrilled that she had a solution. I adored her for being able to make the best of this situation that I feared would be career-ending.

"Thanks, Carol," I looked at her and smiled.

29

My grandmother was quickly deteriorating. She hated being at the hospital, so when it was safe to unplug her from all of the medical devices, she came home. She was much calmer at home than at the hospital, where she could be with the dogs that she loved so much, sleep in her own bed, and eat familiar Romanian food that my mother prepared, although it was nowhere near as tasty as her own cooking.

"Plegh! What is this garbage?" she spat in Romanian at the dinner table one night.

My sister and I laughed in unison at my grandmother's insult of my mother's cooking.

"It's your favorite—stuffed grape leaves, just eat it," my mother replied.

"This is disgusting!" she declared, throwing her fork at her food.

"Mother, please. Look, Dad is eating it," she responded to her mother, as she nodded her head toward my grandfather, bent over his plate, chewing quietly.

"That hog will eat anything!" my grandmother cried out.

"Mom, can you please just try . . ." I could detect the weariness in my mother's voice.

"Ugh, I just want to die! Oh, God! Please, just take me now! I am so sick of this miserable life!" my grandmother wailed.

"OK, Mom, time for bed," my mother got up to help her out of her chair and take her to her bedroom.

"Girls, you can go watch TV when you're done with dinner," she said.

"Yes!" we exclaimed as we picked up our plates and rushed to the TV in the living room.

A few days later, my grandmother was back in the hospital. She was in and out of the hospital until the following spring.

One day after school, after my sister and I had arrived home, we found my mother on the phone, sounding rushed and worried. My grandfather was holding my grandmother's hand as she lay on the couch, tears in his eyes.

"Girls, pack her things, I am trying to get the doctor on the phone!" she shouted to us.

"You pack, I'll help her get up," I told my sister.

"Tati, can you help Baby pack?" I asked him in Romanian. He looked weary and exhausted. My sister and I were fresh from school, but he had been dealing with my sick grandmother all day, and the past few years. We had the energy to help.

"Nanni, time to get up," I said as I took her hand from my grandfather.

"Victoria? Is that you?" she asked, looking straight through me.

"Yes, it's me, can you sit up?" I asked, as I hoisted her frail ninety-pound frame into a seated position on the couch. I had either grown strong from riding, or she had lost a lot of weight, because I felt as though I could easily pick her up.

"Oh God damn it! What now?" she barked as she opened her enraged eyes. My grandmother had green-hazel eyes, which usually blazed with rage. I avoided eye contact.

"We're just going back to the hospital," I said calmly, as I pulled the covers off of her.

"I'm not going ANYWHERE! Leave me alone!" she spat.

I heard my mother's footsteps approaching as soon as she heard my grandmother scream at me.

I turned around and told her, "It's OK, Mom, just call the ambulance."

She rushed back to the telephone in the dining room.

"OK, Nanni, you have to get up now," I said as I slid my right arm under her back and my left arm under her legs. I started shifting her legs towards the edge of the couch.

"Get off me!" she screeched. She was defeated, and started to cry.

"I can do it myself," she said finally.

I slipped her dress over her nightgown, got her shoes, and called my mother to get her coat. As we sat, waiting for the ambulance to arrive, she turned to me, looked directly into my eyes and said, "I'm going to die."

"You're not going to die, Nanni," I said, slightly drained.

"Yes, I am going to die today!"

I was too tired to respond, and also knew she would challenge anything I said, so I simply sat with her, stroking her back.

When the ambulance arrived, my mother grabbed her keys. "Girls, take care of the dogs. Order takeout. I might spend the night. I'll call later."

"OK, Mom," we were looking forward to the distraction of homework and then dinner in front of the TV.

Both my mother and grandfather spent the night at the hospital. The dogs wailed and whimpered, as they did whenever my grandmother was gone. We tried to distract them until we were exhausted, and fell asleep with all of them on the couch.

The next day was Friday, and I was elated. It had been a draining week, and I was looking forward to escaping to the farm.

"Hey Sandra, you going to the farm after school?" I asked her at lunch.

"Yeah, want a ride?"

"That would be great."

"Sure, no problem!" she said.

I called my mother at the hospital to let her know I had a ride to the farm, and that my sister was going to her friend's house after school. She didn't pick up, so I left a message.

The day was uneventful, which I appreciated. I took comfort in the dull routine of being in school. I was tired. Sandra's mother picked us up after school and drove us out to the farm. When we arrived, Sandra went to her pony at the far end of the barn, and I went directly to Moonshine's stall to greet him.

After my ride, I was untacking Moony in the aisle of the barn, just outside his stall. He had a pile of carrots on the floor to keep him busy while I took off the saddle, bridle, and leg wraps. As I removed the last wrap, I saw someone appear under the barn's fluorescent lights from the darkness outside. It was my mom. Just as I was about to greet her and ask her why she was at the barn when I had a ride, I saw my grandfather come in after her. He looked smaller than ever. I knew that his being at the barn meant something was wrong. But my mind didn't let me immediately go to the worst case scenario—death. Maybe they got into a fight? Maybe she was in one of her moods. Maybe he wanted some fresh air and to be away from the hospital and the house.

"She's gone," my mother said, somber.

"Oh, Mom, are you OK?" I asked.

"Yes," she lied, her face red and weary.

"Your grandfather is heartbroken," she added.

I didn't say anything to him. I knew there was nothing I could say that would ease the pain of having lost his spouse of over fifty years. I simply went to him and hugged him.

"Do you want to pet Moonshine, Tati?" I asked. This was the first time he had seen Moonshine.

"No," he said, looking straight through Moonshine.

"Mom, I need a few minutes before I can go, want to wait in the car?"

"Yes," she said flatly.

"Come on, Dad," she said, taking hold of my grandfather's elbow, and leading him back outside.

I led Moonshine into his stall, and gave him all of the carrots I had with me. I ran to Sandra's pony's stall, where I was sure I'd find Sandra and her mom.

"Mrs. Turner, my mom's here, I have to go," I breathed out as I saw her.

"Sure, Victoria. Is everything OK?"

"Not really, my grandmother passed away."

Just as I said "away," a lump choked me, and I realized what had happened. She was gone. I would never see her again.

The funeral was held a few days later. It was small. I had never seen my mother cry so much. My grandfather sobbed as he stroked his dead wife's hair while she lay in the casket. That was the first time I ever saw a dead person. She looked the same as she did when she was alive; she just looked asleep. The lines of the tubes up her nose left marks all over her face. Even my sister was crying. I didn't. As much as I wanted to cry, I didn't want to upset my mother even more. She didn't need that.

The day we buried my grandmother was a crisp, spring day. The ground was mushy from the early rain. I watched the casket sit suspended above the hole in the ground. All I could think about was how miserable she always seemed. I wondered if she was in a better place now.

After the funeral and burial, my grandmother's absence was palpable. My mother and grandfather were a combination of devastated and empty. Everything was suddenly silent. The house was quiet. The dogs whimpered. The house was no longer filled with aromas of rich Romanian cooking. It was empty, quiet, and sad.

The farm continued to be my relief from reality. Other than the time my grandfather showed up at the farm, my regular life was totally separate from my farm life, which I loved. The barn was a sacred place that my home life couldn't invade.

30

I was eager to turn sixteen, because it was one step closer to seventeen—the year I could finally drive myself to the farm. I would no longer have to depend on someone else for a ride. I would no longer have to beg my father for money on the long drives to the farm. I would no longer have to listen to my mother's endless worries about making ends meet. I would no longer have to ask my sister's classmate for a ride. I could just be alone. And then I could be at the farm, with my horse, for as long as I wanted.

"So, you're learning how to drive, huh?" Carol said as I headed out to the parking lot where my father was waiting.

"Yeah, I'm really excited!" I said, smiling.

"Well, normally I'd be worried about having another teenager on the highway, but if you drive like you ride, you'll be fine," she said.

"Thanks!" I was uplifted. Carol's confidence in my driving gave me an even greater sense of confidence.

Things were looking up, my sophomore year was coming to an end, summer was fast approaching, and I was driving. A few months had passed since my grandmother's death and we had been forced back into our daily routines.

I was especially eager for summer to arrive because it was 1996—a summer Olympic year. Not only that, but the Olympics would be in Georgia! We had driven down to Florida several times when I was younger, so I knew it was a drivable distance. The biggest, most prestigious sporting event would be in my country, within driving distance! I was giddy. By the time May rolled around, I could no longer contain my excitement. All I could talk about was how close the Olympics would be. How my idol, Michelle Gibson, who was from Georgia, would compete for a medal in her home state, and how extraordinarily special that was. It was so poetic—who gets to compete in the world's greatest athletic event in their own home state? And beyond that, the opportunity was given to Michelle Gibson, a superstar, who worked her way to the top. She deserved to win. I wished I could be there to watch history unfold.

On one of my drives out to the farm with my mother, I said, "Hey Mom, you know the Olympics are going to be in Atlanta this year?"

"So?" she said, disinterested, obviously not sharing in my obsession.

"Well, you know they never televise dressage; wouldn't it be cool to go see it live since it's so close?"

"What? You want to go? It's only two months away! I don't think we would be able to get tickets now."

"I know. Just thought it would've been cool to go," I said.

In my lesson that day, I told Carol that the Olympics would be in Atlanta, and she was just as disinterested as my mother.

"Do you know the Olympics are going to be in Atlanta?" I said to her at the end of my lesson.

"Yup," she responded.

That was it. Just "yup." Why didn't anyone care about this monumental event coming so close to home?

School finally let out in the second week of June. My mother picked us up on the last day of school. I was first to the car, so I opened the door to the passenger seat. As I was about to sit, I noticed two airline tickets, and two envelopes with the Olympic logo on them. I picked them up as I sat.

"What's this?" I asked my mother.

"What you wanted," she replied.

I tore open the envelopes—inside were tickets to all four of the dressage events!

"Oh my God, Mom! The *Olympics*!" I whispered. I couldn't say the word out loud. It was too special.

"How did you even get these? I thought it was impossible."

"Nothing is impossible if you want it badly enough," she replied.

I was too elated to be annoyed by her spiritual talk.

"Mom, I don't even know how to thank you for this. This is a dream come true," I said, still in shock.

"I know," she said. After a long pause, she began, "There's more, though."

"What?" I said, still looking at the Olympic tickets in my hands.

"Well, you know how I was a jumper rider in Romania?" she started.

"Yeah?"

"Well, in Romania, during the war, it was a different system for equestrians. There were not a dozen barns from which I could choose to ride. There was only one barn, on the army base. Since it was the only barn around Bucharest where everyone could ride, it had both jumper and dressage riders and trainers. The best trainers in my country trained at this army barn," she said.

"I know, you told me before," I reminded her, hoping she would cut to the chase.

"Well, one of those trainers was George Theodorescu."

"No way!" I exclaimed, "You *knew* George Theodorescu?"

George Theodorescu was an incredibly famous and successful dressage trainer. Not only was he an accomplished rider himself, being an Olympian, but he was also a highly sought after trainer. He had trained hundreds of top riders, including Robert Dover. I had researched and memorized the biographies of almost all of the American, German, and Dutch equestrians, so I knew that most of the riders who had qualified to compete in that year's Olympics had trained with Mr. Theodorescu.

George Theodorescu had a distinctively Romanian name, but he lived and trained in Germany, where all of the best riders, trainers, and horses were. Germany had won every single individual and team gold medal in dressage in the Olympics since the early 1900s. The Germans dominated the sport, and Americans frequently flocked to Germany to train with the best.

The Theodorescu legacy lived on, after Mr. Theodorescu retired from competition, through his daughter, Monica. She was often featured in the equitation magazines I read. I saw pictures of her magnificent steeds, and read about her success—two World Cup Championships, multiple Olympic Team gold medals, and several individual Olympic silver and bronze medals.

I was astounded when my mother announced that she knew this dressage icon.

"Yes, I knew him. I mean, not well, since I was just another kid who did jumping, and he was this elegant, sophisticated dressage trainer, but we would say 'hello' in passing," she continued. "Anyway, after World War II, during one of his international competitions, he escaped communist Romania and fled to Germany. He left everything behind—his home, his friends, and his horses," I sensed her tormented nostalgia from reminiscing about her youth in Romania—her home and her prison.

"So he has been living in Germany ever since then, and now his daughter is also an Olympian," she continued.

I scoffed, "Yeah, Mom, I know. Monica Theodorescu."

"Yes, well Mr. Theodorescu goes with her to all of her Olympics, of course, and this year he is also the team coach for the French dressage team."

"So?" I wondered where this was all leading.

After a long pause, she said, "I have arranged for you to meet him in Atlanta," she concluded.

No WAY! I thought. I was screaming in my head. A hurricane of excitement and disbelief rushed over me. I was dumbfounded. It was as if I had just been handed the impossible on a silver platter. Just as I was about to shriek with glee, she added, "The only catch is I can't be there for the whole week because I have to work and take care of the dogs and your sister," she stated. "I will be there the first couple of days, but your father will be there the whole time."

"Oh, *Mom*!" I whined.

"Enough!" she interrupted. "He is your father, and he loves you."

"But he's such an *asshole*!"

"You are the only person in the world he actually likes; you'll be fine."

I sat back and remained quiet. *Who cares who I'm going to be there with? I'm going to see the Olympics! And meet George Theodorescu!* I thought.

I couldn't wait to tell Carol.

The next day, when I saw her in the barn, I rushed to her and gushed, "Carol, guess what? I'm going to see the Olympics in Atlanta!"

"That's great, Victoria! It will be good for you to see the superstars live. I want a full report when you get back."

"You got it!" I said through my wide smile.

31

The Olympic dressage events were to be held over the course of a week. There were to be four events: preliminaries on Monday and Wednesday, then the top twenty from those two days would be invited to compete on Saturday and Sunday.

On the flight, my mother told both my father and me what the itinerary was—Mr. Theodorescu would be busy with the competition on Monday and Wednesday, but he invited us to have tea with him on Tuesday. My mother would be at the meeting on Tuesday, but would fly home that evening. I couldn't believe it. Here was this dressage legend, who had trained half of the world's best riders, taking time out of the Olympics, where he was coaching his own *daughter* as well as the *French team*, to meet *me* and my parents!

As soon we landed, we were immersed in an alternate universe. The Olympics took over every inch of the city. The proud Olympic rings greeted us at the airport, hotel, and every restaurant. It was like stepping into a world I desperately wanted to be a part of, it was like stepping into a fairy tale.

The following morning, I jumped out of bed at 6:00 a.m., hoping to catch the first shuttle bus to the Olympic dressage venue.

"Mom!" I shouted, flipping on the lights. "Get up, get up, time to go!"

She immediately flipped off the bed covers and flung her legs off the bed. Years of dressage shows had trained her well.

I called my father's room. No answer. He was just a few doors down, so I went over and started banging on his door. After a few minutes, he pulled the door open.

"What? What's wrong with you?" he said, annoyed.

"Time to go, time to go!" I chirped.

"Goddamn crazy kid . . ." he muttered, walking away.

"Mom, he's not ready! We'll be late!" I announced, bursting back into the room we shared.

"No, we won't. Stay here," she said, walking out the door. After a few minutes, she brought him to our room and we were all finally ready to go.

We had to take a shuttle bus from the hotel to the venue, and I didn't know how bad traffic would be. We hustled to the bus stop, a five-minute walk from the hotel. A sizable crowd was already there. The shuttle bus arrived a few minutes later and we were on our way.

We arrived an hour before the first scheduled ride. I hurried through the long line of vendors, weaving through people, and leaving my parents behind. I didn't care about anything, or anyone, I just had to get there. There was a gravitational pull drawing me into the Olympic stadium, just as strong as the force that pulled me to Moony's stall every time I arrived at the barn. I had to see it.

I scurried up a long, concrete ramp, and then, there it was—the Olympic arena. The early morning sun illuminated the damp sand so that it glistened like gold dust. It had been perfectly combed, with careful, straight lines drawn up and down the whole arena. Colorful, fresh flowers peppered the perimeter of the ring. The bright white rails of the arena shone in the sun. A huge monitor stood stoically behind the show ring. Everything looked just as I had envisioned, only more magnificent.

A few people passed me to make their way to their seats, which snapped me back to reality.

Oh, right, the seats, I remembered.

Our row was perfect, although quite high up.

No problem, I thought, *Victor brought his crazy binoculars.*

My father wore his tourist outfit today: baseball cap to protect his bald head from getting sunburned, binoculars, video camera, and photo camera. White socks were pulled all the way up his hairy shins. Khaki shorts pulled up over his big belly, and a light polo shirt tucked in. The ensemble was complete with a fanny pack and shoulder bag. He looked like Humpty Dumpty as a tourist.

My mother simply wore a pale yellow button down shirt with a long denim skirt.

They finally arrived, five minutes before the first ride.

"Victoria, we're here!" my father announced, when he spotted me sitting in the stands.

"Shhh!" I hissed, waving my hand to keep him quiet.

My mother slapped him on his back.

"What did I do?" he asked, feigning innocence.

"Just shut it and behave!" my mother hissed at him in Romanian. Astonishingly, he obeyed. I was again amazed. How could he be so vicious in court all those years and now he was a lamb? I had little time to analyze it, as the first rider then entered the arena.

The world around me stopped; I was drawn into that rider's world. I was seeing what he was seeing, feeling how his horse felt underneath him. I heard nothing else, saw nothing else. It was as if *I* were there in that arena, riding that majestic, white

Lipizzaner horse.

The Spanish rider put in a respectable effort; unfortunately, his horse spooked at several cameramen around the ring. I couldn't believe that even in the Olympics, I saw mistakes. He had some minor errors in some movements, something I saw in local competitions at home, but was not expecting to see from *Olympians.* I was expecting these Olympians, these superstars, to be perfect. I was amazed that they made mistakes, too.

"I can't believe he made mistakes in the tempi changes," I whispered to my mother while the audience applauded after the rider had saluted.

"Just because you read about these riders in all of your dressage magazines doesn't make them perfect, flawless gods," she whispered back.

"But they're in the *Olympics*!" I whispered back.

"So what? They are still riders, just like you. They are only human, and they still make mistakes."

After a few more low profile riders, Michelle Gibson finally took the stage. She was the first American to compete. I knew everything ever published about her. She was born and raised right here, in Georgia. She had left home six years ago and moved to Germany, to train and compete with the best. And now, she was one of the best in the world. After years of hard work and sacrifice, she had come home to compete in her first Olympic Games. She was living out her Olympic dream.

Her horse, Peron, was a notoriously difficult horse. I had read that he had been abandoned by his owner, and Michelle started riding him because he was just sitting in a field somewhere. Nobody wanted him. But she saw something in him, and with help from her trainer, she had turned him into an Olympic mount. This horse that no one else could ride simply blossomed under his young rider (she was still only in her twenties, which is considered young for dressage riders). The horse did not look spectacular and gifted in the pictures I had seen, so I knew there must be something extra, something a camera could not capture, for them to have had such remarkable success. I couldn't wait to see this extra element to the pair that was making America competitive with Germany, for the first time in the history of the sport.

This twenty-seven-year-old girl could change the sport today, I thought as I watched her enter the arena.

She moved together with her horse as if they were one. He was an unimpressive mover, but he seemed to read her mind as if they shared one consciousness. It even looked like they breathed at the same time. I had never seen a rider so united with her horse. Peron was so focused on his rider that he paid no attention to the distractions that rattled the other horses—the loudspeaker, the flags, the cameras, the crowd. His ears were pointed back at her, listening to her, for the whole ride.

Everyone waited anxiously for the score; it seemed that the whole audience knew that Michelle might be the first American since 1932 to win an individual Olympic dressage medal. Other than the previous Olympics in 1992, the last Olympic medal brought home to the US was a team bronze, secured by Hilda Gurney and a Thoroughbred that she owned and trained herself, Keen. Even though her monumental win happened before I was born, I knew her story well, and was inspired by it—she and her racehorse dared to compete in dressage at the Olympic level, and came home with a bronze medal. I was confident that this US team in Atlanta could also win a team medal, but I really hoped Michelle would win an individual medal.

The score was posted—75.853%, a solid, high score. The crowd—Michelle's home crowd—went wild. I joined in the jubilation.

"Do you think she can do it—get an individual medal?" I asked my mother.

"I think so," she said, as she applauded.

If Michelle could win an individual medal, I would have a renewed sense of hope for my own dressage career. If an

American girl with a horse from a field could compete with the Germans, Dutch, and Swedes, the long-time dominators of dressage, my world would change. I would no longer assume that judges wanted to see fancy horses with impressive pedigrees and famous riders. I would believe that judges were scoring the rides they saw, not the history they knew. I would hope that they rewarded good training rather than impressive bloodlines. After all, "dressage" was a French word that translated to "training;" it seemed only fair, therefore, for the judging system to evaluate the horses' and riders' training, rather than their backgrounds.

I also saw the reigning Olympic champion compete on her brilliant horse, as well as the reigning World Cup champion. Neither had the magic or the power in their performances that I saw in Michelle's. I was astounded to see some minor mistakes in each of their rides.

"I can't believe it," I whispered to my mother.

"I told you, they are just human—*all* of them," she whispered back.

At the lunch break, an older gentleman appeared in the walkway between bleachers and started up, toward our row. He was small, fragile looking, with white hair sprouting out of his dark, tan head. He was wearing an Olympic team jacket for Germany, and a VIP pass draped around his neck. I gasped when I recognized his face—Mr. Theodorescu! He was coming over to us!

Oh my God, Mr. Theodorescu is here and my hair is a mess! I panicked.

My mother waved at him and bounded down the aisle stairs like a teenager. I followed behind her.

"Hello, Mr. Theodorescu, it's so nice to see you after all this time. Thank you so much for taking time out of your busy schedule to meet with us," she began in Romanian, as she shook his hand. "This is my daughter, Victoria."

"Hello, young lady," he said in Romanian as I shook his hand.

"Hello," I replied automatically.

"Hey everyone, say cheese!" My father suddenly yelled from the stands.

Oh my God I am mortified! Please let that be it, please shut up, Victor! I pleaded in my head.

"Yes, well," he continued, "I wanted to come over to meet you today. I will actually be tied up tomorrow, so we can't do tea. Can you come to the Olympic village tonight, after 6:00 p.m.? Meet me at my hotel," he said, as he handed my mother a piece of paper with the address.

"Of course, thank you," she replied in Romanian.

He turned to walk away.

"I can't believe he's taking time out of the *Olympics* to talk to us," I gushed to my mother as we turned to go back to our seats.

"Yes, me too. He is a good person," she said.

The afternoon of competition came to a close. Michelle's first ride was good, but she needed a second good score to land her in the finals, where she could compete for an individual medal. It was so exciting; I thought, *I might witness an American win an individual Olympic medal!* And I would soon sit down with one of the icons of dressage. My stomach was in knots.

"Victoria, can you please calm down," my mother sighed on the shuttle bus to the Olympic village, while I bit my nails and furiously shook my legs in my seat.

"How am I supposed to calm down? I'm about to talk to George Theodorescu!" I reminded her.

"Yes, I know. But remember, he is just another human being, like you and me," she reiterated.

"Oh darling, he's just another little horse trainer. He's not a *lawyer*," my father chimed in, priding himself again on being an attorney.

"Actually, he *is* a lawyer. He just spends all his time training horses. And he speaks five languages, just like you," I corrected him.

"He's a lawyer?" my father was dumbstruck. At least now I knew he would be respectful to a fellow attorney.

"By the way I speak *eight* languages!" he corrected me.

I rolled my eyes. I let him have the last word because I needed to rehearse what I would say to the dressage legend I was about to meet.

We finally arrived at the Olympic village. Mr. Theodorescu met us at the entrance of the hotel and led us to his room. My mother began the conversation, starting with memories of their time at the army stable in Romania.

"Well, I thought horses were out of my life when I gave up jumping to practice dentistry and moved to America. But then this one has been obsessed with horses since she was little," she nodded at me accusingly, in a teasing way.

"Is that so?" the legend interjected.

"Yes," my mother continued. "When she discovered dressage, she was hooked. When she got her first dressage saddle, a used little one from a local tack store, she would oil it in her room for hours, and then she sat in it, and did her homework on it. Her room was filled with the smell of saddle soap, but she was so happy," she told him.

He was visibly amused. I felt my cheeks flush with embarrassment.

"So forget it when she got her first horse. I would have to pull her out of the stall to go home," and just when she was about to delve into another embarrassing story, he interrupted.

"What kind of horse?" he asked

"Appendix," she replied.

"Not a warmblood?" he asked, amazed.

"No," she now flushed slightly with embarrassment.

"She cannot ride dressage without a warmblood," he said conclusively.

Then my father jumped in.

"Look, Mr. Theodorescu, before we throw millions of dollars out the window, how do we even know she is worth it?" he asked.

The legend, who was impossible to read due to his total lack of facial expressions, lifted one eyebrow.

"Excuse me?" he asked, bewildered that my father so blatantly questioned investing in my passion.

"Well, horses are expensive, but how do we even know she's good enough to go really far?" my father continued.

"I would have to see her ride," Mr. Theodorescu said, "we can arrange to go to a local barn in the area."

This busy dressage trainer, here to coach not only his own daughter, but also the French team during the Olympics, was going to take time out during this monumental week to see *me* ride?

"Come back here tomorrow, we will go to a local barn together, and then talk," Mr. Theodorescu concluded.

"Excellent," my father was pleased with the verdict.

"I have to go back to New York, so I will not be able to be here," my mother interjected.

"I don't have to see *you* ride, do I?" Mr. Theodorescu replied, in the Romanian sarcasm I knew all too well.

He's funny! I thought.

"Well, we are extremely grateful, thank you so much," my mother said as we all rose to leave.

"You are welcome," he said.

Then he turned to me, and said, "I look forward to seeing you ride, young lady."

"Thank you, Mr. Theodorescu," was all I could muster.

The next day, I met Mr. Theodorescu at his hotel. I wore

my jeans and sneakers, instead of my breeches and boots, not having anticipated that I would ride this week. We drove to a local barn where only western saddles were available.

This is ridiculous, I thought. *I'm riding in front of a dressage legend, and I'm not even in an English saddle. He's going to laugh at me.*

I nonetheless hopped on a horse, and gave it the cue to trot. I sat deep in the western saddle, to demonstrate my fluid seat, which may not have come across on the short strided horse I was riding.

"Change direction, please," he said in English.

"Canter, please," he then said.

I did as he ordered.

"Stop, enough," he said.

That's it? I thought.

I slowed the horse to a walk.

Mr. Theodorescu said to my father. "Your daughter has talent. But a good rider can go nowhere without a good horse."

Then he turned to me and said, "You can ride. If you want to train with me, you are welcome to come to join my training program in Germany."

I couldn't control the smile that broke across my face.

My father flustered and stammered, "She is in school!"

Mr. Theodorescu replied calmly, "Will she be in school forever?" then he looked at me and smiled.

"You are welcome to come to Germany and train with me when you are done with school," he told me. "I have to get back," he said, and the conversation was concluded.

I knew my father had no intention of spending a dime on me or my sister, and definitely not on what he considered to be our temporary hobbies. I knew any kind of discussion about pursuing dressage on a larger scale, like going to Germany to train, was off the table. But I had an ally—my mother.

I called her that evening to tell her that Mr. Theodorescu thought I was talented and had invited me to train in Germany.

"Oh, honey, I am so proud of you!" she said.

"And he told Victor that I need a good horse and to go to Germany if I wanted to be really good," I continued.

She was silent. "Can you put your father on the phone?"

I handed my father the phone. "She wants to talk to you."

He walked over to the phone and took the receiver.

"What?" he asked.

Silence.

"Yes, he said she was talented."

Silence.

"So?"

Silence.

"I don't care, she is just a child. She needs to finish school. And then she has to go to college, are you crazy?"

Silence.

"I don't have that kind of money!"

He slammed down the phone.

"Your mother is still crazy," he said as he went back to watching basketball on the TV.

I dialed the number again, and she picked up. "Sorry, Mom."

"Why are you sorry?" she asked.

"Because he hung up on you," I said.

She laughed. "Don't worry, honey. We will figure something out," she comforted.

If I weren't in Atlanta, watching the Olympics live, and I hadn't just met one of my dressage heroes, I wouldn't have believed her, but now I did.

32

The next day of dressage competition would determine who would compete in the finals. Michelle and Peron had again risen to the occasion and turned in another stunning performance. I was elated. The German team had all put in solid performances, including Mr. Theodorescu's daughter, Monica. They had all been awarded high scores, and all four Germans qualified to ride in the finals on Saturday and Sunday, as everyone had expected. The Dutch team met the expectation that they would be right behind the Germans—they had also qualified, although their average score wasn't as high as the German score. Finally, three of the four American riders had qualified. This meant that they all had to put in stellar performances, because all three scores would be counted; there would be no fourth score, known as a drop score, to throw out. The Finnish and Swedish teams suffered the same fate as the American team. I knew that the team and individual gold and silver medals would go to either Germany or the Netherlands, but the team and individual bronze medals were up for grabs.

I desperately wanted Michelle to win an individual medal.

She was a beautiful rider; a hard worker who had plucked an unwanted horse from a field, and turned him into an Olympic mount. The perfect way to punctuate her Cinderella story would be with an individual Olympic medal. I thought that if Michelle won a medal, she would erase the outdated notion that only those with perfect pedigrees could be serious dressage contenders. I hoped Michelle would open the door for me.

Saturday, the day of the individual qualifying competition, finally came. If Michelle qualified to compete in the individual round, she would have a chance to make history, and compete for an individual medal.

In the stadium, I sat on the edge of my seat, rocking back and forth with anticipation for her ride. She appeared on Peron. I sat on my hands to keep from biting all of my nails. *We are so close to a medal!* my thoughts raced.

She put in another stunning performance. The crowd erupted. The score was posted—she had qualified to compete in the individual round on Sunday!

"She did it! She's going to get it!" I clapped my father multiple times on his shoulder in my excitement.

The final individual competition was the freestyle, where she would ride to music. I knew she had an impressive freestyle, because so many magazine articles reported it to be a stunning routine. I also knew that freestyle scores were often higher than regular competition scores, so I was convinced that Michelle would be the first American to win an individual Olympic medal in dressage.

I couldn't eat or sleep that night. I was too excited for the next day, too anxious to watch history unfold. I was wide awake and glued to the television until the early morning, when I drifted off. I woke up at five in the morning and shoved my father awake.

"Get UP, Dad!" I shouted into his ear.

Half of his face was buried in the pillow. One eyebrow lifted to open one eyelid. He looked at me and closed it.

"Come ON!!" I was shrieking now, pulling his arm.

"OK, OK!" he said, irritated.

As he shuffled to the bathroom, he muttered to himself, "Thank God this is the last day of this damn torture . . . crazy child . . ."

I sat on the edge of the bed, and flipped on the television as I waited for him to adorn himself with whatever special outfit he had picked out for today.

The morning competition was filled with the lower profile riders. All of the superstars, including Michelle, Monica, and the reigning Olympic and World Cup champions, were scheduled for the afternoon.

I sat in the bleachers during the lunch break, not wanting to miss the afternoon rides. The two women who sat to my right were speaking loudly between themselves.

"What time is Michelle riding?" one said.

"Two thirty," the one closer to me replied. "Poor girl, I hope she makes it, terrible what they did to her."

I was normally quite shy, but I couldn't stop myself.

"What happened to Michelle?" I asked.

She turned to me and said, "You haven't heard? I thought everyone knew by now."

"No, what?" I was going to explode if she didn't tell me immediately.

"Yesterday, Peron's owners told her to drive out to their house two hours away, even though she had to train. They said it was urgent, so she went. Then they told her that today would be the last time she would ever ride him because they wanted to turn him into a breeding stallion here in the States. Everyone's saying how she can't stop crying. She's devastated, poor thing."

My mouth dropped.

"Those idiots," the other woman interjected. "They couldn't wait until *after* she rode today to break her heart? They ruined our chance at a medal!" she huffed.

"She can still do it," I said, hopefully.

"I doubt it. Everyone knows how much she adores that horse. After riding him for the last five years, I am sure she is devastated now," the closer woman said.

I turned back to watch the empty arena. One of the Swedish riders entered, and the music began. The performance was respectable, but the score was not high enough for an individual medal. Then a Finnish rider, British rider, Dutch rider, and then Michelle entered the arena. My heart raced. I couldn't see her face, which agonized me.

The music began. *She'll do it, she's so close, she has to take it,* I told myself, squeezing my hands until my knuckles turned white. In the middle of her performance, she turned the corner to begin one of her trademark moves on this horse—the piaffe, where the horse trots in place, showcasing the highest degree of collection in dressage. This was her strongest move, so I was confident she would nail it. It started out rhythmically and steady, but then, out of nowhere, Peron bolted sideways, and then backward! There was a unified gasp throughout the stands. Michelle was noticeably shaken; the rest of the performance was lackluster. I was devastated; I knew she was America's only chance at an individual medal and we had just lost it.

I rose, with the whole stadium, to give her a standing ovation.

The score was posted. I looked up—it was too low for an individual medal.

Nothing else mattered now. I watched the rest of the competition that afternoon, apathetic. The results were posted. I didn't have to look up to know what they would be. This Olympics was no different from previous ones—team gold went to Germany, team silver went to the Netherlands, team bronze went to the US. Individual gold went to Germany, silver and bronze went to the Netherlands.

I was disappointed for so many reasons. First, I knew I lived in a country full of talented riders who didn't have the opportunity, the chance to prove themselves, because they weren't paired with equally talented horses. I was jealous of German riders, because the sport's expenses weren't as high in Germany, where there were many more talented horses to choose from, many more experienced and knowledgeable trainers, and smaller distances to drive between shows. I had also learned that the German government provided some funding to dressage, unlike the US, where dressage is a little-known sport. There are very few sponsors for Americans, and without any financial support, even the most talented American equestrian can be forced to leave the sport they love and get a regular job, just because they can't afford to ride.

If Michelle had won a medal, despite all of the factors working against her and other American riders, she would have been catapulted to superstar status in the dressage world. I would always respect and admire her, and, in a way, I felt that because of all of the sacrifices she had made, she should have been given a medal. But medals were special because they weren't handed out to those who sacrificed the most to compete for them. Medals were special because they were earned.

When I was back home, I was eager to share my experience with Carol.

"Carol, you know what I heard?" I couldn't resist sharing my inside knowledge of Michelle's performance at the Olympics.

"What?"

"I heard that Peron's owners told Michelle *the day before* the freestyle that this Olympics would be the last time she would ever ride that horse," I started.

"Yeah, I heard that, too," she interrupted.

"How?" I was stunned.

"Gunilla was there, and she called and let us know as soon as she found out," Carol answered.

"Why?" I asked.

"I don't know, maybe so we wouldn't get our hopes up about an individual medal," she concluded.

"This sport is impossible," I said. "If you *are* lucky enough to get a sponsor to pay for a horse that you can compete with, there's always the risk that they can take it away from you whenever they want. But then if you *own* your own horse, you'd have to get a regular nine to five job to be able to pay for it, and then you wouldn't be able to ride as much because you're at work all day, trying to pay for it. I don't know how anybody makes it in this sport," I concluded.

"I guess some people just get lucky," Carol replied.

"So the people competing for the highest honors in the sport aren't necessarily the best dressage riders, just some riders who caught a lucky break? That's not fair," I said.

"Well, we don't have enough time to think about what's fair and not fair. That's just the way it is. Pick up a rising trot around me." And that was that.

It was sad. If she had a decent horse, Carol would have been competing in the Olympics. I wondered how many more Americans like her were out there. Able, but unable to compete at the highest level.

33

The end of summer was fast approaching, and this year's show season proved just as mediocre as last year's, although Moonshine and I did advance one level. Carol insisted that her students first have fun with their horses, and then let that show in the competition arena. She must have sensed my and a few others' disappointment at again not qualifying for the Regional Championships, because she organized a group trail ride, including all of her thirty students (she was the busiest trainer at the farm, even busier than Gunilla). We would load our horses into all of the farm's trailers and those boarders who had their own trucks and trailers would bring them as well. Moonshine now walked into any trailer, following in step right behind me. I think he liked to travel and see new places; or maybe he craved all of the extra attention he got when we went away. After all, at shows I would spend the entire day with him since we usually stayed at a hotel nearby. When we weren't showing, I only saw him for a few hours, three days a week. I'm sure he realized that any time he got into a trailer, it meant we would spend all day together, with some competing thrown in.

It was ideal for both of us.

Our trail riding destination was only a quick, half-hour drive away. As soon as we got there, I jumped out of Jean's car, since she had offered to drive me, to be one of the first to get my horse out of the big, six horse trailer.

I led Moony out of the trailer, and easily slipped on his bridle after all the horses had been unloaded. He was calm and confident, unlike many of the other horses, who were animated by the new surroundings. Moonshine was the only horse that kept his head low, so that I could make the usual adjustments to his bridle. He was totally unimpressed and unaffected by the other horses' whinnies, and anxious hopping around. It was only when I positioned myself to get on, that I learned he was just containing himself—just as I slipped my foot into the stirrup, he trotted off with me hanging off his side! I grabbed his mane with my left hand, pulled my body up, and threw my right leg over his back. I yanked him to a stop with the reins. Nora was in front and had witnessed my graceless mounting spectacle.

"I guess Moony's ready to go!" she hollered.

"As always, with or without me!" I laughed back, now that I was adjusted in the saddle. I could only imagine how hilarious I looked trying to climb onto Moonshine's back as he happily trotted off.

Moonshine loved to be the leader of any group, and hated when a horse walked shoulder-to-shoulder with him or passed him. He especially hated when a bigger horse was anywhere near him. If any such larger horse ever dared to approach Moonshine, he would pin his ears back, bare his teeth, and dive into an attack. I was usually quick enough to pull the reins in the other direction, so he hardly ever got to actually bite his would-be victim.

On this particular day, however, he was surrounded by warmbloods, all of which had strides twice as long as his own. He couldn't keep up with them. We eventually fell to the back of the long line of horses. To my surprise, Moony wasn't rushing to stay with the herd, he seemed to enjoy being alone with me at the end of the line. I trusted him so much, that I let him have the rein, riding with loops, and dropped my feet out of the stirrups.

Carol turned to see where we were and when she saw that Moony and I were at the end of the line and not rushing to stay close to the pack like everyone else, she called, "Are you guys relaxed enough back there? Do you want a piña colada or something, Victoria?"

"I'm good for now, maybe later though!" I called back to her.

It was getting hot and we were approaching a clearing, which was the small beach of a lake. When all of the horses saw that the land in front of them disappeared into water, they spooked. As the line of horses came up to the water, each shied away from it and ran back to the trail. But when Moonshine saw the water, his ears perked up and he charged through the crowd of horses. He shoved his way through, and ran right into the water. Instantly, my horse was submerged in water up to his shoulders, and my boots and saddle were in the lake with him. But that wasn't good enough. Moony insisted on swimming to the middle of the lake! When he got shoulder deep, I pulled him back, and then he started pawing and turning, like he always did, before he was about to roll. Then, everyone started screaming, "Get out! Get out! He's going to roll!"

Carol kicked her horse as hard as she could to come in and help me, but her horse reared up and ran backwards.

"Victoria, he's going to ROLL! GET OUT OF THE WATER!" she yelled.

"I'm TRYING!" I was caught somewhere between amusement and genuine concern. I was worried because everyone else was visibly agitated. But seeing how determined Moony was to roll in water just struck me as hilarious. I kind of wanted to let him roll since he was so determined and I figured it would make him happy. But I had once read in one of my horse magazines that if horses go under water, they can't hold their breath like humans, since their nostrils are so huge, and they might drown. So, I reconsidered letting Moony have his way. Plus, everyone was screaming at us to get out of the water.

But Moony was just as stubborn today as he was on every other day. The harder I pulled on the reins to direct him back to the beach, the further into the lake he went! So now the water was above my knees, and quickly going up my thighs. Moony was gleefully in shoulder-deep, and heading for deeper water. I was kicking him as hard as I could, and pulling his head one way or another, any direction but straight ahead. Finally, when I saw the water rise to my thigh level, a wave of strength took over my limbs. My right arm whipped his head to the right, and just as I got his head turned, my legs kicked with such force that I created a wave under the water. Moonshine was infuriated that I thwarted his plans to go deep sea diving, so he angrily about-faced and charged the beach—where everyone else was standing! He slashed through the herd of horses, and tore back on the trail. I sat back and pulled the reins with my whole body, and he stopped short. Then, he shook off like a dog.

"Good thing you don't have expensive tack!" Carol joked as she trotted her horse up to Moonshine.

"He's so mad right now!" I laughed to Carol, pointing at his ears, flat on his head, and the menacing head-tossing and gnashing teeth he was threatening Carol's horse with.

Moonshine's antics on that trail ride were the talk of the farm for a while after that.

34

I wanted to spend every waking minute at the barn. But when I started my Junior year, I knew that was the year I needed to excel in school; it would be the year that would set up my whole life. I had to get a good SAT score and GPA so that I could get into a good college. Ignoring boys was easy; ignoring Moonshine was not. I decided that when I wasn't at the farm, I would not be there mentally, either. When I barricaded myself in my room to study, I would *study*—no more staring out the window, daydreaming about making it big with Moonshine. I soon realized that controlling my mind was one of the hardest things I had ever done. How do I not think about what I wanted most?

The morning of the SAT soon came. I couldn't remember ever being so anxious. I had found a good seat in the classroom, close enough to the door but not too close. Once seated, I couldn't stop tapping my pencil and wagging my crossed leg. I had never been so jumpy, not even at my biggest horse show. I had been judged by famous and respected judges, I had ridden in front of an Olympic trainer, and I wasn't nearly as nervous then as I was that day. *What's the big deal?* I reasoned with myself, *it's just a test, like everyone keeps saying. No, actually it's not. This test will shape the rest of my life. This test will either let me go to a good school and get a good job so I can have horses when I'm older, or not. Stop that!* I scolded myself, *Are you trying to freak out before the SATs and totally ruin your life?* I had to get up and walk around, work off some of the energy that was building. I was in my seat too early anyway, I had a half hour.

The exam was being held in the school's library, at the school's top level. I just went down the stairs to the school's rotunda, and walked a small circle. I went up and down the stairs a few times. It felt good to move a little bit, I felt like I was at the start line of a major race, I had enough energy to run a marathon. I stretched all of my limbs, and took a few deep breaths.

OK, now I'm ready, I studied. I'm ready. I avoided eye contact with everyone. I didn't want to talk to anyone. I stared straight ahead as I ascended the steps. Then, I spotted my chair in the library and walked directly to it. I sat down, picked up my pencil, and put my left hand to my forehead as a shield against anyone's gaze. I was not about to talk to anyone now that I had mentally prepared myself for the test.

The exam passed quickly once it began. It was challenging, but fair. My mother was waiting in the car outside, to take me to the farm.

"How was it?" she asked once I was in the car.

"I don't want to jinx it, but not bad," I said, prompting her to smile. I knew she wanted to know more, but I had recently come up with a rule that I wouldn't discuss major tests until I had the score back, because I was afraid I would jinx it. Living with my mother had finally made me superstitious, like she was. At least she would think I was just superstitious and wasn't failing.

"Do you want to drive?" she asked.

"Not today," I replied, not because I didn't want to drive.

I always wanted to drive. I just didn't want to deal with her gasping and flinching in the passenger seat all the way to the farm.

Everyone at the farm wanted to talk about my SAT, except me. I kept my responses short, but polite. This was the only slightly annoying thing about knowing so many people who knew so much about me—they wanted to talk about *everything* going on in my life. I just wanted to be left alone.

Carol was the only one who would just ask once and never pried into any part of my life. I loved her for that. She was the only person who seemed to understand me entirely. I returned the favor—unlike a lot of her other students, I never asked her about her marriage, her horse, her hopes and dreams. If she wanted to volunteer some information about her life, that was different. Our world together never changed. It was always all about horses.

35

Moonshine and I were progressing; we had advanced to Third Level, which meant he was performing more advanced movements. We were learning more tricks, but we still "fought" occasionally. I would erupt in frustration if a movement was not perfect by the third attempt. Then, I would lose my temper and smack Moonshine on his hind end with the whip to wake him up. But Moonshine wouldn't be reprimanded like any other horse—he always retaliated with a buck. If I then responded with another quick tap, he would throw in another, more dramatic buck. Luckily, Carol was usually around to supervise, even if I wasn't riding in a lesson with her. For years, she had been telling me that I could not ride Moonshine as if he were any other horse, but I ignored her advice, until one random day, it finally clicked.

It's amazing how the days that end up being the most significant are not always the special days I would imagine, not a big competition, or major life event. It was just a regular day, just another Saturday lesson I was having at the farm. Moonshine was in no mood to truly come round and work correctly, despite my best attempts using my seat and leg. So then, to wake him up and engage his haunches, I tapped him on his flank with the whip. I was instantly catapulted onto the pommel of the saddle, which pissed me off, so I tapped him again, and was again launched onto the top of the saddle. I tried hard to keep my cool and just keep riding, but I was getting more and more frustrated. I was hoping Carol would tell me to hop off, so she could fix him, as she had done on so many prior occasions. She simply continued to instruct me, though.

"Carol, it's not working, can't you hop on him and just fix him?" I pleaded, now exhausted from fighting with Moonshine.

"No, Moonshine won't go for me or anyone else, the way he goes for you. He is *your* horse in every sense now," she replied.

"But I don't know how to fix this!" I replied.

"You're too caught up in getting the immediate result, you have to dig deeper than just getting the movement. Dressage isn't about just executing the movements. The movements are there to show the harmony between horse and rider."

"I can't have harmony with this horse, he bucks all the time," I replied.

"He only bucks when you instigate. Remember, he was abused, so he's not like one of these other dressage horses that will tolerate being touched with the whip. It's something that already happened to him that he'll never forget, and you can't change that."

"So, what are you saying? This is pointless?" I asked.

"Absolutely not. I'm saying you have to be smarter than your horse. Since you know he'll buck when you touch him with the whip, forget the whip," she said as she pulled it out of my grip.

"How can I ride without a whip? Everyone rides with a whip!"

"Yeah, but no one else rides Moonshine. He is a different kind of horse, so you have to be a different kind of rider."

I was growing impatient with her theorizing. I wanted her to just get to the point, already.

"Carol, I have no idea what you're talking about," I confessed.

"You have to *persuade* him—*ask* him, don't tell him."

"*Ask* him?" I questioned.

"Yes, ask, don't demand," she insisted. "That is the key to riding Moonshine. You have to make him think everything is *his* idea. If you can play these mind games with him, you'll be amazed at what he can do and how well he can do it."

Not like I don't know anything about mind games, I thought, as I remembered how many times I tried to manipulate my father by fueling his massive ego. I never thought my mind game practice would bleed into dressage, but here it was. Dressage was turning out to be more about mental gymnastics than physical work. I had to break into the mind of an animal, figure out how to communicate with it, and persuade it to dance.

"So, I still don't understand. 'Ask him, don't tell him' sounds like a nice theory, but how does it come into play? What does it mean? Can you give me an example of how I can ask him instead of telling him to do something?" I asked.

"Sure. Just now was a perfect example. We were just schooling tempi changes, right?"

Tempi changes are an upper level movement where the horse canters usually on a straight line across a diagonal line of the arena. He starts the line cantering with one leg leading. For example, if his left front leg leads, it means he is on the left lead canter. In a flying change, the rider recognizes the moment of suspension, when all of the horse's legs are off the ground, and in that moment, asks him to switch to the other lead. So, in essence, he is switching his leading leg in the air, which is why the movement is called a flying lead change. Tempi changes are a sequence of the flying lead changes.

The easiest sequence is introduced in Fourth Level, where

the horse performs three of these flying changes on every fourth stride. The movement gets more difficult as the levels advance. The next level up from Fourth Level is the first of the international levels—Prix St. Georges, Intermediare I, Intermediare II, and finally Grand Prix, the highest level in dressage. Each level has more demanding sequences of flying changes. I knew most of the more advanced dressage tests because I really wanted to ride Grand Prix and I had memorized the required movements in each level. There were more tricks in the upper levels but I found the flying changes most challenging.

Third Level has no flying change sequences; all that was required in Third Level was to do one single change. But I had competed at Third Level, and, according to Carol's philosophy, I had to be training in the movements a level above the one in which I was competing; since Fourth Level introduced the challenge of tempi flying changes, we had to know how to perform tempi changes well before we would compete at Fourth Level. I was excited to be schooling the movements in Fourth Level because I knew Fourth Level was very similar to Prix St. Georges. Carol had the challenge of teaching two inexperienced students—Moonshine and myself—an advanced movement, simultaneously. She was a truly gifted teacher because even though I had no prior experience with tempi changes, I didn't know how to ask my horse to perform them, or how they should feel when executed, she was so clear in her explanations and answers that she was able to overcome my inexperience with her training.

"We need to hammer down these tempi changes if you're going to compete at Fourth Level next show season," she advised.

It was November. I only had five months.

"Do you really think he could learn this by next spring?" I asked Carol, skeptical.

"You would be surprised what this horse could do once you

have him figured out. But it's your job to tap into his brain and persuade him to do what you want. Remember that you and Moony are in this together."

That made sense. I had never really thought about Moony's perspective. I assumed that since I was in charge, my perspective was the only one that mattered. But Moonshine wasn't the kind of horse that would allow me to be in charge. He forced me to be his partner instead of his leader. How could I forget that? I knew he hated to follow, so why had I tried so hard to force him to follow my lead? I had been so thoughtless.

"Be smart when you ride now. When he's good, be obvious about letting him know. He is an egomaniac, so praise will get you really far with him. If he knows what you want, and how happy it makes you, he would do it so easily. He loves praise, you know that," she continued.

"But what if he's bad, then what do I do?" I asked.

"If he's bad, first, don't get emotional about it. Everyone learns best by the mistakes they make. Let him make the mistake, then correct it. Don't try so hard to prevent it. If you never let it happen in training, he'll never know what *not* to do, but if you *do* let it happen in training, and show him not to do it, then he probably won't do it again. Think about what caused the mistake, rather than the mistake itself. Usually, an error in a movement is the result of something deeper, so you will have to be sort of like a technician or engineer and dig for the core of that problem," she instructed.

"What does that mean?" I asked.

"Here's a perfect example—the flying lead changes. He can just barely do them, and they look chaotic. It's messy and out of control because you aren't setting him up to do the flying change perfectly, you're sort of just throwing him into it. Every movement in this sport is about *preparation. Think* about it before you do it. Think about how you have to ask. Think about whether he is all set up and ready to do it. You have to think now. The higher up the levels you go, the more mental the game becomes. Eventually, you'll be able to ride him with just your mind."

"Cool," I said.

"Yeah, it's really cool—that's pretty much the essence of dressage," she corrected.

"OK, so how do I fix the flying changes then?"

"For starters, you have to be able to canter a straight line, keeping him round, collected, and controlling the rhythm with your seat. Exaggerate your aids for the lead you are on, so if you are tracking left, coming onto a diagonal to change direction, really sit down on your left seat bone, and keep your left leg on snug, right at the girth, and your right leg one hand's distance behind the girth. Hold your right rein to keep him balanced, and keep your left rein soft, so he can bend to the left. But he can't change his entire balance to the right with a flying change if he is totally bent to the left, so just before the flying change, you have to prepare for it—make him really straight, but make sure he can stay round at the same time. Test him for a few strides, make sure he can canter super straight. When you feel like you have him there, just switch your cues, imagine your legs are like scissors and just switch their positioning. So, when he is in the air, bring your left leg back, right leg forward, and shift your weight from your left to your right seat bone, and drop your right shoulder.

"The trick in this moment of suspension is in the landing, when he lands on the new lead, you have to keep him from taking off. This is where you've been having problems controlling him. Try first to sit down deep in the saddle, with a really strong seat to control the rhythm. Just because he changes his lead doesn't mean the rhythm of the canter has to change. But if that doesn't work, then make a more obvious correction, like a small circle going in the new direction. If you pull him into a small circle, he can't build up speed because you're breaking his momentum. Eventually he'll figure out that flying changes aren't about getting excited and taking off, they just mean a switch in the leading leg. Once you guys have those down, we'll start playing with adding more on a line, like maybe one change, then another after five strides, then another after six strides. Whenever he feels ready, ask for more. But always ride smart, you have to ride like a trainer now."

Ride smart, I thought. *OK, so basically, I have to turn off my emotions when I ride. How is that possible? How can I not get mad when he doesn't want to do a movement he's done a hundred times before?* I wondered. I would definitely try, though.

That winter, I worked on controlling myself. I was desperate for Moonshine to be famous and for the whole world to know what a special horse he was, so I would do anything to get him there. I don't know why I cared so much what people thought all of a sudden. I usually didn't care what others thought, but when it came to Moonshine, I did. I needed for everyone to recognize that even though he wasn't as talented or graceful as the warmbloods we competed against, he was just as special, and even more special because not only did we dare to compete with horses that were superior, but we sometimes even gave them a run for their money.

I would no longer be controlled by my emotions; I would now be the one in control. Learning how to be in command of my reactions was the biggest challenge I had met thus far in my dressage training. I tried to be more practical, more pragmatic in my training. It was difficult, and I slipped many times in the beginning. But the difference that this new mindset made in training was significant and notable. Whenever we made a mistake, I would correct it, instead of punishing my partner for having let it happen. I realized that he was always reacting to a cue I had given him. Carol was right, all the mistakes really *were* my fault.

If I expected him to be perfect, then I had to be perfect myself—expecting anything else from my horse would have been unfair. After all, from his point of view, why should he do anything for me? He let me sit on his back and make him work and let me put him in trailers and take him to shows not because he shared my ambitions or aspirations. He didn't know the difference between an important show and a training ride, or who was judging a particular class. He simply did everything I wanted because I wanted him to do it—out of the goodness of his heart. When I thought about training from Moonshine's perspective, he hadn't been bad or intentionally malicious. He just didn't know why I wanted him to do the things I wanted, and he would never know why. So, if I wanted him to perform at his maximum capability, I would have to be at my absolute best.

My horse was not a push-button horse; he wouldn't go around an arena doing movements like a robot. I sat on a few horses that were so perfectly programmed. Even though they were easy to ride, I didn't like them—they were boring and uninteresting. I thought I would love sitting on a trained horse, but I preferred my horse, the most difficult horse on the property. I both loved and hated that Moony forced me to be perfect every time I rode. He never let a mistake of mine slip, like other horses did. If I was half a second too slow with my cue for a flying change, Moony would either execute it piss poorly, or not at all. Other horses might have realized what I actually meant for them to do and done what I thought. They would have assumed what I wanted and done it. But maybe the fact that Moonshine only did exactly what I asked him actually made him the best trained horse; maybe that made him the most obedient. And maybe this is what Carol meant when she said that if I could ride this horse, I would be able to ride any horse. No other horse would teach me to be a perfect rider.

Moonshine very much appreciated my new style of riding. I no longer rode with a whip. I no longer rode emotionally. When we were faced with a problem, I stopped to think about it. I was going against my natural instinct to erupt in anger and frustration, and instead analyze the situation before I did anything else, as Carol taught me to do. I would try the movement two more times, and if it still had not improved, I would go back to the basics to figure out where the deeper issue lay buried, just like she said. I was beginning to learn that dressage was not testing the rider's and horse's ability to execute the movements, but rather, that the movements were there to demonstrate how well horse and rider communicated. It really was a dance—we had to perform as one. Maintaining such a high degree of control over my mind and thoughts was the greatest, and also most rewarding, challenge that I had ever faced.

As soon as I changed my mindset, Moonshine and I flew through the levels. Most horses struggled for at least a year to learn how to perform pirouettes at the canter. Moonshine learned pirouettes in two months. Most horses took years to learn how to perform piaffe and passage, the most advanced movements in dressage, Moonshine learned piaffe and passage in two months. It took most horses about four to five years, minimum, to learn all of the most advanced dressage movements. Moonshine learned them *all* that winter.

"Look at you! Pirouettes and piaffe and passage!" Jean exclaimed as she caught the end of one of my workouts that winter.

"Yeah, he's a good boy," I said as I patted his neck.

"He's a superstar!" she emphasized.

When Moonshine and I reached the more advanced levels and began schooling the most difficult movements in dressage, others began to notice us. Our Saturday lessons would draw a small audience. I was perplexed and also flattered that someone else thought they could learn from us. I also noticed that Gunilla was watching.

"Gunilla is bringing over a few horses from Europe, I think

you should sit on some and give them a try," Carol suddenly suggested.

"Why?" I asked. I now had everything I had ever wanted—a horse that knew me inside and out, that did not take advantage of me, and that truly loved me. I had also come to love him more than I had ever thought possible. I couldn't imagine my life without Moonshine. It wasn't just that he was now my horse, my partner, my loyal companion; he had become my life, my reason for being. I wanted to make him as happy as he made me. This bond that we had formed convinced me that he was the only horse in the world for me.

"Moonshine can only go so far. You can't go as far as you want to go with him. He *is* limited, he's not a dressage horse, he's just an Appendix," she tried to reason.

"But he already has come so far, Carol. We're schooling almost all of the Grand Prix moves," I reasoned.

"Yes, but he's not an Olympic-level horse. Just because he can do the movements doesn't mean he's Olympic material. It's not just being able to do the movements, it's the quality of the movements and the horse. You need a horse that can match your talent."

"I don't think it's just about talent, Carol. I think anyone can make it if they really want, even if it's a horse. You know how Moony loves the spotlight, how he puffs up if he knows he's got a big audience. He's a show horse," I countered.

"You're not listening. I didn't say he's not a good show horse, I never said he's not a good horse. I said he's just not a talented horse, are you going to argue with that?"

"No, I just think there's more to it than that," I argued back.

"OK, how about this—how many Appendix horses did you see at the Olympics in Atlanta?"

"None," I answered, deflated. I knew had lost.

"Right. Let's just see what you look like on a warmblood—no strings, no commitments. I'm not telling you to give Moony up. I'm just curious to see how you sit on a warmblood, so just humor me, alright?"

"Fine," I had to agree.

Gunilla brought back so many horses from Europe that Richard built her a whole new barn. She now had two barns full of her exclusive European imports.

"Hi, Kiddo!" Gunilla greeted me one Saturday. "Listen, I spoke to Carol, and you're going to ride one of my horses after your lesson on Mr. Moonshine." I was irritated by the way she referred to my horse, like he was a cute little pony, not a serious dressage contender. I was tempted to correct her, but was sure I would simply end up in an argument trying to defend Moonshine—probably a bad idea, being that she was the farm's owner.

"OK, which one?" I asked.

"Don't worry which one, Tracy, my groom will get him ready for you and bring him to you in the indoor, right after your lesson."

"But what about—" I wanted to know what would happen to Moonshine while I was forced to get on this new horse. But she knew before I asked.

"Don't worry about Moonshine, she will take him and take excellent care of him, cool him off, untack him, hose him. He'll be fine without you."

I did not agree with her last statement, but understood its context, or at least I thought I understood.

After my lesson, Gunilla appeared in the indoor from the office, and Tracy appeared with the new horse. Carol told me she would give me a mini-lesson on the new horse. I hopped out of the saddle and rolled up my stirrups. Moonshine turned his head, not understanding this break in our usual routine—I always walked him for about ten or fifteen minutes to cool him out. He knew I was betraying him.

Tracy brought the new horse to me just then.

"Can you walk Moonshine for about ten or fifteen minutes? He's still pretty hot and needs to cool down," I said to

Tracy as she appeared.

"Sure," she said casually. "This is Angelo," gesturing to the new horse.

"Thanks," I said as I took his reins and placed Moonshine's reins in her hands. I turned my back to Moonshine, to try to avoid the questioning look in his eyes. I also knew that he watched me walk away with a new horse and I would have to deal with a jealous, angry horse later.

"Just take your time in getting to know him," Gunilla called from the center of the arena, where she stood beside Carol. "He is trained to Fourth Level, and you could probably qualify to do Young Riders with him!" she enthused.

I knew Young Riders was a prestigious competition where riders ages 17 to 21 had to qualify at a test that was the equivalent of Fourth Level. The qualification criteria were competitive, and only twenty young riders in the country were invited to compete. Beth had gone twice.

"*Moonshine* is schooling Fourth Level," I started.

Gunilla scoffed loudly.

"Ha! Kiddo, there is no way you can do Young Riders with *that* horse! You need a *real* horse if you want to go to the real shows."

Now I was furious. Again she tried to rob me of any hope of achieving greatness with Moonshine, again she was completely ignorant of the incredible progress we had made, not just in the last two years, but also particularly in the last few months. The self-control I had learned to maintain on Moonshine had vanished. I almost felt sorry for this new horse; he was innocent, and did not deserve me and my wrath. But I was overcome with anger now, and incapable of rational thinking. I rode by instinct. I gave the horse forceful cues, and he was accepting. He did not object or even have an opinion. He was submissive and obeyed. It was like sitting on a robot.

"Wow," I heard from the center of the arena, as well as from the sides, where various spectators had gathered. I imagined it was quite eventful to see anyone other than Gunilla riding her horses, especially when she watched from the ground. As more and more people crowded around the sides of the arena, I realized that besides Tracy, no one else had ever been seen riding one of Gunilla's horses, not Carol or Beth, or any of the other best riders from the farm.

The more people gathered, the angrier I became that they only came to watch Gunilla's fancy horse. They didn't all come to watch Moony; only a handful of people were impressed with Moony's progress.

This is so unfair, I thought. *Just because this horse was born into the right label, he's automatically 'better' than Moony. He'll never have to work as hard as Moony, and probably never will, and he'll still always win if he competes against Moonshine.*

Sitting on one of Gunilla's horses, a 'fancy' horse, should have been a thrill for a young dressage addict, but it only broke my heart all over again. It reminded me of what people wanted to see—everyone wanted to see the talented horses, and no one had any interest in Moonshine, except me. I still believed Moonshine would be great. He had advanced too quickly, he performed his tests too solidly, and he was too well trained. There was still something I wasn't doing to show everyone how extraordinary he was.

"OK, good job, Victoria, come to the middle for a chat," Carol waved me in.

"So, what do you think?" Gunilla asked, through the widest grin I had ever seen on her face.

"He's nice," I said. The horse was indeed a good horse, obedient and polite.

"Nice enough to buy?" Gunilla asked.

"*Buy*?" I almost choked on the word. "I can't buy another horse, no way . . ." I began, but Gunilla interrupted me.

"Isn't your father a lawyer?" she asked.

"Ha!" Now it was my turn to scoff. "He'll never pay a dime for any horse," I concluded.

"Not even for a horse like *this*?" she asked.

"Not for *any* horse," I repeated.

"Doesn't he know you want to go to the Olympics?" she asked.

"Sure, he knows. He just doesn't care," I said plainly.

"Can't be!" she exclaimed.

"Can be," I corrected. Carol nodded in agreement.

"Bring him to the farm, I will talk to him," Gunilla decided.

"I don't really think that's going to do anything," I warned.

"You never know until you try," she said.

"Oh, trust me, I've tried!" I almost laughed.

"Well, *I* haven't tried," she ended.

"OK," I said, my voice rising to warn her of the futility of her new project.

After she turned to head back to the exit, Carol and I exchanged a look of disbelief and anticipation of what we were sure would be a memorable show. Carol and I no longer needed words to communicate—a look was enough.

I called my father every week, asking him to be my designated driver out to the farm. I had my learner's permit, so I could drive, but I needed a licensed driver to supervise.

"Victoria, are you nuts? It's winter! It's too cold! Who rides horses in the winter?" I heard from the other end of the phone.

"You know there's an indoor," I grumbled back.

"Don't be ridiculous!" he exclaimed as he slammed down the phone. Having telephone conversations with him was increasingly irritating because he had a habit of hanging up on me. He was the only person I knew who was fine with not concluding a phone conversation with any kind of "goodbye," "talk to you later," or "I love you." Apparently, I was done talking when he was done listening.

The following weekend I arrived at the farm with my mother, as usual.

Gunilla found me in Moonshine's stall.

"Where is your father?" she asked, seemingly surprised I had not obeyed a direct order.

"Hibernating," I replied.

"What?" she asked.

"It's too cold for him," I explained.

"Are you kidding me?" I could detect the anger and frustration in her voice.

"Nope, sorry," I replied, somewhat relieved that someone else was experiencing firsthand what a deadbeat father I had.

"Well, we'll make the best of it. You can try out all the horses I brought over from Europe, then by the time spring comes, you will know which one you want, and I can have that discussion with your father," she decided, out loud.

I already had the horse I wanted, but it would still be entertaining to watch Gunilla try to persuade the cheapest man on Earth to indulge his teenage daughter in what he considered a stupid hobby, so I simply agreed with her.

"Alright," I said with a smile.

"Unbelievable," I heard her mutter as she walked away.

For the first time, I was somewhat grateful for my father not believing in me, it had at least bought me a few more months of Gunilla being forced to acknowledge Moony as my horse, and stop trying to get me to buy another one.

36

My birthday was in March. I had never been so excited for a birthday. I had taken a driver's education course after school so that I could get my license when I turned seventeen. My mother was actually looking forward to it as well so that I could drive myself out to the farm, and she could work more. She had observed my driving for the last year as my designated passenger and I had earned her respect with the way I handled myself in heavy traffic, around other drivers' interesting navigational choices, and in bad weather. I was more comfortable driving than she was, so I drove almost every chance I got since turning sixteen. I was genuinely surprised that she was so calm about such a monumental event in my life; after all, she seemed to get excited over virtually everything. It didn't matter. I knew what driving meant—freedom. I would be free to go anywhere at any time, or at least whenever she didn't need the car. Since my mother was the only licensed driver in our household, we only had one car. My grandfather, sister, and I had been totally dependent on her to take us where we needed to go. But that would now change.

"Honey, we need to talk," she told me a month before my seventeenth birthday, fast approaching in March.

"I know you are excited about driving by yourself, and being able to get to the farm without asking anyone to sit in the car with you, but I will still need the car sometimes."

"OK, so what are you saying, Mom?" I asked impatiently. I wanted to know what she was getting at.

"Can you please try to talk to your father about helping you get your own car so you can be totally independent? It would be so helpful," she asked delicately.

"Of course!" I exclaimed, jumping up to hug her. Nothing would have thrilled me more than to be completely independent.

"Are you sure you're up for it?" she said, apparently remembering the last time I had asked my father for a large sum of money, when I asked him to help in the purchase of Moonshine.

"Yeah!" I let out gleefully. Nothing would stand in the way of my pursuit of total independence. I was willing to do anything. My father hung up on me on a regular basis now, so that no longer bothered me. Petitioning him for money was now almost a hobby, so I was immune to his perpetual rejections. I would just pester him until he couldn't take it. I had nothing to lose.

I thought I would have fun on my first try, so I called him that night.

"Da," he answered in Romanian.

"Dad, I need a car," I said.

"No." Click.

I laughed.

My mother was in the same room and had correctly guessed the outcome.

"He said no?" she asked.

"Of course, don't you know what a cheapskate you married?" I teased. I could not stop grinning.

Just as she was beginning a rant, I stopped her to say, "Mom, relax, you didn't really think he was going to say yes on my first try, did you?"

"That's what a normal father would do!"

"Well, we already know he's special," I joked. Then I said, "Seriously, Mom, don't worry, I have this soliciting him for money act down to a science. I just bring it up, he rejects me, and then I keep pestering and badgering him until he's almost out of his mind and starts talking about how he wants to kill himself. Then I tell him not to do that because he would be depriving the world of one of the greatest legal minds in the world."

She scoffed in disbelief.

"Mom, it might work. He really believes he is the smartest lawyer alive. All I need to do is feed that already massive ego and tell him that if he bought me this car, I would never bother him again because he would never need to sit in the car with me ever again. I would just drive myself out to the farm all the time if I had my own car. Don't you think he would love that idea? For just a small chunk of change, he would never have to see or hear from me again. He would totally jump at the idea!" I declared.

"Well unfortunately, you might be right. Where did you learn how to do all this scheming and manipulating anyway?" she asked.

"From the greatest legal mind in the world!" I exclaimed.

She laughed.

I pestered my father for a new car relentlessly. I called him every day, both at home and at work. In the spring, he finally agreed to drive out to the farm with me, I jumped at my chance to nag for the whole hour that I had him trapped in the car. It was one of the few times I actually appreciated living so far away from the farm.

"Dad, I need a car," I began.

"No."

"Dad, come on, I *have* to be able to get out here," I whined.

"Drive your mother's car," he answered.

"Mom won't always be able to give up her car for the entire weekend. You know she works weekends too," I explained.

"Victoria, I am not buying you a new car!" he huffed.

"Who said anything about new? I don't care if it's new or old, I just want something on four wheels to get me out to the farm," I stated.

"Well, you still want too much. You want a horse, a car, it's just too much!" he exclaimed.

"Dad, I don't want a car just to have a car. I want a car so I can drive myself out to the farm and not have to depend on anybody. Wouldn't you like it if I stopped calling you to waste your entire Saturday just to drive out to the farm with me?"

"Yes! I would love that!" he declared.

"So then get me a car!" I persisted.

"Ugh, Victoria, you are exhausting," he sighed.

I worked on him tirelessly. I continuously dropped hints that a car for me would make his life easier, and I would stop asking him for things. I told him that most of my classmates' parents had gotten them brand new cars. He also knew of my infatuation with Beth, and I made him well aware of the fact that her parents bought her a brand new car for her seventeenth birthday.

When Gunilla saw him at the farm, she pounced. She broke from the conversation she was having with another boarder and approached my father. She greeted me dismissively, "Hi, Victoria," she said as she brushed past me and went straight to my father.

"Hello, there," she began, as she took him by the elbow and led him out of the barn. I watched from Moony's window as she walked him up the steps into the office.

Well, here it goes I guess. I knew she was as determined to get my father to buy me a new horse as I was for him to buy me a new car. Having her nag him for a new horse only worked in my favor, though, because he would soon grow tired of being solicited for money and would do anything not to come to the farm anymore—maybe even buy me a car.

After my ride, I walked back to his car, where he waited, reading the newspaper.

"Finally," he said when I got in, as he always did after he had waited for me to finish up with Moonshine.

"So, did you have a nice chat with Gunilla?" I asked innocently.

"All you women ever want from me is money, money, money!" he exploded.

I kept my cool.

"I can't take it anymore!" he let out.

"Well, if I had a car and you didn't have to drive out to the farm with me, no one would ask you for money," I said confidently.

"OK! Alright! I will get you a damn car already! I can't stand this torture anymore!"

"Oh, thanks, Dad!" I leaned over to hug him, overdramatizing, but sure he wouldn't notice. "You're the best!" I exclaimed.

"Yeah, when I give you money, I'm the best," he replied.

I ignored him, and simply reveled in the fact that my scheme had worked.

A month had gone by when I was home one Saturday morning, getting ready to go to the farm, and all of a sudden I heard an unfamiliar car horn being blown relentlessly. I followed the noise to the driveway. I saw my father sitting in a white Jeep Cherokee sport. I burst from the house and ran to the car.

"Say hello to your new car!" he beamed, as he got out.

"Oh my God, Dad! This is amazing!" I said as I jumped into the driver's seat.

My mother then came out of the house after me, and asked, "What's all this? What is going on?"

"I bought the child a car," my father said, proudly.

"Dad, thank you so much, thank you!" I gushed from inside the car.

"Where did you get it?" my mother asked my father, skeptically.

"New Jersey," my father answered evasively.

"Where? Is it new or used?" she asked, suspiciously.

"The child does not need a brand new car," he said matter-of-factly.

"Did it pass inspection?" she asked, suspecting that he purchased it for very little money at one of the car auctions he frequented in New Jersey.

"I just bought it today and drove it here, so you handle those things. But I bought the car for her, not for you, so you better not drive it," he warned.

"I am not putting my daughter in a death trap. It has to be safe for driving!" my mother said.

"Well, I just drove it myself, so it's safe enough," he said.

Just then my sister bounded toward the white car in the driveway.

"Oh my God, Vicky got a new car?" she exclaimed.

"Yes, *I* bought it for her," my father informed. "Let's all go out for a spin!"

Before my mother could object, everyone was in the car. She finally gave in and got in the back seat with my sister. My father was in the passenger seat, as he couldn't fit in the small back seat.

I backed it out of the driveway, but when I went to turn, the front wheels didn't follow the direction of the steering wheel. I kept quiet, knowing that if my mother detected any problems with the car, she would end the ride and take the car away. I managed to wrangle the wheel and not hit any parked cars.

"Is everything OK, Victoria?" my mother asked, noticing my spastic driving.

"Yeah, Mom, I'm just not used to driving a Jeep and being so high up. Don't worry," I tried to assure her.

"OK, turn here and let's go down Union Boulevard," my father directed.

"OK," I said, still trying to adjust to the loose steering wheel.

I turned down Union Boulevard, where traffic usually traveled at about forty-five mph. The north and south sides of the highway were separated by a concrete divider. My father directed me to the left lane, where traffic was fastest. Just as I entered the left lane and was about to straighten the wheel, I heard a clicking noise come from the steering wheel, and then felt something pop. I turned the wheel slightly to the right to continue traveling straight in the left lane, but the car still drifted to the left. I noticed we were quickly approaching the concrete divider.

"Oh my God, we're going to hit the wall!" my sister screamed from behind me in the backseat.

"Turn, Victoria!" my mother screamed.

"I can't!" I shouted.

"Oh, shit!" I screamed as I turned the wheel as hard as I could to the right, and pushed it down to connect it again. I slammed on the brakes, but we were going too fast to come to a full stop. My new car hit the wall. The car continued to travel forward, and it grazed the wall on my side.

I had slowed down to about twenty mph and was greeted by angry motorists, shouting and gesturing out of their windows as they passed by.

I ignored what was going on around me. I pressed the steering wheel down hard to feel it connect again with the rest of the car. I managed to turn it into the middle lane and then the right lane. Then I turned down a local street and pulled over.

My mother jumped out of the backseat and went to yell at my father in the passenger seat.

"*This* is the car you buy for your daughter?" she accused. "How *could* you? She could have been *killed*, God forbid! How *dare* you! What kind of father *are* you?"

"Woman, it didn't do that when I drove it! It's probably the kid's bad driving!"

"You know she is a good driver!" she replied. "Why would you get her a death trap, *why*?" she continued.

As they argued, my sister and I also got out. Luckily, the impact on our side of the car wasn't severe enough to trap us in the car.

"You OK?" I asked her.

"Yeah, you?" she asked me.

"Yeah," I said. I then inspected the scrape alongside the car. It was sizeable, but not too obvious, given that the car was white to begin with.

My father hailed a cab to get back to his apartment in the city. My mother went looking for a pay phone to call AAA.

The Jeep was my mother's responsibility to repair, as my father would not return her or my own calls after that. She took it to my neighbor's auto body repair shop, around the corner from our house. "Where did you get this piece of trash, a junk yard?" he asked. I was surprised by David's aggressive tone, he was usually calm and relaxed. I had never seen him so animated.

"No, her father gave it to her," she said, gesturing to me.

"Her *father*? What kind of father would do that? Do you have any idea how dangerous this car was when I first saw it?" he asked.

"No, what was wrong with it?" she asked.

"The alignment was shot! How did you even steer the car?"

he asked me.

"Not very well!" I said, stifling a laugh.

"How bad do you want this car?" he asked me.

"Really bad," I said.

"OK, then I'll need at least another week," he said to my mother.

"Thank you, David," my mother said.

Within a week, I had my car. The steering wheel now controlled the front wheels. My mother, however, still did not trust the car completely, so she insisted on driving with me in it for at least a month until she was sure it was safe.

37

That month, Carol suggested that I submit an application for one of the Young Rider clinics, with Conrad Schumacher, a renowned German trainer.

"Are you sure I'm good enough to apply?" I asked her.

"I know you're good enough—you *and* Moonshine," she replied.

"No, I mean advanced enough?" I clarified.

"The selection criteria aren't only based on show scores, Victoria. They're also based on recommendations of each rider's ability, potential, commitment, and experience," Carol said.

"Yeah, but the primary factors are show scores, right?" I asked.

"I suppose," she replied.

I knew that would diminish my chances.

"Just send in the application. Stop being such a pessimist, you never know how something will work out unless you try," she said, slightly frustrated.

"OK," I said, not believing I had a chance to take a lesson from one of the most well-known Olympic trainers in the world.

I nonetheless took the application from her, filled it out that night, and dropped it in the mail the next morning.

The next day, Carol told me that since Moonshine and I were progressing so smoothly and would soon be competing at the higher levels of dressage, that I would need new equipment.

"First, you need a double bridle. They're pretty expensive, so until you can put together enough cash to buy one, you can borrow my old one," she generously offered.

"Thanks, Carol!" I was relieved.

"The only problem will be finding the right bit," she cautioned. "Since Moony is smaller than most warmbloods, finding a Weymouth bit small enough to fit his mouth might be tricky. I don't think they sell pony-sized dressage bits, but you should look into it."

Finding a bit small enough for Moonshine's mouth was tricky. None of the tack stores around the farm sold pony sized dressage bits. I also called some of the catalogs and none of them had pony sized dressage bits. So, I bought the smallest horse size dressage bit and crossed my fingers while I waited for it in the mail.

Meanwhile, the mailman brought me an unexpected package from the United States Dressage Federation.

"We are pleased to inform you that you have been selected as one of the eight young rider participants in the spring Conrad Schumacher Young Rider Clinic series."

My mouth dropped open. I looked up at my mother, watching me with hopeful eyes.

"I got into the clinic," I said softly.

"Oh my God!" my mother burst as she hugged me tightly.

When she finished hugging me, she called Ava to share the good news.

When she was done gushing to my godmother, she suggested calling Carol and letting her know.

"Mom, she's probably riding or teaching, we can tell her on

the weekend," I tried to calm her.

But she had already dialed the number and was waiting for an answer on the other line.

Jane, the secretary, answered.

"Jane, hello, this is Victoria's mother," she started.

I was amused by the fact that not only did everyone else at the farm identify my mother as "Victoria's mom," rather than by her first name, but that is how she now identified herself as well to people at the farm.

"Is Carol around?" she continued.

There was a pause.

"OK, well then, please tell her that Victoria got into the clinic!" she gushed.

"Thank you!" she said as she hung up the phone.

That weekend, Carol congratulated me as soon as I saw her.

"See? You never know until you try!" she said as she winked at me.

"I still can't believe they picked us."

"You'll do great. Just give it your all in those lessons and don't take everything he says to heart," she warned.

"They might ask you to ride in a double bridle. Have you found one yet?" she asked.

"I ordered the smallest horse size Weymouth bit I could find. I couldn't find pony-size Weymouth bits," I informed her.

"Well, hopefully it arrives before the clinic, you need some time getting used to riding Moony in a double bridle before you go to this clinic," she said.

"I'll let you know as soon as I get it," I said.

Two weeks later, my bit arrived. I brought it to Carol for her to examine before I latched it into the double bridle she had given me. She walked with me to Moony's stall so that she would be the first one to put it on him and be able to adjust the straps.

"Hmmm," she said frowning, as she looked at it from both sides of my horse's mouth.

"What's wrong with it?" I asked.

"Well, you see how I can fit in two fingers between his mouth and the end of the bit on each side of his head?" she asked as she demonstrated.

"Yes," I said.

"That means it's too big," Carol said.

My heart sank. This was the smallest bit available and it was still too big. Moonshine had the typical Quarter horse nose—small and delicate.

"Do you think I can ride with it anyway?" I asked hopefully.

"You can definitely try. Just try not to hold the curb rein—try to hold onto the snaffle rein instead. Maybe if he doesn't feel the curb, the fact that it doesn't really fit won't bother him too much," she said optimistically.

"Worth a shot," I said.

Moonshine did not need much time to adjust to the double bridle; most other horses required at least a month to get used to such new equipment. I was thrilled that Moonshine was still improving, despite the fact that I was asking him to work at his best in ill-fitting equipment.

Then it was time to go to the clinic, which would be held at the United States Equestrian Team headquarters in Gladstone, New Jersey. I was familiar with the headquarters, having already been there last year, to watch the US Olympic trials. Moonshine would be stabled in the same historic barn as my idols when they competed here last year. I was also excited because the Young Rider participants were going to stay in the grooms' quarters above the barn, for the duration of the three-day event. I was thrilled that I would be so close to Moonshine, instead of always being an hour away. I could be with him whenever I wanted, all hours of the day, with no other obligations or time limitations to take me away. Nora had a two-horse trailer, so she drove Moonshine down, with my mother and I following behind her. My mother did not trust the Jeep, so we took her station wagon. She also would not stay;

she had to stay home with my sister, sick grandfather, and dogs.

Since my grandmother had passed away, my grandfather had deteriorated. He had been overweight for as long as I had known him, but now he looked gaunt, with hollow cheeks, and his big belly had vanished. He was quiet most of the time now, which was a drastic difference from how loud he often was in the frequent arguments he had with my grandmother. I was always intrigued by the fact that they had been married for most of their lives, but seemed to be able to communicate only in explosive argument. And yet, for all the years I had known them, they were always near each other; if they weren't in the same room, they would be soon. I realized after my grandmother passed away, and my grandfather seemed to cease existing, that they had not intensely hated each other at all; they had instead been bonded by so many degrees of intensity—love, passion, hatred, friendship, and partnership.

38

On the drive down to New Jersey, my mother asked me, "Are you sure you will be OK, all by yourself?"

"Mom, please, are you kidding me?" I said.

I was extremely excited to be on my own, even if it would only be for two nights and three days.

"I'll be fine, I'll be in the grooms' quarters with all the other riders. I won't be alone, don't worry," I assured her.

She smiled with relief.

Finally, we arrived at the USET headquarters. As we drove down the long driveway to the barn, I saw the same competition arena that I had seen the year before. Then, I saw the entrance of the historic barn just in front of it. I had not noticed it before, maybe because there were so many tents and banners at the Olympic trials last year. It looked magnificent, and I thought it would make a beautiful picture. I was glad that I had packed so many disposable cameras; I would take pictures of Moony standing in the threshold of the barn, and then at the entrance of the arena.

Nora parked the trailer in front of the barn, and I backed

Moony down the ramp and out of the trailer as soon as she opened it. Moonshine looked to his left, then to his right, to take in his new surroundings, as he always did when I took him to a show. Then he started toward the barn, perhaps smelling the other horses, or maybe he knew that was where he needed to go anyway. As we entered the barn, he stopped. The floor was unlike any other floor either of us had seen—it was made of peachy-yellow cobblestone. The stalls were shiny waxed wood on the bottom and had dark green bars. The corners of the stalls had brass posts. It was the most beautiful barn I had ever seen.

"Hi, who are you?" I was greeted immediately by a woman who was helping to set up.

"I'm Victoria, and this is Moonshine," I said.

"Oh, great, you're right here, in the corner stall," she said.

I knew Moony would love this stall—it was in the middle of the barn, amidst all of the action. It was across from the wash stall, so he could watch horses getting bathed, and it was just in front of the main entrance, so he could watch people and horses coming and going. I knew he was extremely curious, and being able to watch everything was perfect for him. As I led him into the stall, I was impressed by its massive size. It was almost twice the size of his stall at home. I was glad that I brought extra bags of shavings with me. Nora helped me unload the shavings, bales of hay, and tack trunk from her trailer, while my mother grabbed a bucket and filled it with water for Moony to drink.

Then Nora left to beat the rush hour traffic, and my mother hurried to follow in her car, as she was sure to get lost if she tried to go back without a guide to lead her. She was terrible with directions.

"Are you sure you're going to be fine?" she asked me again.

"Mom, I'm *sure*, just go already!"

"OK, here is your bag," she said, handing me my suitcase. "Can you call me tonight?" she asked, worried.

"Ugh, do I have to?" I whined. I didn't want to stay

connected to reality, I wanted to completely immerse myself in this new world where it was just me and my horse.

"I would really feel better if you did. Just a quick five minutes so I know you are OK," she bargained.

"Fine," I said, giving in.

Then she kissed me on my forehead and left. Now it was just me and Moonshine. I set up his stall while he inspected what I was doing, sticking his nose over my shoulder as I set up his water buckets, nuzzling my back as I set down some hay. I knew he would be easily distracted by food and I could continue with my chores without him shadowing me. I ran my hands up and down the walls of the stall, to make sure there were no loose nails to hurt him, as I always did when I put him in a new stall. Then I threw down all of the shavings I had. I knew he would love this part and roll in the new shavings. I was right. As soon as he saw a pile of clean, fresh shavings in the middle of the stall, he was down, rolling around in them. I think one of his favorite parts of going to shows was the fun of rolling around in fresh shavings.

"Moony, you're such a little freak," I said as he thrashed the shavings around and covered himself in the big white flakes. At least he saved me the job of having to spread them around with a pitchfork.

"Someone's a happy camper," another rider's mother said as she passed by, catching a glimpse of Moonshine's hooves in the air.

"Yeah, he loves to roll," I said, smiling.

Then he got up and shook off the excess shavings, like a wet dog drying itself.

"Happy now?" I asked him. I always talked to him like he was a person. I was convinced he understood everything I said. He grunted and then blew his nose at me.

"Thanks, Moon," I said, checking my shirt to see if he had gotten me this time. He hadn't. I knew this meant, "You can leave me alone now, I'm eating." He liked to be left alone when he ate, so I headed to my room upstairs.

On my way to the staircase leading up to the sleeping quarters where the riders would stay, my eye caught the other barn entrance—the one I had seen from the driveway, with the main competition arena in front of it. I dropped my bag and was pulled in by the magnificent sight. The historic barn had an elegant vaulted entrance right out to the main arena. I stood in the opening, and saw Moonshine and me in the ring.

I walked slowly onto the sand; it was still wet from all of the rain we had been getting that spring. The bleachers where I sat the year before at the Olympic trials were gone, but I knew where they were supposed to be, to the right. I knew the exact spot where I sat, watching the competition. I looked in that direction, and then back to the center of the arena. This is what those competitors saw when they came in here—the audience to the right, the arena straight ahead. I wanted to see what they saw just before they set foot in this ring.

I closed my eyes and took a deep breath. The air was damp and cold, unlike the hot and humid air I remembered from the day of the Olympic trials. The show grounds were so different now. There were no tents, vendors, or crowds. It was empty. But, we had made it here. Moony and I were still going to ride in exactly the same place that I saw the best riders in the country compete for a spot on the Olympic team. I was standing where history was made. I knew we were just at a Young Riders' clinic, and this event was nothing compared to the Olympic trials, but we were still *here*, at the United States Equestrian Team headquarters, and we had *earned* the right to be here. I got lost in the pride I had in my horse—the horse that everyone dismissed as useless and worthless, was the horse that brought me here, to the USET.

"Hey, are you going up to check out the rooms?" I was pulled out of my daydream by a loud voice behind me.

"Yeah, I was just headed up there," I said, as I saw the owner of the voice, another young rider like myself, but with blond, curly, unruly hair.

"Let's go check it out! I'm Katie," she said, extending her hand.

"I'm Victoria," I said as I shook her hand.

She went up the spiral staircase first. This was my first time on a spiral staircase. It went up in the middle of the barn. We were one floor above our horses, and the top floor was perfect. It had a main room, a few bedrooms at the end, and a bathroom.

"Wow," I said.

"Pretty cool, right?" she said in agreement.

"Yeah, you would never think there was a barn downstairs," I said. I was tickled by the thought that I would be sleeping just upstairs from Moonshine. For the first time, I would be able to see him at whatever time of day I pleased.

"I'll take this room," she said, throwing her bag on the bed in the first bedroom.

"I'll take the one across," I said, setting my bag down beside the bed. I looked out through the window—it was the same scene by which I had just been mesmerized—the show ring.

"Is your trainer here?" she asked.

"No, she's coming tomorrow," I said.

"Yeah, mine too. She's so busy," she said.

"Yep," I agreed. This girl was nice, but I had had enough socializing and wanted to be back in the barn.

"OK, well I'm going to get my horse and ride," I said.

"Cool. I already rode. You should ride in the indoor, it's so wet out there," she advised.

"I know. How's the footing inside?" I asked.

"It's good," she replied.

We headed back down the spiral staircase to the barn.

I walked up and down the aisles, looking for a wheelbarrow. As I walked down one end, I saw the horses in the stalls, all bigger than Moonshine. There was no wheelbarrow at that end, so I turned around and walked all the way down the aisle to the other end of the barn. Again, the stalls were filled with huge, dark horses.

They're all warmbloods, I thought.

I finally found a wheelbarrow and cleaned Moonshine's stall before I tacked him up.

As I worked him, he felt just as solid and reliable as he did when we were working at home. Nothing seemed to faze or excite him. I didn't work him too hard, as Carol had taught me to save the energy for the show, and not use it all up on the warm up day. I decided that for a cool-down, we should walk around the competition ring, just in case the weather would be nice that weekend and the clinic would be moved outside. I couldn't resist rationalizing the need to walk around this ring, when I really just wanted to indulge my fantasy.

I expected Moony to step proudly onto the sand where so many famous horses had competed. It didn't take his breath away. Instead, he kept his head down, and simply ambled straight down the middle. I again looked to my right, and instead of seeing the emptiness that was actually there, I saw the bleachers, the flags, the audience. I heard the cheers, the announcers, the scores. Moonshine did one lap around the ring and headed for the barn. I knew he wanted to get back to his stall and finish his hay. All this horse ever wanted to do was eat. He picked up the pace when he realized I wasn't going to steer him away from the exit; I looked back at the ring and saw Moonshine's hoofprints—they had formed a perfect teardrop in the wet sand.

That evening, the clinic organizers had arranged for all of us young riders to dine upstairs in the main room and get to know each other. They also wanted to give us the ride schedule and let us know what to expect.

"For those of you who have never participated in a clinic before, you should know that certain things will be expected of you. First, this is a learning experience. You should make every effort to learn as much as you can. So, when you are not riding, you should be watching. You can learn a lot from watching each other's rides. Second, do not be late. This is a German trainer, with German punctuality. Give yourselves enough time to warm up and be ready to go as soon as your lesson starts. Finally, tomorrow we will dine with Mr. Schumacher, at both lunch and dinner. You will have the opportunity to ask him questions. Your parents and trainers are invited to attend the lunch. He will give a lecture on dressage principles. The dinner is just with Mr. Schumacher and you guys. Be polite and professional, keeping in mind that he works with Olympians," the organizers instructed.

My new friend Katie looked at me and rolled her eyes. I smiled in response.

At the end of the talk, the ride schedules were passed around. I had a perfect ride time—three o'clock in the afternoon. This would give me a chance to watch some of the morning rides and get a feel for the new trainer. It would also give my mother enough time to get here, factoring in time for her to get lost and find her way. I also hoped Carol would be able to make it.

The next morning, I got up early and went down to the barn to give Moony his morning hay and grain, fill his water buckets, and muck his stall while he ate. He still didn't like it when I was in his stall while he ate, keeping his ears pinned back, and whipping me in the face with his tail when I was near his hindquarters. But I was pressed for time. The clinic would start in fifteen minutes and I did not want to be late to watch the first ride. I quickly cleaned his stall while he ate, dumped the wheelbarrow, and headed to the restroom to wash up. I then grabbed coffee and a bagel from the breakfast table and went to the indoor arena. I was one of the first to sit down in the bleachers.

I spotted Katie and sat down next to her.

"Hey, how's it going?" she asked, as she watched the first rider warming up.

"Good, you?" I replied.

"Good," she said as she sipped her orange juice.

Precisely at 8:00 a.m., an imposing figure entered the arena. He was massive—he stood about six feet four inches, with broad shoulders and a heavy build. His voice was deep, as I expected, and he had the heaviest German accent I had ever heard. He had deep blue eyes and not one of his dark gray hairs was out of place.

"Good morning, young lady. Come to the center please, I would like to meet you," he said.

They chatted briefly and then the lesson began. He was demanding, animated, strict, and he forced her to be precise. He was unforgiving, pushing her physically until she was bright red in the face. Her horse breathed so heavily it seemed to hyperventilate. It was still cold in the morning, but the horse was dripping sweat within ten minutes, and was foaming on his neck, where the reins lay. After ten minutes, the instructor gave them a break. The break was short and they resumed the work. She had two chances to do what he said, when she didn't do as she was told on the third try, he exploded.

"I SAID KEEP YOUR LEG ON, WHAT ARE YOU DOING? ARE YOU ASLEEP UP THERE?" he shouted forcefully into the microphone, which was connected to speakers all around the arena. This stung all of our ears and spooked the horse—he bolted to the other side of the arena.

Katie and I exchanged looks. I realized that if he was this tough on a rider with a talented dressage horse, he would be ruthless with me and Moonshine. Katie also didn't have one of the more talented horses at the event, so she was probably thinking the same thing.

The next rider came in with another lovely horse. That was irrelevant to the German. He was still demanding and unrelenting. After repeating the same instruction to the rider several times, he exploded: "You do not deserve this horse! He is too good for you! You had better find another hobby!" Now everyone in the audience was exchanging looks. I felt pained for the girl. I saw tears in her eyes as she left the arena at the end of her lesson.

The German went even further with the third equestrian. After explaining to her that her horse was a hundred times more capable than she could ever hope to be, he instructed her to dismount. We all looked at each other, wondering what his next step would be. He walked to the horse and rider, took the reins from her, and put his foot in the stirrup. He hoisted himself onto her horse. The horse was visibly agitated by the extra weight on its back; the man was easily an extra hundred pounds of weight. Nevertheless, the horse obediently complied with his new rider's orders. After about ten minutes of working the horse, he stopped and brought the horse back to its owner.

"Now, get on and feel how it *should* feel. Try to memorize the feeling before you ruin it," he instructed.

By now Carol had arrived. She spotted me in the audience and made her way to the free spot on the bench to my right.

"So, how's it going?" she asked.

"He's going to tear us apart," I muttered.

Katie smiled sympathetically.

"Why?" Carol inquired.

"You'll see," I said.

He continued to berate his third victim of the day, and Carol fell silent.

At the end of her lesson, the lunch break was announced. Everyone was invited to the lunch lecture.

"What time do you ride?" Carol asked me.

"Three," I answered.

"I'm right after lunch," Katie said.

"If you need to leave early to tack up, I'll let you know if you miss anything good," I offered.

"Thanks," she replied.

As we walked through the barn, I saw that the girls who had ridden that morning were still in tears. They were huddled in corners, bent over tack trunks or bales of hay to hide their grief. I genuinely felt sorry for them, and also dreaded that I would soon share their fate.

The lunch lecture was highly informative. The German was knowledgeable and provided lucid explanations of dressage principles.

He also provided a brief instruction, complete with diagrams, on the ideal dressage horse's conformation. He showed how the croup, or hind end, had to be at least level with the first half of the horse, so that the horse can rock back and take more weight on his haunches as he accepted the higher degrees of collection required in the more advanced levels of the sport. He noted that certain horses are impossible to ride in dressage. I had read certain articles of other famous trainers who had said that any horse can do dressage, regardless of breed and conformation. I sided with that camp of dressage experts. But then he explained why dressage is impossible for some horses.

"Thoroughbred horses, for example, are bred to run, to be fast. Therefore, they are bred to have longer hind legs than any other horse in the world. Having much longer hind legs makes it virtually impossible for them to rock back on those long legs and accept the higher degrees of collection."

"Is that true?" I whispered to Carol.

"Don't worry about it. And Moony's only half Thoroughbred anyway," she encouraged.

Katie got up and rushed out to prepare for her lesson. I wished her good luck and hoped that the German wouldn't annihilate her and her horse. If he had been so brutal on the girls with the beautiful horses, how would he react to Katie and me, the only ones at the event with homely horses?

After the lunch break, we all piled out back to the indoor arena. Katie was still warming up, and as soon as she saw Mr. Schumacher enter the arena, she went over to introduce herself and tell him about herself and her horse. He was just as demanding of her as he was with all of the other girls, but in his final review at the end of her ride, he actually praised her. I was a combination of surprised, thrilled, and relieved. He didn't chastise her because she had shown up on a non-warmblood horse. I hoped that he would take it easy on Moony and me.

Then my mother showed up and sat down next to Carol and me.

"Hi honey, how are you? Did you eat? Did you sleep well?" she began.

"Hi, Mom; everything is fine. I actually have to go and get Moony ready now, though," I said.

"But you don't ride for another hour," she interjected.

"Yeah, but I have to make sure he's clean, and all warmed up before my time," I said.

"OK, good luck," she said.

"Good luck, Victoria," Carol repeated.

"Thanks," I said as I headed back to the barn.

Moonshine was fine, relaxed and calm, as usual. I loved how mentally sturdy he was, I hardly ever saw him rattled, even when all the other horses around him were excited. And I knew exactly what mattered most to him—food. He was always content if he had food. He did not need my undivided attention at all hours of the day. At an event like this, where I had to be away from him except when I had to ride, I was extraordinarily grateful for his independent nature.

"Moony! Time to ride!" I called in his direction as I approached his stall.

His head popped up and his ears flew forward. The shape of his ears always amused me. They were little, a common characteristic of Quarter horses, but they were slightly crooked, so that when he perked them straight up, they actually inverted a little inward, making them look like devil horns, as my mother often said.

"Hi Moony monster," I said as I opened the stall door and patted him on the neck.

He took this opportunity to shove me in my belly, his favorite greeting. He always had to make the point that he was the boss.

I groomed him until his dark coat was gleaming. I also sprayed him with a little shine spray to make him extra shiny. Then it was time to put the white polo wraps on his legs, then the white saddle pad, the saddle, and then finally, the double bridle. He only wore white for shows and special occasions, like this clinic.

"Be good a good boy, OK?" I told him as I fastened the straps on the bridle.

I led him outside, to the competition arena, where I warmed him up for fifteen minutes. Five minutes before my ride time, I headed to the indoor arena.

At the conclusion of the previous lesson, Mr. Schumacher gestured for me to come over to him.

"Come here, young lady," he ordered.

"Hello, I am Conrad Schumacher," he said as he extended his hand for a handshake.

I removed my glove, as my mother had instructed me to do a long time ago, having told me it was rude to shake another's hand with my glove still on. He smiled as I took off the glove and leaned over to shake his hand.

"Hi, I'm Victoria," I said.

"What breed is this horse?" he asked.

Great, cutting right to the chase, I thought.

"Appendix," I replied.

"Vas ist that?" he asked in his thick German accent.

"Half Thoroughbred, half Quarter horse," I replied, bracing myself for a torrent of insults.

"What? A Thoroughbred!" he exclaimed, slightly horrified, slightly amused. "*Thoroughbreds* are not dressage horses," he continued. "Do you know you cannot do dressage with a Thoroughbred, young lady?" he asked.

"I know I can try," I replied, before I realized what was coming out of my mouth.

I heard some scoffs and muffled giggles from the audience. I knew it was probably a mistake to retaliate so assertively to such a famous trainer, but sometimes words slipped out of my mouth before I realized what I was saying.

"Ha! You sure can try!" he repeated.

"So, good, go and *try* to pick up the rising trot, please," he ordered, commencing the lesson.

He pushed Moony and me to our limits. Despite the crisp spring air, I was sweating from every pore of my body. I felt sorry that I was pushing Moony so hard, harder than I had ever asked him to go. But I had no choice, I had to comply with the German's commands.

"Keep your hands together, stop shaking, keep them still!" he ordered.

I had never noticed that my hands shook, but glancing down a few times, I noticed that my left one did vibrate frequently. It seemed to be doing it on its own, like it wasn't a part of me. Nevertheless, I willed it to stop and be still.

"What are you looking at?" he shouted into the microphone.

I don't know why a man this loud had a microphone, he really didn't need one.

"Look UP! *Look* where you are going!" he shouted, animated.

"Now your hands again! Egh! Concentrate, young lady! Keep your hands still!" he commanded.

"The left hand is out of control!" he bellowed.

I was trying hard to keep my left hand still, but it refused to hold the rein steady, like my right hand.

I could feel Moony tense up slightly any time the loud voice screamed through the speakers. I tried to keep my back relaxed, so that he would relax in his back as well. But I was being yelled at by a famous trainer in front of a sizable audience, which included my own trainer. For me, though, when I was highly agitated or upset, the first emotion to surface was always anger.

"Your left hand is a *disaster!*" he roared, in his thick German accent.

That's the last time I hear anything about my stupid left hand, you crazy German, I thought, now furious.

I continued looking up and straight ahead through Moony's ears, but I imagined there was now an invisible rope that tied my hands together. My two hands became one entity. Instead of asking Moony to bend left with my left rein, I asked him to bend with my left leg. I was grateful to Carol for teaching me how to control Moony with my whole body, and not just my hands. I was grateful for all of the lunge lessons she gave me where she forced me to learn how to control my horse with just my seat. Now I realized what an extraordinary trainer I had. "Better," he said calmly, through the speakers.

Then the lesson was over, and I went to the middle to receive my review. I was surprised that he did not begin with Moony and how unsuitable he was for dressage.

"You are a good rider, but you need to work on keeping your left hand still. You have talent, but if you want be a *dressage* rider, you had better find a *dressage* horse," he said, as he petted Moony's neck with his massive hand.

I wanted to tell him that I already had a dressage horse and to get his hand off my horse, but I reconsidered.

I walked back to the barn, somewhat dejected, but not feeling as discouraged as I thought I would. I definitely was nowhere near shedding a tear over what this big trainer thought. I was more irritated than anything else. But I put my emotions on hold to fawn over Moony a little bit, after all, he had worked his heart out for me, and I was really grateful for that.

"You were such a good boy," I said, as I dismounted and petted his neck. Then he shoved me sideways with his head. I knew this meant, "I don't need to hear it, I know I was good, just give me my carrots."

Then Carol and my mother appeared in the barn.

"You did great!" Carol beamed.

"Thanks," I said.

"Yes, honey, you were fantastic!" my mother gushed.

"What did you think?" Carol asked. She usually liked to discuss rides and events for my impression and so that we could exchange ideas and work on issues in our subsequent lessons.

"He's wrong about Moony, how he said that he's not a dressage horse. There are so many people who made it without warmbloods," I started, still angry.

"OK, what did you think about the *lesson*, do you feel that you learned anything?" she asked, still smiling.

"I didn't know my left hand was so bad," I started.

"We'll work on that," she said.

"What else?" she asked.

Then we fell into a detailed discussion, theorizing about the dressage principles introduced at the lunch break, and how they applied to Moonshine and me. We continued our talk as I untacked Moonshine. Then it was time for me to hose him off, and Carol said she had to be off, but that she would come back tomorrow to watch my lesson.

I also told my mother she could go home, because I was

fine on my own. She looked at me quizzically, to which I responded, "Just go, Mom! I'm fine, really!"

Then she kissed me and said she would be back the following day.

I missed the last lesson of the day, spending the hour with Moonshine, making sure he was cooled off and clean. Then I cleaned my tack before the sweat and foam could dry on the leather. Lastly, I looked for a spot to hang my soaked saddle pad.

Before I knew it, an hour had passed and the first day of the clinic was over. Everyone gathered in the barn. I noticed that all of the riders had red and wet eyes except for Katie and me. I was not expecting that, and found it slightly humorous that the two girls with the least talented horses were the only ones who had not shed a tear that day.

We had an hour until the dinner. I dumped Moony's grain in his bucket, threw him some hay and headed upstairs to wash up. I loved this part, just going upstairs to get cleaned up, not having to sit in the car for an hour until I could shower. I also loved that I could see Moony again after dinner.

The dinner was just for us juniors and Mr. Schumacher. I jumped at my chance to pick his brain while he ate, hoping he would be more content if he was eating, and give me the answers I wanted to hear. If I could convince my cheap father to buy me a car, I could surely convince this German that my horse could be a serious dressage contender.

"Mr. Schumacher, I have a question about my lesson today," I began matter-of-factly.

"Yes? What is your question?" he said pleasantly through his accent.

"It was about what you said about Thoroughbreds not being able to do dressage," I continued.

"Ach, ja, you are die girl mit das Thoroughbred horse,

nicht?" he said, slipping in some German.

"Yes," I replied, somewhat dejected that he had identified me, apparently from his "hopeless" category.

"You have a good horse," he said.

I was shocked. I thought he hated Moonshine!

"He is well trained, and he is very responsive to you. He has a strong will to work, which is valuable for a horse to have," he said.

"Thank you," I said, bursting with pride.

"But he is still just a Thoroughbred horse, young lady. He cannot go far at all," he started.

I was deflated.

"Yeah, that's what I wanted to ask you about," I said. "There are lots of people who don't have warmblood horses who do end up going very far," I persisted.

"Maybe in *dis* country, but not in *Germany*," he scoffed. He didn't care at all that he was in a room full of Americans. He was perfectly fine with reminding us that Germans are the best in dressage.

"Well, there have been Thoroughbreds who have gone to the Olympics," I said, grateful that I knew my dressage history.

"Ha! Maybe a hundred years ago. But not now! As I told you before, if you want to be a dressage rider, you must get yourself a dressage horse. You cannot do dressage with a racehorse!" he insisted.

"OK, thanks," I said, even though I was ungrateful for his feedback.

I slunk back in my seat beside Katie; I knew she had overheard my entire conversation with the German.

"Just forget about it," she whispered, "let it go."

But I couldn't and wouldn't let it go. I was grateful that I had two more days to prove to him how wrong he was about my horse. Moony *wasn't* limited by his breeding, he had no limitations at all.

The following day, the German was just as demanding on all of us riders as he was on the first day, but apparently most of the participants had grown a thicker skin overnight, as fewer tears were shed. I was also a lot less nervous. Maybe it was because I knew what he had to say now, and that he thought Moonshine and I had no chance of being a successful competitive team. Or maybe I was still fuming over what he told me the day before. I still rode my heart out, though, trying to force him to eat his words and recognize that Moonshine *was* a dressage horse, despite his conformation and breeding.

"Good job today, young lady," he said as he ended the lesson and petted my horse on the neck.

See, Moonshine can do it, I thought.

I was fully satisfied and gave Moony extra carrots that night.

Sunday was the last day of the clinic. I was ready to make this German rescind his initial comments and recognize that my horse truly was a legitimate dressage contender. That morning, the organizers told me that I would ride earlier than my previously scheduled ride time because some of the other girls had gone home early.

I looked around the barn, incredulous. It was true, the three horses that had been stabled around Moonshine were now gone.

Just then Katie walked by.

"I'm glad you're still here," she said, flashing a bright smile.

"Some girls left early?" I asked her.

"I guess so," she replied as she walked to her horse's stall at the other end of the barn.

I called Nora to tell her that if she wanted to pick Moonshine up earlier than I had previously told her, I would be ready to go. I also called my mother to tell her that my ride time had been moved up. I didn't call Carol because she had told me she wouldn't be able to make it down for the final day of the clinic.

On the last day, the clinic was moved outside, to the show ring. I was delighted. Bleachers were set up to the right of the arena, as they had been for the Olympic trials the year before. By the time I had to ride, the audience had filled all of the seats that were set up outside. The final lesson was just as demanding as the first two. Mr. Schumacher pushed Moonshine and me until we were again breathing heavily and dripping with sweat. I did notice a dramatic improvement in Moonshine, though. He was crisper in his executions, longer in his extensions, rounder, and straighter in his general movement. Even though I disagreed with Mr. Schumacher's final assessment of my horse's potential, I was grateful for the improvement that he had brought out in both of us.

"It was a pleasure working with you, young lady," he said at the end of my lesson.

"Likewise, Mr. Schumacher, thank you for the lessons," I replied.

"I hope to see you again—on a dressage horse," he ended.

I kept my mouth shut and forced a smile.

Don't pick a fight on the last day, don't pick a fight, I coached myself.

39

The following weekend, in my lesson with Carol, she asked me what I thought of the clinic. I knew what she wanted to hear.

"It was a good learning experience," I said professionally.

I could tell from the way she raised her eyebrow that she didn't believe me.

"Yeah, why?"

"Umm. I learned a lot?" I asked. I might as well not even try to hide it now.

"What *specifically* did you learn?" she pressed.

"That my left hand is a disaster!" I bellowed in a fake German accent.

She laughed.

I was relieved that I had thought of a clever way to get out of a sticky situation with my trainer.

"Here's what I think," she started. "I think it was good exposure for you. It was good for you to ride in front of so many people, and in front of someone so famous. Now you'll see that Germans aren't the best just because they have some magic potion that they feed their horses and riders. They are the best because they ride to their absolute limits. They push themselves to perfection. I think you might realize that what you thought was perfect before, is actually only good now. That might explain that just because you can do a movement doesn't mean everything when you compete. The key is how *well* you execute the movement. How round and straight is your horse? Are you maintaining the same rhythm for the entire ride? How perfect is your position? It's not just about doing a shoulder in or flying change, it's about how harmonious and easy that movement looks. Does that make sense?" she explained.

"Yes," I replied.

"Are you just saying that or do you really get it?" she asked.

"I get it now," I assured her.

"OK, so we'll pick up where he left off," she said as she began the lesson.

Shortly after that clinic with Mr. Schumacher, I learned that I would compete in that year's United States Equestrian Team's Festival of Champions—the very same competition that had hosted the US Olympic Trials the previous year, to be held again at very same USET headquarters in Gladstone, New Jersey!

When Carol first told me the news, I thought I was invited to participate as some sort of exhibition junior rider, not participating in the actual competition; the competition was a prestigious event that drew the most advanced and qualified riders from the entire country. There was no way I had qualified to compete in the main event or even the juniors' division because my scores had been consistently mediocre. I asked Carol how it was possible that I had been invited to compete at the Festival of Champions—a national competition.

"You qualified," she simply said.

"How? I never get good scores," I said.

"Like the clinic, it's not just based on scores. They want to show off consistent junior riders, and I guess they looked at all the shows you've done and then word got out about how well you did at the clinic . . ."

I had a feeling that meant that Gunilla had made a call to the United States Dressage Federation and recommended that I represent Junior riders. It was a new youth division that targeted younger riders than the Young Riders. The Juniors' test would be the equivalent of Third Level, while the Young Riders' test was a more advanced test, similar to Prix St. Georges. However, both youth riding divisions would be sponsored by the FEI—International Equestrian Federation—which meant that I would compete in the FEI uniform. I would compete in a top hat instead of a helmet, shadbelly coat instead of the plain short coat, and mandatory white gloves. The horse was required to be in a double bridle, rather than the simpler snaffle bridle. When Carol told me about the required apparel, I was delighted.

"Oh, and I'm riding in the open division, so we'll trailer down there together," she added.

"Really? You're competing too? It'll just be the two of us going down there?" I asked.

"Yep," she said, smiling.

I wondered if she knew how much I adored and idolized her. I had gone to shows with her before, but with the whole team. This time, it would just be us going to show together.

"Oh, and Gunilla has to judge too, so she'll drive us down in her trailer," Carol informed me.

I knew Gunilla was a judge, but I had just recently read some articles in my dressage magazines announcing that she had now achieved international judging status. She never said anything at the farm. I guess there was no reason I should know, because other than a casual greeting in passing, we rarely spoke.

Moony and I trained hard leading up to the prestigious show. I had read an article in one of my dressage magazines where Michelle Gibson's trainer said that if a rider wanted to get a 60% at a show, then in training at home, she had to ride for a 120%, because there are inevitable distractions at shows, which would always bring down the score. I had never heard anything like that, but it made sense and it was my new guiding principle. I pushed Moony as hard as I had at the dressage clinic the month before. The greatest advantage of this upcoming show being at the same USET headquarters as the clinic was that Moony was already familiar with the show grounds, having just been there. I was grateful for this lucky advantage. Then, finally, it was time to go to the Festival of Champions.

I loaded Moony and Carol loaded her horse, Verdi. Both horses walked into the trailer calmly and without any objection.

"I guess Moony doesn't mind getting in trailers anymore!" Carol remarked, remembering how obstinate he had been years before.

"You did a great job teaching him to load," she said to me as we closed up the trailer.

I didn't really teach him, he just started following me in.

"Is your father coming down to watch your national debut?" Gunilla asked as she did a final check of the trailer.

"I doubt it," I said.

"Hmph," she grunted angrily, "he should! You and Moonshine have come really far."

Gunilla was blunt and genuine. If she felt someone was doing a terrible job, she said so. Her insults and compliments were always sincere, so I was really flattered by the compliment she had just paid me.

"Thanks," I said, smiling broadly. I could feel the goofy grin take over my face, but I didn't care. Gunilla's acknowledgment of Moony's improvement was truly satisfying, especially after her insisting for so long that riding him was a useless endeavor.

The ride down to New Jersey was uneventful, and yet I was a nervous ball of excitement and anticipation for the whole trip. I couldn't believe I was shipping Moonshine down to *compete* at the Festival of Champions at the United States Equestrian Team headquarters!

When we finally arrived, I jumped out of the car to get the stabling arrangements from the show management.

"Hi, I'm Victoria, do you have the stabling assignments?" I asked the show manager.

"Horse's name?" she asked.

"Moonshine and Verdi," I replied.

"Lower barn, stalls 56 and 57," she answered.

"Lower barn? Not this barn?" I asked. I didn't even know there was another barn.

"Yep, head on out down the driveway, take it all the way down 'til it ends at the lower barn," she said.

I took the paperwork from her and walked back to the trailer.

"What's the word, kiddo?" Gunilla shouted from the trailer.

"We're in the lower barn," I said.

"Meet you there!" she said as shifted the truck back into drive.

The lower barn was smaller, darker, and much plainer than the magnificent main barn in which Moony had been stabled during the young rider clinic the month before. I hoped that this new barn would not throw him and once he was out in the arenas, he would be comforted by the fact that he had been here not too long ago.

Carol unloaded Verdi and I walked with Moony off the trailer. The stalls were a lot smaller than the stalls in the main barn.

"Why are we in this barn? Why aren't we up there?" I asked Carol as I gestured to the main barn at the top of the hill.

"That barn is for the bigwigs," she said, slightly joking.

"Well then you should be in it!" I exclaimed.

"So should you!" she teased me, as usual.

We unloaded our things from the trailer, and gave the horses food and water.

"You want to ride in an hour or so?" Carol asked me.

"Sure," I replied.

After letting the horses settle in, we tacked them up and headed out. I cued Moony up the hill, toward the main competition arena.

"Where are you going?" Carol asked.

"I want to warm up in the show ring, so he sees everything," I said.

"They closed it off to preserve the footing for tomorrow. Don't worry, Moony knows where he is. Plus, it's not like he ever gets spooked by anything. You'll be fine tomorrow. Let's go to the indoor and see how the boys feel," she said.

"OK," I replied as I followed her to the indoor arena.

The arena was filled with superstars. I was delighted and again in awe that I was in the same arena as them.

I guess this will never get old, I thought, as I watched the celebrity horse and rider pairs preparing for the next day's competition in awe.

"Victoria!" Carol said as she snapped me out of my daydream.

"Don't get distracted," she instructed. "You are not a spectator, you're here to ride! Pick up the reins, working trot," she instructed.

"OK," I said.

"I have to school my horse too, but I'll keep my eye on you, and help you if you need it. But practice being independent, remember to ride smart," she instructed.

"OK!" I exclaimed, excited to ride. She had revved me up and now I wanted to prove to everyone here that this is where Moony and I belonged.

I rode Moony in the double bridle so he had one last chance to get used to it before the big day tomorrow. He still wasn't totally comfortable in it, because I couldn't find a bit small enough to fit his mouth. But I figured that if I rode more with my seat and didn't really use the reins, he wouldn't be in any pain, and it wouldn't be so obvious that my horse's bit was too big for his mouth.

The next day, my class, the Juniors' class, would be the first one of the day, and I was the first rider. Carol wasn't scheduled to ride until much later, but she still got up early to help me warm up. I wasn't relaxed in my back, and my shoulders were stiff. I was nervous. *Just get over it,* I told myself as I walked Moonshine down to the indoor arena to warm up. But the new show attire did not help my nerves. The shadbelly coat was a constant reminder that this was a more advanced show, and I was competing at a more advanced level. The top hat squeezing my head also reminded me that I was about to compete in an important show.

After walking Moony around on a loose rein, as I always did for about ten minutes before beginning the work out, Carol asked me, "Where are your spurs?"

"Spurs? I don't have any spurs. I never ride with spurs," I said.

"You don't have any spurs?" Carol asked me, her tone putting me on high alert.

"You have to ride with spurs at the FEI levels! I thought you knew that!" she said, now panic came through.

"No, I didn't know!" I said in a full panic.

"OK," she said, regaining her composure, "Just warm up, I'll get you my spurs," she said as she ran out of the ring and back to the barn.

Oh my God, this is bad, this is really bad. I've never ridden with spurs before! I hope Moony will be OK with spurs! I panicked.

Then Carol arrived back in the arena.

"Victoria, come over here!" she called.

I headed over and she quickly fastened the spurs over my ankles.

"Carol, I've never ridden Moony with spurs," I said.

"It's OK, just try to squeeze him with your calf if you have to squeeze but really just ride with your seat. If you need to go more forward, ask *only* with your seat—no legs, no hands, just like in the lunge lessons," she said.

"Right," I said, my voice quivering.

"You'll be fine. You can do this," she coached.

I was not convinced.

I spent the warm up focusing on keeping the spurs off of Moony's belly and not taking much contact with the reins. I was trying to ride completely with my seat, but I was tense and nervous, so my back frequently froze. I focused on sinking my heels down in the stirrups to elongate my legs and open up my seat. Then, my number was called.

I walked Moony up the hill to the show ring. It was still early, but I saw several Oakwood boarders and trainers in the bleachers. I couldn't believe they had driven all the way to New Jersey so early just to watch me ride. I was touched. Gunilla stood by the entrance. As Carol, Moony, and I approached, she said, "Go show your stuff, kiddo!"

"Good luck," Carol said as Moony stepped into the ring.

The announcer introduced Moonshine and me. As I made my way around the outer part of the arena, waiting for the judges to ring the bell so that I could start my test, my confidence grew. *This is what you've wanted for so long. You're here now, don't let it go. Show everyone how great Moony really is,* I told myself.

Then the bell rang.

I urged Moonshine forward into the ring, with my seat. I halted and saluted. Moony was a little tense, his short strides were choppier than usual. So, I pushed harder with my seat to get him moving forward and stretching to open up his strides, as he had done in the clinic. I rode forcefully, and in my fervor to make him look spectacular, my left hand accidentally jolted the rein. He flipped his head up.

Holy crap, OK, just push him forward, forget it, let it go, I told myself.

Then my spur must have touched him because he suddenly bucked.

Damn it, Moony! Just be good! I was getting angry that he was being so obstinate the one time he should have been at his best.

I decided I would make up for the mistakes with one fantastic trot extension at the end of the test. Carol and I had trained Moony to do a competitive trot extension, so I knew that if this extension was great, we could possibly make up the points we had thrown away earlier.

I urged him forward with my seat, but just as he started the movement, in my excitement and determination to make up the points, I bumped him with my legs. I had forgotten that I had Carol's long spurs tied to my ankles! Moony grabbed the bit in his teeth, threw his head high up and took off in a bucking gallop to the end of the ring, thrashing his head. When he got to the corner, he slammed on the brakes—he did a sliding stop, but luckily I didn't come out of the saddle. Although I couldn't believe this was happening, I was still riding the test and had to finish it, or else get eliminated. So, I pointed him down the center line, in a canter-trot mix and managed to wrangle him to a stop in the middle, and salute the judge, to end the test.

My ears were ringing, the lump in my throat swelled, and tears pooled in my eyes. I really didn't want to cry but it had been the worst ride of my life. And the most important. This was my first time competing in front of international judges, and that was my first impression. I wanted to crawl into a hole and never come out.

I heard weak, pity applause from the audience. I couldn't bring myself to look at the Oakwood supporters; I had let them down.

I walked to the entrance of the ring. Gunilla and my mother simply stared at me, with gaping mouths.

Carol came to me, and grabbed Moonshine's reins to stop him. She looked directly at me and ordered, "Victoria, *breathe.*" I was in a fog; it was like hearing her while underwater. She said something else that I didn't hear. Then, she released Moonshine and I walked him back to the barn alone.

Once I was by myself, the hot tears poured down my face. I took the long route, around the open field. I was tempted to punish him for his antics, but I knew if I reprimanded him now, it wouldn't turn back time and erase that horrible ride. I tried to make sense of it. How could he be OK with the double in training and now, the *only* time that it mattered, he totally freaked out? How could he jump and buck and toss his head like that when I can't even remember the last time he did that in training? What *happened?* I knew deep down that it was my fault for riding him with poor fitting equipment, which made the sting even sharper—I had no one to blame but myself. Still, I had hoped that his love for me would overcome anything, and he would shine when I wanted him to.

When I got back to the barn, Gunilla, Carol, and my mother were there. I also saw my father, unexpectedly. Carol saw my tear-soaked face. I didn't say anything. She came to me, took the reins out of my hand and gave them to Tracy, Gunilla's assistant.

"Here, sit down," she directed, as she shuffled me to a bale of hay.

"Fafa! Nice to see you, thanks for inviting me!" my father began sarcastically. I didn't invite him because I knew he wouldn't want to come to this show, so I was surprised to see him here.

"Not now!" my mother commanded as she stepped in front

of him, breaking his path to me.

"Outside, NOW!" Gunilla commanded.

I was surprised to hear Gunilla get involved. I didn't think she cared about me or my love for the sport. But here she was, joining forces with my mother to keep my father from upsetting me further, if that was possible.

Carol sat on the bale of hay with me. She put her arm around my back. I cupped my face in my hands, and propped my elbows on my knees. I just wanted to disappear.

"It's OK, calm down," she said softly.

But I couldn't calm down. That was it, this was my last show with Moonshine. The vet said we couldn't show anymore after this year because of Moonshine's Navicular disease. And that performance was the impression we would leave. Everyone was right, we really didn't belong.

My mother and Gunilla forced my father out of the barn. While they spoke outside, I confided in my coach.

"I can't do this anymore. I am so sick of always crying, always losing. I just . . ." I trailed off.

"I know, it'll be OK," she began, but then we heard Gunilla shouting outside.

"You see that girl in there? She is your *daughter*! And she is crying because of *you*!" she reprimanded loudly.

"*Me*?" I heard my father say in his playful, innocent voice.

"Oh cut the shit! None of this would have happened if you had listened to me and just bought her a decent horse! She can't do anything with that ridiculous little horse she rides, you know that! Don't you love your daughter?" she said.

"Of course I do!" he said, now sounding offended.

"Doesn't it hurt you to see her crying her eyes out time and again, trying to get somewhere with a horse that is clearly incapable? Do you *like* to see her like this—crying on a bale of hay? She should be on top of a podium, not crying in the barn!" Gunilla lectured loudly.

"Well, I just don't think it's worth it to invest so much

money in this," my father said seriously.

"Not *worth* it? You don't think she is worth it? What is wrong with you? How many times do I have to tell you that she *is* worth it! She has the talent, the drive, and now the training. The only thing she doesn't have is the horse! With the right horse, she could be a champion—try and get that through your thick skull!" she declared as she stormed off.

My father and mother were left outside, stunned. My father looked at me and then turned his back. He and my mother walked away from the barn in conversation.

After a while, I calmed down, my breathing was regular again. My mother came back, and Carol got up to give her the free spot on the bale of hay.

"Aren't you hot, honey? Let's take off the coat and boots and everything, huh?" my mother said.

I had forgotten that I was still in my full show attire: shadbelly, white breeches, boots, and the top hat. "Why don't you go change into a T-shirt and some jeans?" she said, knowing it was always best to distract me when I was upset. I sighed heavily as I got up. I passed Moonshine in his stall as I went to get a new set of clothes. He was wet, someone had hosed him off. I was grateful that someone had done that for me and I wouldn't have to deal with him for a while; I knew my anger and distress would not subside quickly.

When I came back in clean, dry clothes, my mother was alone in the barn. Carol and Verdi were gone, so I assumed she had taken him out to warm up before her ride.

"I can't believe Gunilla yelled at him like that," I said to my mother.

"I know, she was really mad," my mother replied.

"I didn't think she cared," I said.

"Oh, she does," my mother answered.

"He went home?" I asked.

"Yes," she replied.

"I'm going to go see if Carol needs anything," I said, grabbing a water bottle for her in case she was thirsty.

"I'm right behind you," she said, still putting things away.

I walked to the indoor. Carol saw me. I held up a water bottle, she shook her head no. I headed up toward the stands, lowering my baseball cap over my eyes so people wouldn't recognize me.

"Victoria! Come here, sit with us!" my heart sank when I heard familiar voices calling.

Damn it, I cursed to myself. I just wanted to be alone to watch Carol's ride.

"Hey kiddo!" Jean exclaimed. I was relieved Jean was here, she supported us no matter what, and was always happy to see me.

"Hey Jean," I said weakly.

"Sit down, right over here," she said, gesturing to the free spot next to her.

As I sat down, she put her arm around me, "You'll get 'em next time," she whispered.

"Did you get your score?" Edith asked me.

"No, I never want to see that score sheet, Edith," I said.

"Well, then I'll get it for you," she said as she stood up.

"Edith, sit down!" Jean snarled.

"How else is she going to learn?" Edith asked her.

"She's learned plenty today, leave it alone," Jean commanded.

"So, what happened out there?" Beth asked.

"I don't know," I said, defeated. I was done talking about it.

"Look, here comes Carol!" Jean interrupted.

Carol put in a precise and accurate test, as we all expected. She placed sixth, in the top ten of today's preliminary round, which meant she qualified for the finals tomorrow. I excused myself to help Carol with Verdi when she got back to the barn.

"Guys, I'm going to go help Carol untack and cool out, see

you tomorrow," I said.

"You got it!" Jean replied through her wide smile.

I was struck by her unending kindness and support. I couldn't understand why she believed so much in Moonshine and me, especially after today. We never won anything; it was like she got a kick out of rooting for the loser. Whatever it was, I was grateful for her and her ability to always know what to say, or not say.

"Congrats, Carol!" I said, meeting her back in the barn.

"Thanks!" she said.

"Want some help?" I said, unfastening Verdi's bridle straps.

"Sure," she said as she unbuttoned her shadbelly coat.

"I'll hose him off," I said as I slipped off the horse's bridle and replaced it with his halter.

"Thanks, I'll go get our score sheets," she replied.

Don't bother with mine, I thought, *I know what it will say. "You are a lost cause; you are making a mockery of this sport."*

Within a half hour, she was back with ribbons and score sheets.

"You got a ribbon!" she declared.

"What place did I get?" I asked.

"Oh who cares, you got a ribbon!" she repeated as she pinned it to Moonshine's stall door.

I knew that meant I got last place, and there just happened to be such few competitors in my class that I would get a ribbon.

"Do you want to look at your score sheet?" she asked.

"No," I said.

"Get over here," she said playfully.

"Wow, forty-three, I think that's my lowest score, ever."

"What did they give you on your position?" she asked, as she held the score sheet in front of me.

"It says seven," I replied.

"Great! That means they thought you're a good rider! Now, what do the final comments say?" she asked.

"Nice pair, unfortunate disobedience at end of test," I read from the score sheet.

"See? They thought you were good!" she encouraged.

"Right," I said pessimistically.

Just then Gunilla came back in.

"Good job, girls! I am very proud of both of you," she declared.

My mother did not come to the show the last day. She called to let me know that my grandfather had passed away that morning and she couldn't make it to New Jersey.

"Oh, Mom, I'm so sorry. Is there anything I can do?" I said.

"It's OK. Can you drive back by yourself?" she asked, her voice breaking.

"Of course," I said, grateful that I had driven myself down to the show and wasn't dependent on her to drive me back home.

"I know you will be alright driving, you are such a good driver," she said through her sobs.

"Mom, I can come home now, if you want," I said.

"No, no, there's nothing to do now, it's all over. Just stay with Moony and get him in the trailer and back to the farm. You can come home when you are all done," she said.

"Are you sure?"

"Yes. I love you, see you later," she said, and then hung up the phone.

I was stunned; my grandfather hadn't been sick for years like my grandmother, so at least he didn't suffer like she did. I was grateful for that. But I knew my mother was devastated. I wished I knew the right thing to say.

Carol competed and won fourth place in her class. I was relieved that we got to go home so quickly.

40

In my first lesson back, Carol said the United States Dressage Federation was going to create a national competition, just for Junior riders, ages fourteen to eighteen. Since I was seventeen, I was eligible to try and qualify for that show.

"I don't know," I said, hesitantly, not wanting to ever repeat the disaster from the Festival of Champions show.

"If you want to make it as badly as you say you do, one little show wouldn't change your mind," she said.

"It wasn't one little show—it was the biggest show of my life!" I declared.

"How are you ever going to get anywhere if you give up?" she said.

"I won't," I said.

"Exactly, you won't give up," she clarified for me.

"We'll do the Oakwood shows and then some little local shows over the summer. If you don't have the scores you need by September, we'll go to Connecticut, where they have some more shows. The Juniors show is in October, so at least that buys us some time," she strategized.

"One thing we really need to do though, is to find Moony the right bit, and you need to get a set of spurs, and ride in them every day," she instructed.

"OK," I said.

I had discovered a company that specialized in tack of all sizes. I ordered the smallest bit and spurs they sold, and crossed my fingers.

When the bit arrived, I found Carol and asked for her opinion on how it fit. She slid it into Moonshine's mouth. "Hmm . . . looks like I can put in one finger on each side. The port doesn't look too high or low. It's not hitting his bars . . . looks like we have a winner!" she said.

"Really?" I asked in disbelief.

"Go get your bridle, take off your bit and put this one on, let's see how he likes it," she instructed.

I ran to the tack room, unfastened the buckles of the old bit and attached the new bit to the bridle. I hurried back to Moony's stall, where Carol stood waiting. I handed her the bridle.

"OK, let's see if this fits," she said as she slid the bridle on Moonshine's head.

"Looks good to me," she said as she checked it on both sides, and lifted the corners of his mouth to see how the bit looked inside.

"Tack up, I'll meet you in the indoor," she said.

I tacked him up quickly, got on, and we walked to the indoor, where she waited with Gunilla by the office.

"Pick up the contact," Carol called to me.

I picked up the reins, shortening them gradually. Moonshine did not object. He simply chewed softly on the bit, a sign that he accepted it.

"Super!" I heard Carol say from the office. "Warm him up

as usual, I'll be right back," she said. I warmed up. Moonshine felt soft in the contact, and light off of my legs, but still reaching for the bit. This was the feeling I had been reading about for years in all of the dressage books and magazines I read.

"Wow," Gunilla said as she came out of the office with Carol. "Looks like we finally have a bit!"

I kept Moonshine working, but a smile took over my face. I had to try again, I couldn't quit now.

"OK, Victoria, take a break," Carol called.

As I brought Moonshine back to a walk, I looked over to Carol and asked, "So when is our first show?"

That summer, both trainers were determined to help me and Moonshine reach our highest potential. I was allowed to work as Carol's working student again, so that I could practice on other horses, and improve my seat. Sometimes Carol gave me mini-lessons on those horses, but I still got my hour-long lessons on Moonshine. When I wasn't riding Moony in a lesson and Carol wasn't around, Gunilla appeared to give me tips and pointers. Gunilla also had me ride the sale horses she hadn't sold yet. There was no more pressure to buy; now the focus was to feel the movements on trained horses and translate that to Moonshine.

That show season, Moonshine and I consistently earned respectable scores, never getting scores lower than 60%. I knew we had a chance to qualify for the National Juniors Championships that fall.

Then, one day, at the end of the summer, I tacked Moony up for a lesson with Carol. I walked him for ten minutes, like I always did, before I asked him to pick up the trot to warm up. But as soon as he started trotting, I felt him limping. I sat back in the saddle to stop him, "Whoa, Moon."

But he grabbed the bit in his teeth and wouldn't stop—

he actually sped up. At the higher speed, the limp was more obvious.

"Hey, Victoria! Your horse is lame!" Gunilla shouted from the barn.

"I know! He won't stop, though!" I yelled back, hoping people wouldn't think I was asking him to keep trotting.

"Just stop him!" she yelled back, more forcefully.

I understood the concern, if he kept trotting on a bad leg, he could do more damage, possibly career-ending damage. But Moony was so stubborn, he wouldn't stop. I had to pull back with all my weight, and steer him into a corner to stop him.

Jean saw the spectacle, as she was hand-grazing her horse just outside of the ring, and said, "Poor guy, he still wants to go! What a heart!"

"I know," I said, touched that my horse still wanted to do his job, even though he was in pain.

"Well, there goes that pipe dream," I said to Moonshine as I slipped off the bridle, sure that this lameness ended any possibility of us going to the Juniors' Nationals.

Just then Carol appeared in the barn.

"What happened?" she asked.

"He's lame," I replied.

"The Navicular must be acting up. Alright, we'll just give him a few days off, but get him out of the stall and walk him as much as you can. We'll give him some meds, and see how he feels on Thursday. I'll tell Kim about the meds," she offered.

"OK, thanks, Carol," I replied, grateful that she was always around.

"Why don't you walk him for a little bit, wrap his legs for the night, and when you're done, come to the office," she said.

I had done as Carol instructed and when I finished with Moonshine, I headed to the office. Carol was chatting with Gunilla. I went over to them.

"How's the horse?" Gunilla asked.

"Lame, vet's coming tomorrow."

Carol started,"The plan is for you to ride Moony in the Junior's Nationals. Since you got a bunch of qualifying scores, we'll stop competing him. I think you got enough scores to earn a spot on one of the teams, but we'll have to wait and see the scores that the other Juniors get, since there are only twelve spots. So, he'll get a week off, and we'll see how he is after that."

"But you need to keep riding. So I'm lending you Gerry until Moony is back on track." Gunilla interrupted.

"Gerry?" I repeated, unsure if I heard her correctly.

Gerry was Geronimo's barn name. He was one of Gunilla's highly trained warmbloods. I was shocked that she volunteered him for me to ride.

I was afflicted by a mixture of gratitude and concern. I was struck by Gunilla's generosity in lending me her horse. But I was also concerned about Moony—would this lameness end it all, right now? Would we never get the chance to redeem ourselves? Would I ever be able to prove that Moony was just as good as a warmblood?

I was grateful for the back up horse that Gunilla offered, but I wanted more than anything to make it with Moonshine.

"Thank you so much," I said.

With that, summer ended and I began my final year of high school.

41

I couldn't believe I was finally a senior. It was time to apply to colleges. My school's college advisor drew up a list of colleges to which I should apply—Brown, Dartmouth, and UPenn. I told her I couldn't go away, that I had to stay in New York, because this is where my horse and trainer were.

"You can take your horse with you, Victoria. A lot of these schools are in rural areas, and have stables on their properties," Ms. Frost said.

"Yeah, but I can't take my trainer with me," I replied.

"I hope you understand what's at stake here. You have had an excellent GPA all through high school. You also have a respectable SAT score. These are prestigious colleges and I'm confident they would accept you, if you apply. Do you know what you are giving up?"

"There are good schools in New York, too, Ms. Frost," I replied.

I had anticipated this lecture, and had come prepared with everything that I had learned about New York University. I had even visited the campus once with my parents. I loved the culture and diversity I saw, and I knew I would learn and grow there. But most importantly, I felt free there. Nobody seemed to care how others looked or what people wore. From my short visit, I even felt slightly liberated myself, a welcome change from what felt like a lifetime of wearing a uniform and following rules. I knew this school would be a perfect fit.

"What did you have in mind?" she asked.

"Well, I visited NYU and really liked it," I replied.

"Oh, well sure, you can apply there too," she said.

"Actually, that's really the only school that I want to go to," I said.

"Oh, really? Why is that?" she asked.

"Because I visited once and I know it's the right fit for me," I said conclusively.

Ms. Frost had known me for years, as we had discussed the college path all through high school. She must have recalled how stubborn I could be, been tired of arguing, or actually agreed with my decision, because she simply said, "Well then, you will have to do early admission and submit your application before everyone else. But remember, that means you cannot apply to any other colleges until *after* you get a response from NYU. So, if NYU rejects you, that might also hurt your chances with other schools, as it would delay your ability to apply to any other school. Is that a chance you are willing to take?"

"Yes," I said confidently.

Then she told me what to do, where to find an application, and how to fill it out. It wasn't as a bad as I thought it would be—I finished it the following weekend, and brought it back to her the next week.

"Good girl, now I know you've been riding forever, but what is your biggest riding achievement? You should put that down here," she said.

"Well, I hope it will happen in October," I said.

"Why? What happens in October?" she asked.

"Well, there's this show—the National Junior

Championships . . ."

"Why, that's marvelous!" she lit up. "You *must* put that down!"

"But I don't know if I qualified to compete in it yet," I said.

"Well, we can always send them an addendum, but if your mind is set on NYU, we should send the application in as soon as they open the early admissions application process," she advised.

"That sounds good," I agreed.

Moonshine benefited tremendously from his time off. He was sound again! Even when I started riding him again, I was easy on him. As much as I wanted to go to the Junior Championships with him, it was more important for him to make a full recovery and have a long, happy retirement. I owed him at least that much, since he had given me so much, taught me more than I could learn in any classroom, and made me happier than anyone had ever made me. Nothing and no one could compare to my prickly, obstinate little horse. He was the best thing that ever happened to me.

Now that I had my driver's license, and had applied to NYU, I was at the farm at least three days a week after school, and on the weekends, as usual. I was over the moon. But every time I drove home, I was anxious about what would be in the mail. Would it be a big or small envelope from NYU? Would I get any envelope at all from the United States Dressage Federation?

I was eating lunch with my friends in the senior lounge, when suddenly, the door flew open. It was Mr. Conners, the principal. His face was bright red, and his eyes frantically scanned the room.

"Turn off the radio, Mike!" he commanded. "Where is Victoria?"

Oh, God, my father did something big this time, I thought immediately, remembering the numerous times that he tried to take my sister and me out of school whenever he lost a custody battle.

He rushed to me, with a piece of paper in his hand. I was scared.

"Kiddo, you did it! You did it! You're going to the *Olympics*!" he jumped, crumpling the paper in his right hand as he threw up his arms in jubilation.

I stifled a laugh, but knew what he was too excited to say.

"You mean the Junior Nationals?" I asked.

"Yes! Yes! You did it! I am so proud of you! You did it! Everyone—she did it! Victoria is going to the Junior Olympics!" he shrieked, as he handed me the paper he had crumpled and skipped out of the room.

I had never seen our principal so animated before. It was amusing to see a man I had known for the last six years lose it like that. He had always been so composed, to the point where he often looked somber. Plus, he looked really old, and it was strange to see such an old-looking person bounding around a room with the energy of a teenager.

I was more affected by the delivery of the news than the news itself. Then I looked down to read the paper. It was a fax from my mother to the school. I realized she had received the package in the mail and wanted me to see it as soon as possible.

"So, what's going on?" some of my classmates gathered around me on the sofa.

"Oh, just this show I got into," I said, having learned to contain my enthusiasm for dressage at school.

"Victoria, you got into the Nationals! Congratulations!" my friend Michelle declared, hugging me.

I couldn't wait for the day to end so I could hop in the car and drive to the farm. I thoroughly enjoyed that drive. I rolled all the windows down, blasted the radio, and sang to the music on the radio at the top of my lungs.

When I finally got to the farm, I ran to the office.

"Hi Jane, where's Carol?" I asked the farm's secretary, sitting at the computer.

"In the back," she said.

When Carol heard my voice, she came out.

"Carol, I got in! I'm going to the Juniors!" I said.

"Congratulations! I *knew* you would do it!" she said as she hugged me.

After we hugged, I ran to the barn to hug Moonshine for making it all possible.

42

I had still only received one response in the mail, so now I really wanted to know if I got accepted to NYU. I kept myself busy with school during the day and riding at night. This rigorous schedule made the time fly. Before I knew it, the leaves were changing into bright yellow, vibrant orange, and deep red. The weather was perfect. It was the best time of year: colorful with perfect temperatures for riding.

I had one more week before it was time to go to the Junior Nationals. I got up late the Saturday before the show, tired from the driving and riding during the week. My mother had set breakfast for me on the table. There was a big white envelope in the middle of the table.

I looked at her.

"It's from NYU!" she exclaimed.

We both knew a big envelope was good news and a small envelope was bad news. This was a big envelope, and heavy. I held my breath and my heart started to race.

"Open it, open it!" she chanted as she clapped her hands.

I silently said a quick prayer that my grandmother had

taught me, stuck my finger in the corner, and ripped it apart at the crease. I looked for the cover page.

"'We are pleased to inform you,'" I read out loud, and then my mother grabbed me violently, giving me an uncomfortable sideways hug.

"Oh, honey! Congratulations! I am so proud of you!" she said, as she held me tightly and rocked me from side to side.

"Mom, can't breathe," I gasped. She had twisted my neck, cutting off my air supply. As she undid her grip on me, she yelled, "Baby! Your sister got into NYU!" My sister was still sleeping.

My sister's door opened suddenly. She was cranky.

"That's great," she said as she sat down at the table.

"Thanks," I said, taking a sip of the orange juice.

My mother was already on the phone, calling everyone she knew.

When she was done, she sat down at the table and announced that she was coming to the farm with me.

"Why?" I asked suspiciously.

"Just because. Who wants more eggs?" she said.

I knew this meant she was going to tell everyone at the farm that I had just been accepted to NYU.

"Mom, please don't tell everyone, OK?" I asked.

"Aren't you proud of your achievement? People should know!" she said adamantly.

"Mom, people don't really care."

"Yes, they care!" she said conclusively.

"Good luck with that," my sister said. We both knew my mother would follow through with her intention of telling everyone the good news; when she made her mind up, that was it.

We arrived at the farm. I drove and managed to tolerate my mother's flinching, squirming, and back seat driving because I was still happy and relieved that I had gotten into my first choice college.

She was out of the car as soon as I had parked it, and in a blink, she was in the office.

And she's off, I thought, smiling.

As soon as I was on Moonshine, I was congratulated by everyone I came into contact with.

Man, she's fast, I thought.

Then it was time for my lesson. Carol met me in the outdoor arena.

"Congratulations! I just heard the good news!" she called as she entered the ring.

I'm sure everyone has by now, I thought.

"Thanks, Carol," I replied.

43

I knew we were ready for the big show, and couldn't wait for the drive down. The week dragged by. Nora would take us in her trailer. I loaded Moony into the trailer, and then drove down to DC behind the trailer with my mom in the passenger seat. I found it poetic that this show was being held at the same show grounds as our first away show, four years ago. I couldn't afford to pay Carol the training fee for the whole weekend, so it was just us. But that was fine with me. I knew Moony would be great.

The trailer rattled as usual, from Moony's incessant kicking. When we finally arrived and I unloaded him, I noticed one side of Nora's trailer was covered in blood. Then I looked over Moony's body and saw that he had worn off most of the hair on his hindquarters, and blood was dripping down his legs. I rushed him to the nearest hose, and ordered my mother to find his stall, and then the on-site vet.

Nora observed the huge bald spot on his haunches. "Talk about a severe case of monkey-butt!" she said, and erupted into cackling laughter. "Maybe you can cover it up with some black spray paint!" she laughed again. I usually appreciated her humor, but not this time. I smiled politely as I rushed Moonshine toward the barn.

The friend I made from the Schumacher clinic greeted me immediately.

"Hey, Katie!"

"Victoria! Good to see you again!"

"Hey, do you know where the vet is?" I asked, pointing to Moony's bloodied butt.

"Oh, gosh, no. Wow! That doesn't look good," she replied.

"Mom, hang out with him for a second, OK?" I asked her as I put him in his stall.

I sprinted to the office to find medical help. I knew how to treat a surface wound, but Moonshine was limping.

"Oh boy," the vet sighed when he saw Moonshine standing in the aisle. "That doesn't look too good," he said as he put down his emergency kit and examined Moonshine's haunches.

"Yeah, but he's also limping," I said.

"Was he kicking in the trailer?" he asked me.

"Yeah," I confessed.

"He's probably just a little sore from the kicking. Just alternate cold hosing and walking him for ten minute intervals for about an hour. I wouldn't ride him today, though," he said.

"Thanks, doctor," I said.

I was grateful that we had arrived two days before we were scheduled to compete. It was Thursday; we weren't set to compete until Saturday and Sunday.

"Looks like you get a day off, monster," I said to him as I petted his neck.

Surprisingly, I wasn't too worried about missing a workout before the championships. I knew he was familiar with the tests and the movements. I was more concerned about Moonshine.

After I cold hosed his leg for ten minutes, I decided to walk him to the arena where we would compete—the stadium.

I walked him down the ramp. It was October, so the entire arena was adorned with colorful Halloween decorations—scarecrows, pumpkins, and hay bales, all around the ring. They were cute, but all that stuff would spook even the calmest horse.

"Remember this ring, Moon?" I asked him as we descended the ramp and entered the magnificent arena.

"This is where we won our first class, little man," I whispered to him. He pushed me to the side, disinterested in the arena.

"Not afraid of any of these decorations?" I asked him. He wasn't, marching forward, clearly on a mission of getting around the arena so the walk could be over and he could be back in his stall, eating his hay.

Even though I was annoyed with him for having torn up half of his body in the trailer, I was grateful for his confidence. If anything ever caught him by surprise, he never ran away from it, instead, he would turn around and attack it. After having ridden all the horses I had up to this point, I had come to realize this was a rare and valuable trait in a horse. Most horses ran away from frightening stimuli. I had become thankful for the trait that I had detested most in my horse—his aggression.

As I walked Moony around the arena, I noticed Gunilla sitting up in the secretary's stand with all of the other Junior riders. She waved at me to come join the party.

"OK, buddy, let's go back to your stall so you can eat your hay," I whispered to him. As soon as he realized we were headed for the exit, he picked up the pace, to the point where he was leading me back to the barn, as he usually did when he knew where we were going.

I was the last one in the crowded secretary's stand. There was pizza. I realized I had forgotten to eat. But I wasn't hungry.

Gunilla was speaking. I realized she was one of the

organizers of this show. As soon as she saw me, she stopped addressing the other equestrians.

"Hi, Victoria! How is Moonshine?" she said.

"A little sore from the trailer ride down here, but I've been cold hosing and walking him, so hopefully he'll be OK tomorrow," I said.

A look of concern flashed across her usually confident face. This was not training at home; I did not have a back up horse here, and we both knew it.

Nevertheless, she continued explaining the itinerary. She told us that this was a national competition, and that we would be divided into three teams—East Coast, Midwest, and West Coast. Katie and I were on the same team—we smiled at each other.

"OK, guys, I know this is the first FEI competition for a lot of you. That means there are special rules that you must follow. Additionally, this is a Junior National competition, so there is another set of rules you need to know. Because this is a national show, you will all compete before three judges, instead of one, as you might have become accustomed to doing. In FEI competitions, the show begins with the jog. You must each jog your own horse on a flat surface chosen by the ground jury. For those of you who don't know, the ground jury is all of the judges who will be judging you. You must all show up for the jog at the same time, and in business casual attire, such as khakis and a dress shirt. However, being that this is the Junior Nationals, you will be required to wear the team jackets that I have here in this box. You are the only twelve Junior riders chosen out of the entire country who were invited here to compete. You are therefore representing all of the Juniors who couldn't be here this weekend. That means you must always look neat, make sure your horses look tidy, and wear these jackets at all times. Think of yourselves as ambassadors for all the American junior riders. Finally, your hotel rooms will be paid for by the show organizers, as well as all of your meals," she said.

Oh, wow, so cool, Mom doesn't have to pay for the hotel! I thought. I knew that was always one of the biggest expenses of going to shows far away from home.

After the pizza party/information session, I went back to the barn, where my mother was reading a show program outside of Moony's stall. Moonshine was eating his hay.

"How's Moony?" I asked.

"Eating," she replied.

"Please feel better quickly, Moon," I said softly to him.

The next morning, I got out of bed an hour before the time set on the alarm. I couldn't sleep any longer. I wanted to see if Moonshine was sound or lame. I was at the barn at six, before anyone else. I first gave him his breakfast, his grain and his hay. I had to wait twenty minutes for him to finish eating before I could enter his stall. But I saw that his leg was not swollen.

That's a good sign, I thought, optimistically.

"Mom, I'm going to take him out and trot him—let me know if he looks even, OK?" I asked my mother.

"Sure," she replied.

I entered the stall with the halter and lead rope. I knelt down quickly beside his hind legs to feel them for heat, which would be a bad sign. They were not warmer than his front legs, another good sign. I approached his head and slipped the halter over his ears. I then turned to exit, and he followed without any tension in the rope.

I led him outside. The sun was rising. I could see it peeking through the autumn clouds, creating a bouncing light of soft orange and yellow. It was mesmerizing in the surrounding darkness. I turned him down a straight stretch of the concrete road. *Please be sound, please be sound,* I pleaded silently.

"OK, come on Moony, trot!" I cued.

As I started to jog, he pinned his ears and picked up a trot to catch me. When we were shoulder to shoulder, I listened.

Clack-clack, clack-clack. His trot was two-beat, and even! I slowed him to a walk, turned down the same road, back to the barn. I had to be sure.

"OK, Moony, again!" I urged.

And again, he delivered an even, two-beat trot.

"He's even!" I heard my mother call from the entrance of the barn.

"Thank you, Moon," I whispered. I was relieved.

"I knew there was no stopping you," I said, patting his neck.

The other riders and their parents began to trickle in.

"Hey, Victoria!" Katie saw me polishing my boots when she arrived an hour later.

"Hey, what's up?" I greeted her.

"How's your horse?" she asked.

"Good," I smiled.

"You ready for the big jog at nine?" she asked me.

"Sure. I mean it's just a jog, though," I replied.

"Yeah, but you have to admit it's pretty cool to do a jog, like we're famous, you know?" she said.

"Yeah," I agreed.

It *was* cool, really cool. We were suddenly important, a brand new phenomenon for most of us, especially Moony and me. We were told that once the jog was over, the official competition would begin. That meant that nobody besides us riders and one additional person, designated by each of us, were allowed in the barn. We were all given two ID badges, and after the jog, each of us and our additional person had to wear the badges at all times. We were only teenagers but were being treated like high profile riders.

At eight o'clock, Gunilla and three other people walked through the barn.

"Guys? Your attention, please. The jog will be held right outside the barn, and will begin precisely at nine. Please come outside with your horses in their snaffle bridles, in the appropriate attire. Thank you," she announced. Then she and her entourage were gone.

Moonshine had been gleaming, but I brushed him again at eight-thirty and gave him an extra spritz of shine spray. I double checked his snaffle bridle for any grime I may have missed the last time I cleaned it. Then, at a quarter to nine, I put it on. I checked myself, to make sure my khakis and team jacket were still clean. I pulled my hair back into a bun. Most of the other Juniors were also tacking up, so I felt comfortable heading out of the barn before nine. I didn't want to be late.

I saw Gunilla down the path, a few hundred feet away, with a much larger entourage. As I approached, I recognized some as the world-famous judges I had read about. I also noticed photographers and a video crew, with massive cameras and equipment.

Isn't this a bit much for just a jog? I wondered.

As soon as I had walked Moony out of the barn, there was a line of equestrians donning their blue team jackets, leading their perfectly groomed horses out of the stable. Moonshine and I were in the lead, and I was grateful, knowing how much Moony preferred being first. He might have been fussy toward the back of the line.

Gunilla gave me a quick tip just before I started to jog Moonshine.

"Just run him down the path there, and turn him to the *right*, not the left, like you would normally do, and then run back, OK? That's how they do FEI jogs," she advised.

Just then, a photographer popped out of nowhere and took our picture. I was startled, and distracted. I was nervous; I hoped Moonshine would trot soundly. If he wasn't sound, we wouldn't be allowed to compete. I petted Moonshine one last time, and then I took the first running stride, hoping he would follow with even footsteps. As I ran, I listened to the footfalls. They sounded even. I hoped they looked even. I was preoccupied with how he looked to the judges. Then all of a sudden, I heard, "Turn!"

Gunilla was gesturing me to turn around. I slowed my horse to a walk, and then pulled him in my direction to turn him around. As soon as I had turned him, I realized I had turned him to the left instead of to the right!

Oh, shit! I hope that's not a really big mistake! I thought, wanting to kick myself.

Before I knew it, we were back with the group of judges.

"Gunilla, I'm so sorry!" I began, but she waved me to be quiet.

"It's no problem," she smiled at me.

How could I forget an instruction she just told me? I thought to myself, frustrated.

"Number 74 is entered in the competition! Next horse, please!" One of her entourage declared. My heart skipped a beat. We can compete!

Since Moony seemed OK, I decided I would get on and exercise him a little bit so that he would be in top form for the competition the next day. I don't know if it was the team jacket I wore or that he was in a more advanced double bridle, or if I had just grown up, but this time in the warm up ring, I was not intimidated. I was again surrounded by the superstars that I idolized, but I was less in awe of them and more focused on my own ride. I also did not feel alone without Carol or Gunilla there to supervise my ride. I rode with Carol's voice in my head. After all the lessons I had taken from her, it was unclear to me now where her training ended and mine began. Was it one and the same? I knew what her corrections would be, so I applied them whenever necessary. It was incredible, she wasn't here with us but her voice still drowned out everyone else's. Her voice was all that I heard.

44

The next day was the first competition day—the team test. Since there were only twelve of us riders, we did not have to compete for a spot to be able to ride the individual test the following day. There was, therefore, less pressure on us than there would have been on the professionals, who would have had to compete for a spot in the final round.

The show organizers were incredibly gracious and took great strides to make us all feel welcome. We were fussed over as though we were celebrities—we were photographed constantly, given goody bags for our horses, and we were always being checked on—did we need water, how were our horses feeling?

The biggest deal for me, though, was walking around with the team jacket. I don't know if it was the radiant royal blue color, or that it was the one clean piece of clothing we all had in common, but it commanded a high degree of respect. If any one of us stepped out of the barn with the jacket on, we made sure to look tidy because we might be photographed, but if two of us walked around the property with the team jackets, we were sure to be photographed. Walking around with the team jacket was like walking around with the Olympic gold medal—everyone knew who we were, everyone smiled at us (including our idols), and had pleasantries to exchange with us. It was as if we had all been inducted into an exclusive club.

Even though Junior Nationals was the biggest show that Moonshine and I had ever been to, I was more confident and at ease at the show that at any other. I was not freaking out about our impending performance. I was just thrilled to be there. I felt like we had already won.

Moonshine and I were scheduled to compete in the late morning of the first day of competition.

"Ready to show your stuff, Moony monster?" I asked him as I brushed him, two hours before my ride time.

"Do you know your test?" my mother asked as I cleaned my horse.

"Of course," I said confidently.

"Do you need anything?" she asked.

"No, Mom," I replied.

"Are you sure?" She was visibly nervous.

"Mom, calm down," I said.

"I know, I know," she was agitated.

"You can shine my boots if you want," I said.

My boots were already shiny, but I knew that having something to do would calm her down.

Once Moony was tacked up, I pulled on my boots and headed out. Every time someone left the barn to compete, everyone else in the barn would wish that person good luck. I thought it was cute.

"Good luck, Victoria!" voices called behind me.

"Thanks!" I replied.

I hopped on and headed to the warm up ring. Moonshine wasn't at his best in the warm up, which only bolstered my confidence. After so many shows with him, I had learned that when we had a lackluster warm up, we would turn in a great performance in the show ring.

I checked my watch, and saw it was time to head to the show ring in the stadium. Moonshine ambled down the noisy ramp like a pro. He seemed to believe that this is where he belonged. Unlike the first time we competed in the arena, when the only people in the stands were my fellow boarders from Oakwood, now there were random people peppered throughout the stadium. It wasn't filled, but this time, the audience didn't consist of just my own supporters. These were strangers, here to watch Moony and me perform.

"Look, buddy, they're all here to see you," I whispered to him. Moonshine loved an audience. He knew when he had large audience—he would puff himself up, and took longer, flashier strides, showing himself off.

The announcer introduced us over the loudspeaker, and the audience applauded. When Moonshine heard how many hands came together to welcome him to his stage, he grew another foot. His trot transformed from choppy and small to lofty and airy.

"You're such a ham," I whispered to him, as I circled the outside of the arena, waiting for the judge to ring the bell so that I could begin the test.

The bell rang. As I approached the entrance, I heard Carol's voice in my head, "Take it slow, don't rush the test. Enjoy it, show your horse off, and *smile.*"

I did as my trainer had told me. Moonshine and I were relaxed but working hard in the ring. I was breathing hard in the trot work. Then, finally, came the walk break in the middle of the test. The movement required the horse to stretch out his neck, and walk across the diagonal of the arena on a long rein. The purpose of the movement is to show that the horse can go straight from challenging trot work to a relaxed walk, where he stretches through his back and neck.

Moonshine must have *really* felt comfortable in the arena because just as he crossed the middle of the ring, he stopped!

I was squeezing him with my legs to keep going forward, but he wouldn't budge. I felt his back lifting, and I knew he had just lifted his tail. He had stopped to poop in the middle of the ring, in front of all three judges! I started to kick him, but he didn't seem to be bothered. He insisted on relieving himself then and there.

Moonshine, are you kidding me? I thought. I couldn't believe he had parked himself in the exact center of the ring to take care of business. I was also dismayed that he had come to a grinding halt, and would not move. He never did this in training! Why now?

Finally, when he was done, then he continued walking.

When we finished the test, I saluted, and the audience applauded. I spotted my mother waiting by the entrance gate. As I approached her, we made eye contact and we laughed at the same time. So many of Moony's antics were amusing, and this was no exception.

When we got the score sheet back, the score was average, having been knocked down by the points we lost for Moonshine's "disobedience." This was the one time I laughed over a score sheet.

The next day, I hoped that my horse would at least let me look like I was in control.

"Hey, Moon," I greeted him in the morning, as I dumped his grain in his feed bucket. After I tossed him a flake of hay, I stood outside the stall and watched him eat.

"You going to be a good boy today?" I asked.

He pinned his ears and flashed his teeth at the bars, insisting on being left alone to eat his breakfast. I smiled as I walked out of the barn. He was feeling feisty and confident—a good sign. I went out to the food vendor to get breakfast. The sun was still rising, and the morning dew clung to the grass around the barn. Only a few people were at the show grounds, mostly the grooms. I saw one horse being lunged, another being braided. It was peaceful. I walked slowly, soaking in the quiet, crisp morning. Moony needed a full hour to finish his food, after which it would be safe to fuss over him. Before I knew it, I was at the food vendor, ordering a bagel. I looked down at my watch. *I still have forty-five minutes before Moony's done eating. Now what?* I thought, wondering how to kill so much time. I wandered to the stadium.

I sat down in the second to last row of seats, on the aisle chair. I placed the wrapped bagel on my lap, unfolded the wax paper, and took a bite. Three years ago, the whole Oakwood Farm team sat a few rows down from where I was sitting, cheering and whistling after Moony and I had been announced as the winners of that Junior Equitation class. I smiled at the memory.

I wonder if we could win here, too, I thought. I knew my fellow competitors were skilled riders, and that most of them rode talented dressage horses. Our chances of winning were bleak, as always, but I still hoped.

What if our test was absolutely perfect? What if we entered at A, and Moony landed square into a halt at X and stood absolutely still during my salute? What if he would then jump right into a big, powerful trot, and bend deep into the corners? What if he floated across the arena in the half-passes? What if he had a little extra suspension in the extensions? What if the walk was relaxed and full of forward moving momentum? What if the walk to canter transition was light and crisp? What if the flying changes were straight and rhythmic? What if the last halt and salute were as perfect as the first? What if the whole test was perfect? Could we win?

"Programs! Get your programs!" I heard someone shout.

Oh crap! What time is it? I checked my watch, and it had been just about forty-five minutes. I wrapped up the uneaten part of my bagel and hurried to the barn.

I mucked out Moony's stall and gave him fresh water. I

then grabbed a bucket, turned it upside down, placed it by his shoulder, stepped up on it, and began braiding his mane. The barn now was abuzz with the other Junior riders feeding horses and mucking stalls. I wanted to run through my test in my head as many times as I could, to make sure I had it memorized. An hour later, I was done braiding and I knew my test. I then curried and brushed him vigorously. I wanted to give him a massage, but also get him spotlessly clean. After I was done brushing, I spritzed some shine spray and smoothed it into his coat with a towel. He glistened even under the barn's fluorescent lights. I was satisfied. Then I saddled him before I pulled on my shiny leather boots, strapped on my spurs, and fastened my stock tie. After I was dressed in my show attire, I slipped his double bridle over his ears, and he opened his mouth, accepting the bits. I offered him a peppermint as soon as I had the bridle on his head, which he promptly sucked in, like a vacuum. After I secured the noseband and buckled the throatlatch, I led him out of the stall. I grabbed the hoof polish, painted some on, and led him out of the barn.

"Good luck!" voices called after me.

"Thanks!" I yelled back.

I put my left foot in the stirrup, and found my place in the saddle. I kept the reins loose, looked where I wanted to go, and Moony turned toward the warm-up ring.

I looked straight ahead. I didn't care who was riding around me. I was riding Moonshine. And Moonshine had qualified for this show; Moonshine had earned the right to be here.

I let him walk around on a free rein for fifteen minutes, like always. Then I gathered the reins, and he instantly collected himself and picked up the trot. He knew the warm-up just as well as he knew the test. As I worked him, people gathered around the fence.

Our warm-up was lackluster. He didn't try his best, and I didn't push him. As I put on my shadbelly coat, ten minutes before my ride time, I was confident. A bad warm-up usually meant we would have a great test.

I steered him toward the stadium. He ambled down the ramp, and stepped out onto the sand. I was surprised by the size of the crowd in the stands. There were a lot of people peppered throughout the seats. I picked up the reins, and Moony not only collected himself, but also puffed up his body a few inches. He knew he had an audience and was ready to strut his stuff.

As soon as the judge rang the bell, Moonshine entered the arena with a dominating trot. He halted sharply and squarely, and stood frozen while I took my right hand off the reins to salute the judge, and start the test. As soon as I held both reins again, he launched into a powerful trot. I had practiced this test so much that he had memorized all of the movements. He knew exactly when to start bending for the half-pass. But he didn't just set himself up for the movements, he gave me more. At the start of each half-pass, I could see his leading leg—he was reaching more than he ever had. His body stretched more than ever in the extensions. His flying changes were smooth and straight. His pirouettes were perfectly balanced, as he lifted me and his front end easily with each turning stride. He danced like never before. It was the ride I had always wanted, the ride I dreamed about. But before I knew it, I was saluting the judge, and the test was over. The audience erupted.

"Such a superstar," I said, petting him on his neck after I saluted. A tear escaped my eye. This was our last show. I knew it was time to retire Moony. As hard as it was to get here, though, I also knew I would miss it. I would miss it all—the fights we had, the backaches, the heart aches, the thrill of going to our first show and winning the equitation class, the joy of earning his trust after he started following me into trailers, and the satisfaction of becoming a team, when we competed in a hurricane and he wouldn't let me fall.

"Thanks, Moony."

I didn't need to see the score sheet or know what place we

had won. He had proven himself. All of the hours, days, weeks, months, and years of work and struggle culminated into just six minutes we had in the arena. But those six minutes were a dream come true. Moony was now a competitive dressage horse. We had finally shown that we belonged in this world that had rejected us for so long.

Back at the barn, I gave him a whole bag of carrots. An hour later, the loudspeaker crackled to life. It was the first time I had been in a barn with a loudspeaker in it. The riders didn't have to scurry out to hear the results. But all of the activity came to a grinding halt, and everyone shushed each other.

"Ladies and Gentlemen, we have the results of the 1997 National Junior Dressage Team Championships!"

I continued to brush Moonshine. I didn't care what place someone else tried to put us into. It didn't matter to me if those judges thought Moony belonged in third, second, or first place. Moony had already won.

"The bronze medal winning team is the team from Region 1!"

That wasn't us. We were Region 3. So, we had won either first or second place.

"The silver medal winning team is the team from Region 3!"

"And the winners of the 1997 National Junior Dressage Team Championships is the Region 2 team!"

We won second place. Not only were we one of the top 12 best in the country invited to compete at this prestigious event, but we were also the second best out of those horse and rider pairs. Moony, a horse that had been discarded and dismissed, had won second place in the country.

At the end of the day, it was time for the awards ceremony. We were instructed to go to the stadium in our show attire, but were told to wear our team jackets instead of our competition shadbelly coats, and enter with white wraps on our horses' legs. We entered in a line. There was a large podium in the middle of the arena. Gunilla, along with some of the other judges and multiple photographers, waited for us to approach. They applauded as we entered the arena. My team was instructed to line up on the right side of the podium.

"All riders dismount, please, and approach the podium," the announcer said through the loudspeaker.

We did as instructed. Each of our horses had a handler there who would hold our mounts as we made our way to the podium.

I handed the reins to the man assigned to hold Moony. "Don't stand in front of him," I warned. Moony was sure to try to dominate the man and head-butt him. Once all of the riders had assembled atop the podium, one judge began adorning us each with our own medal.

He approached me, and I bent down so that he could put the medal around my neck.

"Congratulations," he said, as he shook my hand.

"Thank you," I replied.

I looked down at my medal and then at my horse. He was pushing his handler around, just as I thought he would.

"Hey, Moon," I called.

He froze, and his ears flew up. I admired how handsome my horse looked. I smiled at his ears. No other horse had ears that curled inward like Moony's. They were just another trait that made him different, unique, special.

"Good boy," I called again.

When he knew where I was standing, his head dropped to a relaxed position, his ears rotated outward, and he stopped fighting with his handler.

I smiled again, knowing that he had found the other end of the invisible rope that kept us tied together.

Epilogue

Moonshine retired from the show ring after the 1997 Junior Championships. The following summer, Victoria trained with George Theodorescu at his farm in Germany. It was through Mr. Theodorescu that she acquired a four-year-old Dutch warmblood/Thoroughbred cross named Luino. She came home in the fall to attend college at NYU. Mr. Theodorescu wanted to keep Luino in Germany for one year to establish some basic training with the horse. The following year, Luino came to the US. Moony did not enjoy sharing Victoria's attention, and would frequently bite and kick at Luino, but he eventually accepted Luino as part of the family.

Victoria spent her college and law school years training and competing with Luino, acquiring her USDF Bronze and Silver medals, as well as qualifying for the Regional Championships. Meanwhile, Moony enjoyed his semi-retirement. Victoria would occasionally ride Moonshine without a saddle but with a simple snaffle bit, to let Moony execute the movements of upper level dressage. She was sure that after all of the attention showered on him as a show horse, he would not appreciate full retirement. She was right—Moony was delighted when it was "his turn." He swelled with pride when others watched him perform tempi changes in a simple snaffle bridle, and without a saddle on his back. He taught many other riders the upper level movements such as tempi changes, piaffe, and passage.

It was during Moony's semi-retirement that Victoria met her future husband, Brian. Victoria really liked Brian, so she gave him the key to unlocking Moonshine—he needs to think he's the boss. Brian played along and endured head-butt after head-butt, Moony's signature move announcing he's in charge. Brian was quickly accepted.

Victoria retired Luino from the show ring when she became a busy practicing attorney. Both horses enjoyed retirement at a small family farm in New Jersey.

At the age of twenty-eight, Moonshine suffered a serious colic at the farm in New Jersey. Due to his advanced age, the vet explained that, even if he did perform the colic surgery, Moony's chance of survival was only 30%. The vet further warned that even if the surgery were successful and Moony survived it, he needed to overcome the next hurdle of waking from anesthesia. Many horses thrash and break their legs while coming out of anesthesia. Victoria was not ready to say good-bye to Moony, so she told the vet to perform the surgery.

Moony's intestine had necrotized and the dead tissue had to be cut and removed. When the surgery was complete, the vet came up and warned that Moony would be coming out of anesthesia. Victoria held her breath. Later, one of the vet's assistants came up and told Victoria that she sat on him while he woke up and Moony waited until he was fully conscious to even try to get up. The healing process was long and slow but Moony eventually recovered completely.

The thought of losing Moony shook Victoria to her core. She and her husband had been discussing buying a house, and they decided to look for a house with a barn and some land.

After a year of house-hunting, Victoria and Brian found

their home. The house was nice, although it needed multiple improvements. When Victoria saw the barn, though, she easily envisioned her horses there and realized she had finally found her home. The barn was full of trash, had broken doors, the stalls had uneven ground, there was no hot water, and the windows and stalls were boarded up. But the foundation was solid—it was made of cinderblock with a concrete floor with drainage and a metal roof. Also, each of the large paddocks had run-in sheds. Victoria could picture Moony and Luino running wild and free in the paddocks—larger than they had had in the twenty years she had owned them. So, Victoria and Brian bought their home.

They moved in and tackled the barn and property first. They cut down overgrown weeds and trees, slashed vines and poison ivy that strangled a storage shed behind the barn, leveled the stalls, laid down rubber mats, put up fencing, and installed a hot water heater (Moony cannot take cold showers, for the safety of all involved, he must be bathed in warm water). Every Saturday morning was spent loading up the truck with cut down weeds, trees, or debris from the barn and sheds and taking it to the local dump. The house also needed major work, in the form of a new roof, new water system, a repaired septic system, and indoor and outdoor paint.

After two months of fixing the place up, the horses moved in. They gobbled up the lush, green grass in the paddock. Victoria tucked them in every night, tossing them extra hay and fluffing up their bedding. She was beyond content that she, her horses, and her husband were all finally together.

Olivia Jane Shade was born August 3, 2015. Olivia met Moony when she was two weeks old and continues to visit him regularly. She laughed happily when she petted him for the first time, while he kept his head low and steady. He has always been tough with adults, especially men, tossing his head and sending their hand flying, perhaps head-butting them in the stomach whenever someone tried to pet him on his nose.

But he is a completely different horse with babies and children. When Olivia delicately caressed his nose, which he kept carefully still, his eyes softened.

Victoria and Moony see each other every single day. He still has his attitude, always insisting on being the first one to come in from the paddock. He is also tough with those who try to pet him. But when someone wants to ride him, he takes care of his rider. He still enjoys the spotlight.

When Victoria isn't in the barn, she often looks out the kitchen window and watches Moony grazing in the paddock. He frequently pops his head up at the same time and looks back.

Moony and Victoria with their 2nd place ribbon at the AHSA/ Cosequin 1997 Junior Dressage Team Championships.

Moony meeting Olivia with Victoria and Brian, 2015.

Moony and Olivia bonding, 2016

About the Author (and Moony)

Moonshine retired from the show ring in 1997, and became a beloved family companion.

After college, Victoria went on to graduate law school, and is licensed to practice law in New York and New Jersey. She focuses on animal law and personal injury protection. She is a member of the New York State Bar Association Animal Law Committee, as well as the Animal Law Committee's Legislative and Publications subcommittees. Victoria also sits on the board of the Hudson Valley SPCA, is a member of the ASPCA's Horse Action Team, and is a district leader for the Humane Society of the United States.

She earned her U.S.D.F. Bronze and Silver medals aboard Luino, and competed with him at the Regional Championships. Victoria then met her future husband, Brian, another horse-lover.

The pair purchased a house on a horse farm, where Moonshine and Luino were retired—Moon Shade Farm. They then adopted two dogs, Rex and Daisy, and were later adopted by two cats, Sochi and the Kitten. In 2015, they welcomed a beautiful baby girl into the world, Olivia Jane, who had her first ride on Moony when she was in mommy's belly.

Tragically, Luino passed away on June 17th, 2016, just three days after his 23rd birthday. Victoria was with him when he passed. He was a treasured member of the family, and he will be sorely missed. He was affectionate and loving, a loyal companion who was happiest enjoying the retired life with Moony and the rest of the family.